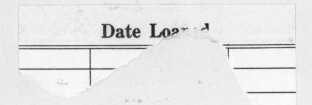

CANON CHARLES KINGSLEY

CHARLES KINGSLEY
IN HIS STUDY AT EVERSLEY

by Lowes Dickinson

Canon
Charles Kingsley

A BIOGRAPHY

By

UNA POPE-HENNESSY

The Macmillan Company
NEW YORK

PUBLISHED BY
The Macmillan Company
NEW YORK
1949

MADE IN GREAT BRITAIN

Contents

Acknowledgements

IT is only the reading of unpublished letters that has made it possible to infuse this book with such psychological and human interest as it may possess. I am indebted to Lady Cope for the loan of many letters and other documents, and to Miss Cope for local information; to the Marchioness of Crewe for permitting me to make use of the Kingsley correspondence among the Houghton Papers; to the Hon. Mrs. Henry Cust for showing me letters written to her mother by Mrs. Charles Kingsley and Dr. George Kingsley; to the Earl of Hardwicke for a document; to the Countess of Iddesleigh for making known to me such inhabitants of Eversley as can remember 'the Canon'; to the present rector of Eversley for showing me over the Rectory; to Mr. E. G. Stapleton, the grandson of the Augustus Stapleton mentioned in this book, who has lent me several bundles of letters and has been kind enough to discuss difficult points as they arose. I wish to thank the officials in charge of the Manuscript Room at the British Museum for producing the many letters they have in their keeping and for arranging to make photostats of Charles Kingsley's drawings for 'Elizabeth of Hungary'. These have never been reproduced before and are of great interest. To Sir Eric Maclagan I tender my thanks for reading the typescript, and to my son John Pope-Hennessy for reading the proof. A special word is due to Mrs. Thorp, who appends to her excellent thesis, *Charles Kingsley*, a most useful bibliography.

U. P.-H.

TO
RICHARD

List of Illustrations

it was second nature for them to beguile trout from their lairs, and to practise a sport that could then be indulged in so cheaply. Charles Kingsley wrote best when describing natural scenes and becomes startlingly dramatic in dealing with sea-slugs and the like, for they seem to have provoked him to terse and directly expressed appreciation. If only he had been able to devote himself to such writing and could have put aside his preachings, social, theological, and philosophical, he would have been esteemed by posterity more highly than Richard Jefferies, or, indeed, any other descriptive lover of nature.

Sporting rectors have always been stock figures in our national life. They were treated in a friendly spirit by landlords, who in the nineteenth century were dependent on them for knowing what went on on their estates and in the parishes of which they were patrons. Buffers between the owning class and the landless class, they also acted as distributors of bene-factions in kind, such as blankets, flannel, or coal. As a rule the clergy could be relied on to support the landed system, but occasionally from their docile ranks a hot-head like Kingsley would arise and scandalise landlords by demanding better hous-ing conditions and a wider ownership of property. No one can overrate the importance of the rectors of England as hinges in the mechanism of country life: the contentedness or otherwise of the poor rested on their shoulders and so, though far less directly, did that of their patrons. It was largely owing to the cushioning ministrations of an educated clergy that no large-scale agrarian revolution took place in early or mid-Victorian days. Where, as in France, these hinge-men did not exist, the aristocracy were liable to feel the full impact of a *jacquerie* that the village *curé*, himself deriving from the *tiers état* or the actual people and in no sense a supporter of the château, was powerless to mitigate.

The rectors of England went to the same schools and colleges as the patrons of their livings, and it used to be said of the original edition of *The Dictionary of National Biography* that more than half the names in it were those of the sons of the clergy. The rector's family could usually be counted on to play a unique and honourable part in social life; its members dealt simply with neighbours of every station and set an example of friendliness that was recognised by those among whom they

Chapter 1

THE ENIGMA OF PERSONALITY

As Manfred says, 'I am of an order of mortals who do become old in their youth and die in middle age.'

CHARLES KINGSLEY

FOR many English people the name of Charles Kingsley conjures up bright memories of water-babies, lays of buccaneers, refrains of sad songs, and a vision of Nature as a kind old nurse. Generations of children have shared the adventures of little Tom the chimney-sweep, and at least one of Kingsley's six novels must have been read by every English-speaking boy alive, for the school editions of *Westward Ho!* may not be numbered. *Westward Ho!*, a greater success than *Hypatia*, placed him for all time in the front rank of English historical novelists. It is not, however, as a novelist that Kingsley is memorialised in Westminster Abbey. His bust there stands on a high ledge in what is now called 'the chapel of the minor poets' near the west door. It is companioned by that of Matthew Arnold, a far richer versifier, and by that of Kingsley's mentor, Frederick Denison Maurice, who never wrote verse at all.

A man of country tastes, who in spite of a severe speech-impediment chose service in the Church of England as his profession, Charles Kingsley is more pleasingly approached in his instinctive role of naturalist and fisherman than in his adoptive role of social reformer, for as a naturalist he remained perennially young and happy, whereas as a reformer he became harassed, irritable, and frequently depressed in spirit. His zeal in the pursuit of flowers, ferns, insects and wild birds would have endeared him to Gilbert White, and his devotional praise of chalk-streams to Izaak Walton. One of the purest delights he ever enjoyed was a day's fishing at Bemerton, where saintly George Herbert had fished before him and, just possibly, John Donne.

Many clergymen of Kingsley's day were addicts of fly-fishing. Brought up in country rectories or on family estates, moved.   It is important to do justice to their usually stabilising influence in order to appreciate what a firebrand Charles Kingsley at one time appeared, not only to his colleagues but to those in authority over him.

With instincts and interests that were human rather than humanitarian, he could lament over the dull squalor of a labourer's life in Hampshire, press on his behalf for the enclosure of common lands, shed tears over a sweated tailor, read patiently to a blind parishioner, and yet go out of his way to express approval of the killing of Dyaks in Borneo, Chinese in Canton, and negroes in Jamaica.   His career seems to have depended on spasms of sympathy, and not to have been determined by any process of intellectual development.   As far as actions and words go, he bristles with apparent inconsistencies which indulgent friends were apt to attribute to a defective memory. A more credible explanation may lie in the fact that all events, great and small, were mirrored for him in some past or present emotion and thus were in their very nature evanescent.   We cannot hold on to an emotional experience as we do to a principle because it is, and of a sudden is not, whereas a principle supports us in consistency just as long as we choose that it should.   In an effort to sum up Charles Kingsley's character, Justin McCarthy said that he had a disproportionate amount of the female in his make-up, and that 'despite his rough voice and vigorous manner he was as feminine in his likes and dislikes, his impulses and prejudices, as Harriet Martineau was masculine in her intellect and George Sand in her emotions'.   Leslie Stephen, who knew him in his professorial days at Cambridge, thought him an attractive but far from strong man.   'His character', he said, 'had charm, but his intellect weakness.'

In speaking of himself, Kingsley blessed the intensity of a nature that enabled him to throw himself into work or play with no thought of anything but the matter on which he was at the moment engaged.   In other words, feeling not observation, instinct not logic, hurled him headlong from one activity to another in bursts of ardour.   This native endowment cut both ways.   It enabled him to steep himself in whatever he was doing with an absorption so complete as to be unreflective and to some degree unintelligent, since he never anticipated what effect his action might have on the persons round him.   For example, when he took occasion in a casual book review to attack the good faith of Catholic priests in general and of Dr. Newman in particular, he was at first surprised and then scared at the uproar he had caused.   Likewise when at a meeting of working men he suddenly declared himself a Chartist as well as a parson, he did not realise what implications would be read into his utterance till repeating his convictions in a church pulpit he was called to order by an irate London vicar and suspended from preaching by a bishop.   His actions, being the result of violent impulses, were unco-ordinated and each faded into oblivion when succeeded by another.   It would be unreasonable to expect a person of Kingsley's temperament to act consistently, more especially as he was in the beginning that rarest if most incalculable of all human beings, a completely unworldly person.   Later in life he lost this pristine quality and, as a family man, sought to advance his own interests in well-recognised ways.   Bigoted and testy in religion, he loathed everything 'Romish' and idealised everything 'English'.   His wife, his children, and his friends adored him, but he managed to raise up for himself a number of implacable enemies who saw to it that he got no preferment till within five years of his death.

Most authors learn to take the rough with the smooth when man-handled by reviewers, and, if they are not, like Keats, cut off by untimely death, devise their own methods of armouring themselves against the pricks and proddings of unfavourable publicity.   Charles Dickens, who was every bit as thin-skinned as Charles Kingsley, ignored his critics and affected to regard them as lice on the body of literature, but Kingsley mortified himself by reading what his reviewers had to say and allowed himself to be unutterably cast down by the cruelty of their attacks.   Both his first novels *Yeast* and *Alton Locke* were pilloried because the opinions of which they were the vehicle were held to be dangerous.   *Westward Ho!* on the other hand was welcomed as a powerful incentive to recruitment for the Crimean War and served to re-establish its author in the esteem of his own class which had been forfeited by the allegedly subversive trend of his earlier books.   *Hypatia* had the misfortune

to be labelled 'immoral', and was the ostensible excuse for with-
holding from him the honorary degree of D.C.L. at Oxford.
Over and over again in moments of depression did Charles
Kingsley resolve not to write another novel. In this resolve
his wife was always quick to second him, for not only did she
spend hours in taking down his words from dictation, but in
some cases made fair copies of his script. In addition to this
secretarial work, she had to endure all his neurotic misery and
disappointment at the way his first books were received, and nurse
him through the complete physical break-downs that followed.
These recurring crises often obliged the rector of Eversley to
reside for months together outside his parish at some health
resort like Torquay or Ilfracombe, but as soon as he felt tolerably
well again he would break his resolve not to write another novel
and start on a fresh book. Reading the Dickens serials and
noting the penetrative influence they exerted on people of every
age and class had convinced Kingsley that a novel of popular
appeal was the only effective form of propaganda. Moreover,
like Charles Dickens, he was under the necessity of making
money. He knew that a novel of almost any kind would
bring in more than the annual output of anonymous articles he
contributed to *Fraser's Magazine,* to say nothing of reaching a
far wider public. It was a great age for reading sermons, and
Mrs. Kingsley, a most practical woman, saw to it that her
husband's were published, either collected in volumes or singly.
She at one time maintained a surreptitious connection with
Good Words which absorbed his slighter effusions, sometimes
without the knowledge of their author.

Sir Francis Galton, who had been at Cambridge with Charles
Kingsley, often expressed interest in his heredity. Charles had
told him that on his mother's side he was 'descended from a pure
West Indian family of I am afraid to say how many generations'.
Local records show that his mother's father, Judge Lucas, was
one of the fifth generation of his name to be born in the Island
of Barbados. Charles, who hated the dry heat of meridional
France, mentioned to Galton that he revelled in 'the damp heat
of the tropics as in a climate congenial to his nature'. There is
nothing much in Fanny Kingsley's idealistic biography of her
husband to throw light on this matter, but embedded in it is a

letter, an appeal from a society proposing to help 'freedmen', which drew from Kingsley a protest peculiar for its bitterness and warmth of feeling.   It was written to his trusted friend, Tom Hughes.

> I am very glad these slaves are freed at whatever cost of blood and treasure.   But now what *do* they want from us? . . . What do they ask our money for, over and above.   I am personally shy of giving mine.   *The negro has had all I ever possessed; for emancipation has ruined me.*   And yet I would be ruined a second time, if emancipation had to be done over again.   I am no slave holder at heart.   But I have paid my share of the great bill, in Barbadoes and Demerara with a vengeance; and don't see myself called on to pay other men's.[1]

There is no way now of explaining this letter except by recording that Charles Kingsley's mother's mother brought plantations and slaves into her marriage settlement, and that his mother, on the death of her only brother in 1818, became sole heiress to the Lucas estates which included a Georgian house and land in Barbados, and property in British Guiana.   We may also note that Charles's younger brother, Henry, when trying to borrow money after his marriage, used to inform those he approached for assistance that on the death of his mother he would inherit £12,000, which for a youngest son was a fortune.   Even if we were able to accept Henry's statement, it would not serve to elucidate the meaning of his brother Charles's letter to Hughes, for as far as we know he never at any time owned money drawn from West Indian estates.

On his father's side Charles Kingsley's antecedents were New Forest squires deriving from Sir Ranulph de Kingsley of Delamere Forest in Cheshire whose 'bugle strung sable' they bore in their arms, but with his mother may have come in strains of a perhaps more mondial nature.   Apart from his grandfather's name, Nathan Lucas (which may or may not suggest a Jewish origin), there is a passage in a letter written by Charles Kingsley to a Jewish student in Edinburgh, saying that he is delighted to

[1] *Charles Kingsley*, vol. II. p. 258.

hear that his writings have been of use to any man, and above all to a Jew.

> For your nation I have a very deep love, first because so many friends of mine—and in one case a near connexion are Jews. . . . Moreover I owe all that I have ever said or thought about Christianity as the idea which is to redeem and leaven all human life . . . to the study of the Old Testament, without which the New is to me unintelligible; and I cannot love Hebrew books without loving the men who wrote them.[1]

The 'near connexion' may possibly have been his mother's father who had married Barbadian-born Mary Crookenden, or just conceivably it may have been an allusion to one of the Grenfells who came to London from Cornwall, where they seem to have been regarded locally as the descendants of Jewish emigrants from Portugal in the days of the Roman occupation of Britain. But this is too far-fetched to be seriously advanced as a solution of the riddle.

Among the causes that Kingsley at one time and another championed was that of equal rights for women. The experience of a blissful marriage to an exceptionally devoted and capable wife had convinced him of woman's eligibility to full partnership in business and in public affairs, while the reading of John Stuart Mill's treatise spurred him to advocate the emancipation of women in general. In the political position of women in his day he was quick to sense the nefast influence of monastic teaching. So obsessed did he become with this notion that he came to believe that a blow struck for equal rights was a blow at the heart of the 'Romish' Church.

It is interesting to note that some of the chief upheavals in Charles Kingsley's life were caused by books. Prominent among these were Montalembert's *Life of St. Elizabeth of Hungary*, F. D. Maurice's *Kingdom of Christ*, Darwin's *Origin of Species*, Newman's *Apologia*, Mill's *Subjection of Women*, and *Essays and Reviews* by a group of writers. Though unrelated to each other in theme and objective, all these books vitally affected his personal life and each produced its peculiar reaction.

In spite of his embracing love of nature in all her moods and

[1] *Ibid.* vol. I. p. 353.

metamorphoses, a love that welcomed such pets as natterjacks, slow-worms, soldier crabs, red-legged cockles, and other of the less demonstrative forms of animal existence, Charles Kingsley seems to have sat rather lightly to his personal life and to have had no love of living for its own sake. It was at a very early stage in his career that he began to regard 'a bed beneath the turf' as the most desirable of all resting places. Cordy Jeaffreson noted the same trait in Henry Kingsley when at Oxford. Henry seemed always to be longing for what he called ' "cheesy" death in the moment of a victory', such as winning 'the Diamond Sculls at Henley'. Over and over again did Charles wish his life were ended. Everyone will call to mind the last quatrain of his song, *Oh! that we two were Maying*, from his play *The Saint's Tragedy*. He was but twenty-three when he wrote it.

> Oh! that we two lay sleeping,
> In our nest in the churchyard sod ;
> With our limbs at rest on the quiet earth's breast,
> And our souls at home with God!

This detached attitude of mind may not in itself be an exotic characteristic in an Englishman, but combined with the form of collapse to which he was prone it suggests a strain not altogether northern. No one could say that Charles Kingsley was a physical weakling, for he managed to maintain his seat in the second Magdalene boat and could walk from Cambridge to London without undue fatigue, but when he put forth anything that was not physical energy, he soon became what he termed 'de-magnetised'. It was a condition he recognised as one to which he must immediately yield by taking refuge in the hammock ready slung in his study in winter and to the fir trees on the mount in summer. The resultant lassitude, which sometimes lasted for weeks or even months, might oblige him to rush off to breathe the life-giving air of his native Devonshire.

The assertion that Charles Kingsley was the prop and stay of muscular Christianity, 'the fear God and walk a thousand miles in a thousand hours' school, in the sense that Tom Hughes was, cannot be sustained. He detested the phrase and complained bitterly that it had been attached to him as a label when he took part in the Christian Socialist campaign. All Kingsley's fighting was carried on with a pen, and his combative resources may be seen at full strength in *Letters to Landlords* by 'Parson Lot' and in the anonymous pamphlet *Brave Words for Brave Soldiers* issued during the Crimean War. He had rushed moments of enthusiasm which involved him in unforeseen activities, but no staying power. By the age of fifty-six he had worn himself out in controversy, and a witty contemporary on hearing of his demise made an entry in his diary, 'So poor old Kingsley has row-ed himself to death at last'.

Chapter 2

THE PARENTAL BACKGROUND

*Our destiny is really nothing more than our character; our
character the result of our active and passive being, the sum,
the combination of all our capacities and gifts.*

RAHEL

IN viewing the career of Charles Kingsley's father, we should
perhaps remind ourselves that service in the Church of England was in Georgian days esteemed more as a profession than
a vocation. Being a state establishment directly under the
patronage of the government of the day it was accounted by the
more worldly clergy almost as a branch of the civil administration, leading, provided the approval of those in authority was
earned, to appointments under the Crown such as canonries,
bishoprics, and other dignified and well-paid posts. If other
openings failed, a graduate of Oxford or Cambridge could
always read for Orders and, assuming that he had any county
standing or other interest, might be certain of getting a living.
Charles Kingsley, senior, of Barttramsley House in the New
Forest, was a recruit to clerical ranks of this type. Brought
up to believe himself heir to a small fortune on which he could
live out his days as a country gentleman, he found after passing
through Harrow and Oxford that most of his inheritance had
been squandered by trustees and that there was little left to keep
him in comfort. Having spent the residue, he married Mary
Lucas, six years his junior, and at the age of thirty began looking
for a salaried job. Too old for the army, he decided on the
Church, sold his Barttramsley estate, and went up with his wife
to Cambridge to qualify at Trinity Hall as a clergyman.

At Cambridge, because of his interest in German, he attracted
the attention of Dr. Herbert Marsh, Lady Margaret Professor of
Divinity, soon to become Bishop of Peterborough. Dr. Marsh,
on the strength of having studied at Leipzig, and of having
written *A Comparative View of the Churches of England and
Rome*, had a great reputation for learning. Though he was

homely in appearance and wore a 'welsh' wig, many people stood in awe of him as he had a turn for vigorous and rather coarse pamphleteering. Opposed to Catholic Emancipation, he was what was called a Broad Churchman, did his utmost to keep men holding evangelical views out of his diocese, and yet was dead against the brightening and popularising of church services by the introduction of music. When appointed to the bishopric of Peterborough he and his wife did their best to humanise the cold, empty palace which they had to occupy. That they only managed to furnish a room or two, and those scantily, is evidence that the problem of making such huge houses habitable was almost as acute then as it is now. Ordinands visiting the bishop for interviews reported that they found him sitting rather miserably at a small writing desk in the middle of a vast apartment. The discomfort in which he was forced to live did not affect his health, nor prevent him from making use of the privilege of power. While tutoring Charles Kingsley at Cambridge he had marked him down for special employment, the first step in his deliberate plan being to ordain the elderly graduate to a curacy in the Fen district from which he was transferred after a short apprenticeship to be curate-in-charge of Holne-under-Dartmoor.

Charles Kingsley's eldest son, Gerald, was born before he went to Devonshire, but his second son, Charles, made his first appearance in the thatched parsonage at Holne, a cosily sheltered house overlooking Dartmoor Chase. The little clerical family were next moved to Burton-on-Trent and then to North Clifton near Newark. While at Newark the rector received notice of appointment to the best living in the Peterborough diocese, Barnack near Stamford. The appointment carried with it the condition that Mr. Kingsley must vacate the cure as soon as the bishop's son, at the time aged seventeen, had taken Orders. This in effect meant keeping the place warm for six years at least, and in the long run was to mean a good deal more than that to one member of the Kingsley family, for Barnack was on the edge of the Fens and into the consciousness of Charles the younger seeped the mystery, charm, and unique atmosphere of the horizonless fenlands. We may see the outcome of this experience in a novel published nearly forty years later, *Hereward the Wake*, as well as in *Prose Idylls* wherein he recalled halcyon days spent by 'dark alders and pale green weeds, wherein the coot clanked and the bittern boomed', where he had watched the ruffs trampling the sedge, listened to the trumpet-note of the wild swan and pursued that 'most exquisite of English butterflies the great copper', while high overhead 'hung motionless hawk upon hawk, buzzard upon buzzard, kite upon kite as far as the eye could see'.

Barnack rectory, a rambling fourteenth-century house, had its ghostly legends and a certain remoteness from common-place life that made it the ideal cocoon for a sensitive boy to develop in.   But Charles in his twelfth year had with the rest of his family to leave this nest of contentment to make way for the incumbency of young Mr. Marsh, and he was next to find himself in lodgings at Ilfracombe.   The fenlands from being a playground became a background, but never were the meres, the reed-beds, the water-fowl of that undrained wilderness forgotten.   His father did not share his regrets for the mists of summer, or for the clean winds that swept so coldly across the marshes, for he suffered from ague and had with a feeling of intense relief jumped at the living of Clovelly tendered to him by Sir John Hamlyn Williams of Clovelly Court.

By the time they left Barnack Charles's elder brother, Gerald, had joined the Navy, and Herbert, the next to him in age, was eighteen months his junior.   Younger still were George and Charlotte who, according to Mary Kingsley, indulged their wild jealousy of their new baby brother, Henry, by placing him in a wheelbarrow and pushing the wheelbarrow into Barnack pond whence it was recovered just in time by the gardener. Henry, born in 1830, had no memories of the fenlands, since at a few months old he was bundled off to Devonshire.   When grown up it was on Chelsea that his imagination played, for from six to eighteen it formed the background of his life.   We may see in reading *The Hillyars and the Burtons* how lovingly he recalled the river banks, the excursions to Penge Wood to catch butterflies (a site selected later on for the Crystal Palace); to Kew Green to gather 'wild tulips' (*fritillaria*); to the Norwood fields for mushrooms; to the lonely pond at Clapham where water-lilies floated, and fishing from a punt at Battersea

Bridge, close to the old Tudor houses that are a feature of his novel.

Charles's mother, a lover of sunshine and warmth, was as delighted as his father to quit East Anglia and settle at Clovelly, where she found much to admire in the singular beauty of the place and the good looks of the parishioners. Both, to her mind, were tinged with something of romance and poetic feeling. In after years her girl, Charlotte, described the steep stair-like street of Clovelly, and the toy-like terrace of four or five houses garnished with myrtles and fuchsias from whence, four hundred feet below, the sea could be discerned breaking and shimmering while across the bay gleamed yellow sands. Charles was also to describe the place in one of his earliest articles in *Fraser's Magazine*.

The two older boys devoted themselves during that first summer, under their father's guidance, to the study of seaweeds, shells, and wild flowers, and the younger children, instructed by their mother, did the same. In her preface to *Ferny Combes*, Charlotte speaks of the deep pleasure she had derived from 'the awakening and fostering within her as a child of the love of nature', and adds that it was to her beloved parents that she 'owed this life-long happiness'.

At the close of an enchanting holiday Charles and Herbert were packed off to Clifton and placed in the charge of the Rev. John Knight, keeper of a small preparatory school there. Charles, after the first term, was reported by his master to be of a very gentle disposition and to prefer spending his spare time in the company of his daughters and their governess than in playing with his schoolmates. He highly praised the boy's translations of Latin into English verse, an accomplishment drilled into him by his father. Herbert seems to have been a much more normal type of boy and to have taken kindly to games and other diversions. Charles was already beginning to feel himself what he told his mother he really was, 'a unique kind of person, utterly unlike others'.

One of the indelible family memories of Clovelly was that of a wrecked ship being pounded by mountainous waves. The Kingsleys first sighted it in daylight as a great barque, foremast and bowsprit gone and with a few rags of sails fluttering from the mizzen mast.   Clovelly fishermen, essaying a rescue, were watched closely from the beach by women and children who clung to rocks or warped themselves to posts for safety from the waves.   Darkness increased the excitement and tension. Sudden breaks in the scudding clouds let through gleams of moonlight and candles stuck in the bayonet sockets of coast-guards lit the faces in the crowd up fitfully while the ship creaked and crashed against the rocks.   Every one of the writing Kings-leys—Charles, Charlotte, and Henry—made use of this incident in a novel, but it was not the only sea tragedy on which they had to draw, for men of the herring fleet from time to time struck a patch of bad weather and, abandoning their nets, would run for home which they sometimes reached as corpses cast up on the pebbly beach.   Henry worked these episodes into *Ravenshoe*, Charlotte into *Over the Cliffs*, and Charles into *Two Years Ago*.

Almost inadvertently, in the autumn of 1831, Charles was drawn into the vortex of the Reform Bill riots in Bristol, an experience that coloured and conditioned his mind to an extent unrealised at the time, but which became self-evident in maturity when he became the champion of Rajah Brooke and the defender of Governor Eyre.   One Sunday afternoon, sullen with rain, he watched a fog-cloud hanging densely over the lower parts of the city of Bristol.   His curiosity gave way to utter astonish-ment when the fog-cloud appeared to be shot through by flames which, increasing rapidly, met and merged into a sheet of fire. The 'mass of the burning', he tells us, seemed to come from just behind Brandon Hill and gave that mound the semblance of a volcano 'from the peak of which the flame streamed up, not red above, but delicately green and blue, pale rose and pearly white, while crimson sparks leapt and fell again in the midst of the rainbow'.   Bristol, of course, was out of bounds to the boys of the Clifton school, but Charles, too excited to think of rules, slipped off to the dock quarter of the city and for a time watched the soldiers sitting motionless on their horses, while blood streamed from their heads and faces.   Though the sight infuriated the boy, it implanted in him for ever a sense of the high value of discipline in an emergency.

Three weeks earlier the Reform Bill had been rejected by the House of Lords, and the reformers of Bristol, like the reformers of Nottingham, decided that the moment was opportune for a protest. Responsibility for maintaining order in the city appears to have rested uncertainly on two sets of shoulders, those of a Colonel of fifty known as 'the inspecting field officer' and those of the Mayor. The Mayor's authority, however, was at the moment cramped by the presence in Bristol of the Recorder of the city, Sir Charles Wetherall, who had just arrived to hold his sessions. Some went so far as to say that it was the advent of this extremely unpopular opponent of Reform on the previous Friday that had provoked the riot. At all events Sir Charles was conscious that his presence was violently resented by the crowds in the streets, and he slipped quietly away on the Saturday prior to the scene described by Charles Kingsley. On the Sunday morning the rioters forced the two prisons open and wrecked them. They treated the Guildhall, the official residences of both Mayor and Bishop and some forty private houses in the same way. No one took it upon himself to control the mob and the colonel on the spot merely instructed his men that no blood must be shed. No one was rounded up, no one arrested, and the rioters without interference set fire to spirit stores and broached the barrels they contained. Drunken people were soon to be seen lying senseless under the drip of the molten lead that began to run from the roofs of the blazing buildings. On the third day some outside authority intervened and the troops were at last ordered to disperse the looters, none of whom, as it turned out, had a firelock between them. The disorder had by that time lasted well over fifty hours.

Charles Kingsley actually saw casks of spirits flowing in the street gutters and half-crazed rioters, who were kneeling to lap up the brandy, suddenly overwhelmed by flames. To the ears of the horrified boy the fiery stream coursed along with a sinister hissing sound as it instantaneously transformed the drinkers into blackened corpses. Many years later people were inclined to gibe at Kingsley for combining the profession of Chartism with the belief that law and order must be strictly maintained at all costs, but those who did so had little notion whence he had derived his 'prejudice' against all forms of social disorder.

On the Tuesday afternoon when the rioting was over,

Charles stole back into the Bristol streets and made his way to the ruins on the north side of Queen Square where he saw neatly laid out a row, not of complete corpses, but of fragments of human bodies. The sight of a charred bundle, with a scrap of ragged petticoat adhering to it, haunted him for years. How despicable had been the behaviour of those in authority, of the absconding Recorder, of the terrified Mayor, of the supine field officer! That no one had dared to assume responsibility for reading the Riot Act and giving the order, if necessary, for a volley to be fired into the crowd was to him an astonishing and searing experience, from which he carried away the lesson that the evasion of responsibility in a public functionary was the basest of crimes.

While the boys were at Clifton their parents debated whether to send them to a public school or not. Dr. Hawtrey of Eton would, it is said, have been glad to take Charles and so would Dr. Arnold of Rugby, but for reasons connected with his abnormal shyness and difficulty of enunciation they decided to send both Charles and Herbert to the Grammar School at Helston in Cornwall of which their friend the Rev. Derwent Coleridge, son of Samuel Taylor Coleridge, was headmaster. Charles always regretted this decision, for nothing short of a public-school education would, he believed, have taught him to overcome his fear of people.

One day in the autumn of 1832 Mr. Kingsley appeared at Helston with his two boys, the elder tall, slight, eager, and as the master was to find on closer acquaintance, 'original to the verge of eccentricity', and the younger who had nothing remarkable about him. The impediment in Charles's speech did not at first strike Mr. Coleridge as very noticeable, but as time went on it seemed to become more and more pronounced. The curriculum at the Grammar School was broken into by sickness. Charles caused his parents great anxiety by contracting English cholera, which left him with a lifelong intestinal weakness. Mercifully he escaped the Asiatic species that was also ravaging parts of Cornwall. Hardly had he recovered than his brother fell ill with rheumatic fever. Though the convalescence appeared to the doctor to be taking a normal course, Charles was hurriedly summoned one afternoon to his brother's bedside.

So horrified was he to find Herbert stretched and motionless that he gave an anguished shriek which was heard by the boys in the recreation room. A voice told him what he already understood, that Herbert was dead.

After his brother's death Charles became more solitary in his ways and snatched at every chance of going out alone, geological hammer in hand, to explore gravel pits and rocks. No one who has ever chipped a small ammonite out of a lump of limestone, or picked up fossil oyster shells, cockles, or 'thunderbolts' in quarries, can fail to remember how satisfying such investigations can be. In summer he avoided games and would strap a botanical case to his shoulder and go hunting for flowers and mosses. Occasionally, in bad weather, he tried his hand at writing verse.

Grief for Herbert's loss and fear for Charles's future made his parents consider removing him from the Grammar School before he had completed the full educational course, but in the end they decided to leave him where he was. A schoolfellow, Cowley Powles, tells stories of Charles's endurance of pain, tree-climbing, and bird's-nesting. He also refers to his incompetence at games and general unpopularity.

In 1836 Mr. Kingsley was offered a living in London by Lord Cadogan. It was that of Chelsea, and in accepting it he became answerable for a very large parish and services in two churches. The incumbent, Dr. the Hon. Gerald Wellesley, aged sixty-six, son of Lord Mornington, and son-in-law of Lord Cadogan, was about to retire to a prebendal stall at Durham.

When Charles heard from his mother that owing to the move to London he would soon have to leave Helston, he was rather cast down, for in his own way he was contented in Cornwall since he could do what he liked with his spare time. In a letter of acknowledgement showing that the thought of London was more alarming than attractive, he requested his parents, if they were arranging for him to continue his education there, to find a Cambridge man to coach him in mathematics without interfering with his classics. Not long after Charles had settled in his new home, his ex-master, Derwent Coleridge, was made Warden of the College of St. Mark, Chelsea, an appointment that may be put down to the influence of the new rector on his patron.

Some twelve years before Mr. Kingsley went to reside in Chelsea, a very large new church dedicated to St. Luke had been opened in Sydney Street to supplement the old church down by the river which held but a village congregation. Designed by James Savage, this edifice at the time of its erection was regarded as a striking architectural experiment. Casual sightseers viewing the roof of the church from within could not understand how it was supported, and even architects were inclined to be sceptical about the balance of its strains and stresses and to wonder as to its stability. No greater contrast could be imagined than that between this elaborately buttressed Gothic structure and a church of almost identical date, St. Pancras, an exact imitation of the Erechtheum, so far as London was concerned, and the culminating achievement of the classic tradition.

As soon as the new rector arrived he was shown over the church and told a tale that in ten years had become something like a legend. At an evening service held by Dr. Wellesley's curate, Mr. Sankey, it had been arranged that divine worship should conclude with a hymn to be sung during a special collection. The men on duty in the roof, who were responsible for the lighting, had not been notified of this and began all too soon to lower the six large chandeliers to the aisle so that their lamps could be extinguished. Suddenly the organist, whose fingers were on the keys and eyes on the reflecting mirror, got the impression that the roof itself was coming down. The congregation, which had developed the same fear, sprang to its feet, panicked, and clambered over the backs of the pews to get away, as they did not dare to venture into the centre aisle. Everyone was jumpy and roof-conscious for everyone had heard the church spoken of as a 'paste-board structure'. When the flustered worshippers got to the door they realised what had happened and returned to their seats. The curate, who had been unable to unlatch the door of his prayer-desk, had clambered out and the congregation was amazed to see him gathering up his ample cassock to vault back into his place for the last verses of the hymn. His behaviour was severely commented on by Dr. Wellesley.

To Chelsea rectory, a spacious Georgian house set in a large garden, Mr. and Mrs. Kingsley took three children younger than Charles, George aged ten, Charlotte aged nine, and Henry aged six. They were all delighted with their new surroundings for they had plenty of ground to play in, a mulberry tree that showered down fruit, and close at hand the still rural banks of the Thames. Charles at seventeen found nothing in these amenities to console him for the loss of the wild countryside. From his point of view it was a miserable exchange, and it made him resolve to eschew London so soon as he could choose a life for himself. He was odd man out in the rectory circle, for the children looked on him as just another grown-up and his parents were far too busy taking up their new work to have any time for him. Loneliness and depression, however, had the effect of steeling his determination to work hard and make a place for himself in the world.

Mr. Kingsley was now responsible, not for hundreds of souls as at Clovelly, but for thousands. Chelsea from having been a village was, owing to the development of the Cadogan estate, rapidly becoming urbanised. Both husband and wife took their duties very seriously and set themselves to organise the parish by districts and form classes and committees to carry out the activities they planned. Charles heard no talk other than that about vestries, schools, curates, and clubs: he saw none but what he called 'splay-footed beings three-fourths of whom can't sing and the other quarter sing miles out of tune with voices like love-sick parrots'. Numbers of young women came forward to offer their services as district visitors, and it shocked him to find that they were being sent to 'abominable scenes of wretchedness, indecency and filth in order to read the Bible to the degraded people who live in these slums'. At all hours and at all meals he heard the ceaseless buzz of parochial discussion, an experience he never forgot, for when he had a rectory of his own, he made it a rule that 'shop' must never be mentioned at meals or in front of the children.

So absorbed were his parents in parish work that they had no time left for amusement. It was against their principles either to go to the play themselves or to permit their children to visit a theatre or be taught dancing. Home life was entirely submerged in parish business, a fact that made Charles only too thankful to be entered as a student at King's College. His daylight hours would at least be completely occupied and in the evening he could shut himself up in his bedroom and read. His two years at King's College thus became an opportunity for grinding work and for winning approval from tutors of classics, history, and philosophy.   Mathematics never came easily to him, and, speaking generally, he still made an impression upon his elders not only of awkwardness, but of great timidity.

In the autumn of 1838 he went up to Cambridge and did well enough in the examinations to win a scholarship at Magdalene College.   Writing to his father he said, 'I am first in classics and mathematics also, which has not happened in the College for several years and shall bring home prizes—a very decent portion of honour . . . I am so happy I hardly know what to say, you know I am not accustomed to be successful.'   At Cambridge he took to smoking a clay-pipe which he fancied helped him through his bouts of congenital nervousness, and clay-pipes were to be a great stand-by at Eversley, where almost every hollow tree or rabbit-hole formed the cache for these vehicles of inspirational puffs.

Cambridge meant for Charles escape into a free world and the chance of distinction.   Just after his first term at Magdalene his father exchanged duties for two months with the rector of Checkenden near Ipsden in Oxfordshire and moved with his entire family to its rectory.   This transfer to the country was fraught with important and rather strange consequences for his second son.

Chapter 3

ONE ROAD TO DAMASCUS?

Give me thy wings, thy wings of faith
And I with thee will cleave the skies
And bound on the eternal wheel
My God may take his sacrifice.

IF we knew nothing of Charles Kingsley's personal life, we should, in reading his works, soon come to realise how deeply he believed in the elevating influence of noble passion. He proclaimed in his writings that the love of man for woman was the greatest of all forces for good. He saw love as 'the star for every wandering bark', and the worship of a lofty feminine character as the means given to man for saving his soul. This assurance is really the central point of his gospel, proof of which may be found in *Yeast*, *Two Years Ago*, and other books. He was very young when he made this discovery, just twenty, but by extreme good fortune the vision that dazzled him then dazzled him to the end.

One summer afternoon there came to the Checkenden garden Miss Frances Grenfell, the Spanish-looking daughter of Pascoe Grenfell of Taplow Court. Dark-eyed, raven-haired, self-possessed, accustomed to luxury and the ways of the fashionable world, she that day made acquaintance with a lanky, stuttering undergraduate seven years younger than herself. His manner of presenting himself was gawky, his voice rough, but neither his shyness, his stammer, nor his callowness seemed to affect her immediate appreciation of his real merit. What perhaps is even stranger is that Miss Grenfell's directness of manner and approach did not embarrass the unsophisticated student. As if under some strong inner compulsion he at once responded to her advance and the two of them in an instant fell—in Fanny Grenfell's phrase—into 'a state of complete mutual understanding'. When four years later, after many conscience searchings on her part, they were married, each said to the other, 'The day we first met was our wedding day'. They even called their first glance at each other 'eye-wedlock', and we shall find Charles Kingsley, when he comes to write the story of his own courtship in *Yeast*, making the hero, Lancelot, and the heroine, Argemone, describe their first look at each other in these terms. And all his life Charles was to think his Fanny's eyes the most wonderful eyes he had ever seen. Edmund Gosse tells how as a small boy he peeped in on a party in which Kingsley was figuring as a lion, and heard a slow deep voice saying, 'There is one thing I consider more beautiful than anything else in the world'—silence fell on the expectant company, as the voice boomed on, 'my wife's eyes'.[1]

Frances Grenfell, 'Fanny' to her family and friends, was an orphan and one of eleven sisters. Her father, who was twice married, had died in 1838 and her mother, his second wife, in 1837. For guardian and trustee she had her middle-aged half-brother, Pascoe Grenfell, and for companions her sisters Charlotte and Georgina, both unmarried and older than herself. In describing her first impression of Charles Kingsley she says that his face had 'a hungry, wistful expression of longing as if he were on the look out for the human sympathy no one had, as yet, extended to him'. When they came to discuss religion openly, she discovered a man 'full of doubts and very, very serious'. Nearly every day during those two sunny months at Ipsden did these predestined beings contrive to meet, and as the outcome of their intercourse 'a new life dawned for both of them'. Neither at this time nor for long afterwards did Frances Grenfell entertain any thought of Kingsley as a possible husband. At the time they first met she was a pious High Churchwoman and about to enrol herself in the sisterhood established under Dr. Pusey's care and influence in Park Village, Regent's Park. This, as Charles Kingsley thought, mistaken resolution roused in him all his fighting and rescuing instincts. Somehow or another he must save so clever and beautiful a girl from becoming the victim of a most perverted decision. The mere idea of celibacy in either man or woman was violently irritating to this rectory-bred youth, who soon developed the doctrine that true

[1] G. S. Lanyard, the *Times*, June 14, 1919.

Christianity was opposed to all forms of asceticism and Mani-cheism, the most dangerous of all heresies.

The kind of young men with whom Frances Grenfell had been in the habit of conversing were, it is clear, totally unlike Charles Kingsley. They would almost certainly have looked down on him as rather an unpresentable creature and, just conceivably, a bore. He drove his family mad with his stammering, patient though they were, and strangers were apt to avoid him after a first encounter. It was miraculous that he should meet anyone who thought him 'a rare being' and found it 'a feast to her imagination and intellect to hold communion with him'. He had much to tell her, for to no member of his family had he ever confided his secrets. At no time had he been able to speak frankly to either father or mother, for fear of shocking them by expressing his opinions. Their simple, con-ventional piety had, he explained, choked him off religion and made him hate its compulsory profession. He had no idea what career to follow, it might possibly be the Law, but would certainly never be the Church. What an amazing release and relief to him it was to pour into the receptive, untiring ears of Frances Grenfell the depressing story of his doubts, his solitari-ness, his imaginings, his failings, his longing for rest! Habitu-ally grave, he never at this time, nor indeed at any time, was seen to laugh. John Martineau, his pupil and friend, who never laughed himself, records this as unique in his experience of men. Charles told Frances that he was not only bored and irritated by religious observance, but that he had altogether ceased to believe in the existence of God. 'And if you don't believe in God, you get into bad ways, you know,' he added. He was not doing any work at Cambridge because he didn't believe in anything, and had spent his first year duck-shooting, card-playing, fencing, and 'boxing with a full-blooded negro'. And always Frances listened intently and wanted to hear more. Encouraged by her evident absorption in his story he went on to tell of his fishing excursions before sunrise, of his flighting on Sir Charles Wade's estate, Shelford, of his exorcism of his own private devils in hand-gallops after his geological tutor, Sedgwick. And all his outpourings seemed to draw him nearer and nearer to Frances, for, as she put it, their progressive intimacy partook more of the nature of 'mysterious recognition' than ordinary friendship. In some curious inexplicable way they were affecting each other's fate and faith.

From the moment that Frances learnt that Charles never opened the Bible, never said prayers, and was totally indifferent to all aspects of Christian practice, she knew herself to be the chosen instrument for his conversion and, like the heroine of *Yeast*, set herself to instruct him in the beliefs she so tenaciously held. Every intelligent person, she assured him, went through a rationalistic phase, but every really intelligent person came through it. Could he not, to please her, read a portion of the Bible daily? and could he not put up a prayer that 'Light from above' might be granted him? and can he not cease from railing against asceticism, which, after all, was a recognised means of grace? But through that idyllic summer all the light Charles Kingsley needed he found shining from Fanny's eyes, and so far as celestial illumination went, he parted with her as much in outer darkness as before.

When Charles was back at Cambridge talks were replaced by letters, and letters gave fresh openings for discussion and advice. Though set on saving her from celibacy, Charles found that a young woman of Fanny's character was tough to persuade. She believed in the virginal life and held tenaciously to her conviction. As time went on the situation defined itself as an effort on Fanny's part to re-convert Charles to Christianity and an effort on Charles's part to convince Fanny that marriage was a higher vocation than virginity. They were both very serious, and set to work with a will defining the Trinity, discussing baptismal regeneration, and dissecting the Athanasian Creed. On questions of doctrine Charles was incisive.

I hope you do not hold the Romish Church's views about baptismal purity. Original sin is not done away with at baptism; the Romish Church asserts it is. Our Article denies this, 'The infection,' it says, 'doth remain, yea, even in those that are regenerate,' and if this be the case, baptismal purity is a non-entity, and the Oxford clap-trap, 'Wash your baptismal robe white again with the tears of penance,' a pretty school-boy metaphor.

And as he repeatedly drummed into her, 'In the ascetic view of sacred human ties, I detect principles, which, if adopted, would sap the two divine roots of the Church of England—the ideas of family and national life'. While considering this problem, he fell in with a book that for him contained cogent proof of the truth of his contention. It was the *Life of St. Elizabeth of Hungary* by Montalembert. Though written from the Catholic standpoint, when read by Kingsley with Protestant intention it seemed a wonderful demonstration of the folly, indeed the wickedness, of a system that encouraged a girl to practise asceticism within marriage. Presently Ambrose de Lisle Phillipps, a Roman Catholic, brought out a translation of the *Life* printed as a folio with an illuminated title page. On turning its pages ideas of confutation began to incubate in Charles's head, though for the time being no result was apparent.

Again and again did he assure Fanny that he was honestly seeking for truth and that his dearest Cambridge friend, Charles Mansfield, a scientist, was teaching him not to be afraid of truth 'wherever it might lead him'. Mansfield was what men called a materialist, but to Kingsley his materialism was more spiritual than other men's spirituality. In Charles Mansfield Miss Grenfell scented a rival, maybe a hostile, influence, and perhaps she was right, for Dr. Stubbs, Bishop of Ely, declares that while Kingsley was at the University 'Mansfield was to him what Hallam had been to Alfred Tennyson'. In the end, however, it was Frances who dominated Kingsley despite the entwining friendship that lasted until Mansfield's early death.

Like many young people before and since his day, Charles Kingsley marvelled that out of the translucent simplicity of the Gospel story and the Sermon on the Mount so elaborate a superstructure of theology should ever have been erected. Of what use was theology? Was it philosophically true, and if so what bearing could it possibly have on every-day life and conduct? How could the noblest study of man be man? was that not nonsense? how could it compare with the study of Nature? Would that Fanny would use her senses more and her 'deep and delicate' mind less! Has it never occurred to her, as it has to him, that the brain might almost be a fungoid growth? If one yielded to the promptings of intuition and the inward surge of the soul, was one not compelled to fall on one's knees in sheer worship of Nature? Should we not feed on Nature, study sky, trees, water? and should we not all read geology, the one science that strikes awe into the mind and forces us to reach after and cling to God? In this frame of mind he wrote one of his first poems, *Palinodia*, the last lines of which run as follows

> Oh hear me, Nature!
> Receive me once again: but not alone;
> No more alone Great Mother! I have brought
> One who has wandered, yet not sinned, like me.
> Upon thy lap, twin children, let us lie;
> And in the light of thine immortal eyes
> Let our souls mingle, till the Father calls
> To some eternal home the charge He gives thee.

The reflections embedded in his letters and in these lines remind one how far was Charles Kingsley from John Henry Newman even in his pantheistic leanings. Some may remember that when Newman stayed with the Froudes at Dartington rectory he would not allow himself to be beguiled by the beauty of fields and foliage. Putting all that from him he wrote:

> There strayed amid the woods of Dart
> One who could love them, but who durst not love;
> A vow had bound him, ne'er to give his heart
> To streamlet bright or soft secluded grove.

The books sent by Miss Grenfell to Cambridge included Coleridge's *Aids to Reflection*, Carlyle's *French Revolution*, and F. D. Maurice's *Kingdom of Christ*. The first two works had the rather unexpected result of convincing Kingsley that 'there must be a God eternal in the Heavens to which the world must be conformed'. But it was the *The Kingdom of Christ* that helped to crystallise, if one may truthfully use this expression of anything Kingsley thought, his decision to accept Christianity pragmatically, to accept it in theory that is to say because it seemed to work well in practice. In a letter written in 1851 we find him recommending it as the book 'that settled my mind for me when I was in a very puzzled state and taught me to see good in all sects and parties, Unitarians and all'. *The Kingdom of Christ* was dedicated to Derwent Coleridge and is described by the author as 'Hints to a Quaker respecting the

Principles, Constitution and Ordinances of the Catholic Church'. It covers a great field of controversy and after explaining the failure of the Quakers, the Pure Protestants, the Romanists and the Unitarians to establish a Kingdom of God among men, maintains 'on the authority of Scripture that the Catholic Church he has in mind is a kingdom for *mankind*, a Kingdom grounded upon the union which has been established in Christ between God and man'. After studying the book, which is very long and detailed, Kingsley began to attend chapel daily. Fanny noted 'a great change in him', for soon she began to get rhetorical screeds saying that he felt 'saved' from 'the darkling tempest of scepticism and from the sensuality and dissipation into which he had drifted' before meeting her. For a long while, if not all his life, Charles Kingsley used *The Kingdom of Christ* as his text-book of belief.

From contemporaries at Cambridge we learn that Kingsley was known as 'odd', 'cracky', 'lazy', though carefully praised for the way he stuck to rowing and tried to be athletic. One, Barstow by name, reports that Charles Kingsley did little work and often asked for help in finishing papers so that he might have something to hand in to his tutor. To Fanny he complained of having to drudge at acquiring 'obsolete knowledge and worn out philosophies'. 'How was it', he enquired of her, that 'every woman who had made even moderate use of her opportunities and time was far beyond him in true philosophy?' By degrees he surrendered to soft but persistent pressure and came to think he must 'attain prestige' somehow or other. He even wondered whether Fanny might not be right in saying 'that a clergyman's life was the one best suited to his physique and morale' and whether he might not be capable of becoming Fanny's 'beau ideal, a devoted parish priest'. Once he had begun to think like this little extra persuasion was needed to get him to remove his name from the roll at Lincoln's Inn and turn his thoughts towards a clerical career. 'A change', says Fanny, 'he never regretted for one moment.'

Though Charles had come to rely on Fanny for spiritual guidance and had assured her that if ever he came to believe whole-heartedly in Christianity it would be in the sense in which she believed it, he did not give up his idea of altering her Tractarian outlook. In a letter to his mother he says, 'Help me to wean her from this pernicious superstition. I say *me* because I feel that in Doctrinal and Polemical Theology *I* must hereafter be her guide, while *she* is mine, thank God, in Christian practice.'

By the early winter of 1840, that is some eighteen months after their first encounter, the doctrinal conflict was suddenly resolved, for they realised and had to admit that they loved each other deeply, passionately, unreservedly, for all time and for eternity. Of this transcendent experience Fanny spoke to no one. Despite her silence a new factor in the situation now had to be reckoned with—Grenfell disapproval. Her sisters had not failed to notice that letters from Cambridge arrived by every post, were eagerly snatched at and immediately replied to. To be absorbed in such an intercourse and never to breathe a word about it was more than odd! What was the obsession, the infatuation as they preferred to term it, of which their poor sister was the victim? Georgina and Charlotte alike were deeply hurt at the way they were treated by one who had hitherto given them her confidence. Surely, surely, Fanny could not be carrying on a love-affair with a penniless under-graduate? And yet she bore every sign of doing so, for she no longer cared about dining out and tried to absent herself from all the parties in which she had once delighted. She spent more and more time alone in her room or on solitary walks. Their brother Pascoe when consulted roundly declared that it was the business of the family to put an end to such nonsense in any way that could be devised. What about sending her abroad, he asked; she was fond of foreign travel and Lady Gainsborough might be requested to chaperon her to Germany where she was going to take a cure. The three of them put their heads together and when their arrangements were complete informed Fanny that it was their wish that she should go for some months to the Continent, that she must stop exchanging letters with Charles Kingsley and return to him all the letters he had written to her. To these conditions Fanny for the time being submitted and in a last interview with her lover before leaving England arranged that they should say the same prayers daily at the same hour. These took the form of clauses in the Litany. After the petition ending 'and to turn their hearts', Charles Kingsley wrote:

That it may please thee to turn the hearts of our families and to teach them thy truth!

That it may please thee to allow us to meet in heaven!

That it may please thee to join us together in holy matrimony, in the days of our youth and our health!

That it may please thee to preserve us through the miseries and dangers of celibacy, and to sanctify to us this our great affliction, that by it we may become more worthy both of each other and of thee.

During the summer a portrait of Frances Grenfell was exhibited at the Academy. Charles went to see it and wrote to his mother from Cambridge:

I saw her picture in the Exhibition yesterday—you cannot think how horribly ugly they have made her—he has given her a pair of little staring glassy eyes—stuck close together, a huge heavy red round jaw and the expression one of amazed, impertinent ill-temper. Can I bear such things? And a Scot plaid dress—the ugliest thing possible in make and colour. The worst of it all is that with all this, it is *unmistakably like*. That drove me furious.[1]

Separation acted like fuel on Fanny's passion for Charles. It blazed up into a long series of unposted letters penned between April 14, 1841, and April 30, 1842. Written to commence with on sheets of note-paper pinned together in pamphlet form, at Baden she bought a red note-book in which to inscribe every phase of her love, unhappiness, devotion and complete absorption in her lover. Suddenly she seemed to have no other life, Charles was her life and she would tell him so every day though he would never read what she had written. These vibrating, passionate letters were kept by Fanny till her death and then by the oversight of executors found their way into the bleak publicity of a London auction room. How she tormented herself at Frankfort, Marienbad, Carlsbad and indeed in every place she visited. A few, very few, undemonstrative letters from Charles reached her while abroad; it was almost as if he were trying to break the intercourse off in deference to some representation made to him from outside. For the first time she is not sure of his sympathy and understanding. Someone evi-

[1] Add. MSS. B.M.

dently has caused him to feel that he is regarded as an adventurer luring an heiress into marriage. These rare and
cautious letters upset Fanny very much, for her adoration of
her lover was complete and made her count every day spent
away from him as pure loss. In November she returned to
London and went to Chelsea Rectory to see Charles's mother.
From her she learnt that tutors at Cambridge had reported a
vast improvement in Kingsley's work and that the papers he
had sent up for the classical tripos during the last weeks at
Magdalene were said to be of high quality. Mrs. Kingsley had
her family pride and it was agreed between her and her future
daughter-in-law that no meeting honourable to Charles could
take place. Fanny had screwed up her courage to have an outspoken discussion with her family and that this must be timed
to take place after the examination results had been announced.

In the end, Charles to Fanny's intense relief, took a first in
classics and was senior optime in mathematics, but the strain
he had put himself through in cramming two years' work into
six months resulted in severe pains in the head, to reduce the
agonies of which leeches were applied. When this trial was
over he asked his mother to write to Holne, his birthplace, to
secure a lodging in which he could lie fallow for a while. He
tells her that he feels desperately lonely and expects to be an
old man before he turns forty, because he belongs 'to that order
of mortals who do become old in their youth and die in middle-
age'. He adds:

> God bless you and if you rejoice that you have borne a man into
> the world, remember that he is not one like common men—neither
> cleverer, nor wiser, nor better than the multitude, but *utterly*
> different from them in heart and mind.

It is a great point in Kingsley's favour that Grenfell disapproval put new heart into him and made him realise more
forcibly than before the high importance of showing what stuff
he was made of. With Fanny as the prize there was no race
he could not run.

In talking of his work at Cambridge Kingsley averred that
he had done his utmost to win the title of 'man of promise'.
To use his own words, 'It was obvious that I must attack

Mammon with the weapons Mammon could feel and appreciate, and the only weapon I could at the moment arm myself with was the qualification of a good degree'. He had been decried as a penniless adventurer and at all costs he must prove himself worthy of his bride by showing his mettle to her rich and contemptuous relations. His mother thought he was taking things too hard and was inclined to grieve over his condition, but he told her not to fret; he was strong, Fanny was strong, they could both wait and endure 'and be happy beyond the grave if not on this side'. He treated his mother throughout his love-affair with every confidence, and gave her his exact impressions of Fanny's relations. Charlotte Grenfell, the future Mrs. Froude, seems to have annoyed him a good deal, but he was anxious Fanny should not hear of it. 'If she suspects the truth she dare not believe it and it is not for me to make her miserable by the conviction that her sister is but common clay.'

After coming down from Cambridge Charles continued to work at a secret manuscript designed to shatter Fanny's last defences, the 'Life of Elizabeth of Hungary'—a work he hoped to offer to his love on their wedding day.

Some time in April Fanny, stiffened by the knowledge of Charles's success in his final examinations, made up her mind to tell her brother and sisters what she intended to do. They were far from sympathetic. Georgina told her to break off the engagement at once, and Charlotte did the same. As for Pascoe, he said he would 'never countenance' such a marriage. Between them they made Fanny feel her conduct had been mean and underhand. Such love they told her was like a Jonah's gourd grown in a night and perishing in a night. Her 'high and happy position in the family' had vanished; she was someone to be distrusted, pitied, and even contemned. Every objection they could think of was paraded. Not only had Kingsley no means of keeping himself much less a wife, but he was unpresentable, friendless, unknown and a fearful stutterer. As for her, was it not a trifle indelicate to throw herself away on a youthful fortune hunter? Did Fanny not realise how badly the disparity in age would affect her as time went on? After all she looked old for her years, and how would her lover behave

when his fancy fell on some fresher beauty? It was a highly
mortifying exposure of the situation as it struck them, but it
had the effect of releasing Fanny's conscientious scruples so far
as the family was concerned and making her feel free to forge
ahead, see Charles as much as she could, write to him as much
as she pleased, wear his letters next her heart and think of him in
secret as 'my very own husband'. The one consoling feature
of the interview had been her brother's admission that he could
not interfere with her income or capital; they were hers to do
what she liked with.

One can only assume that Mr. Kingsley senior was doing all
he could to help Charles to secure a livelihood. He had evidently let it be known in the proper quarter that his son was on
the look-out for a living, since in March 1842 Charles was
offered two Hampshire curacies, and of the two chose Eversley.
Mr. Kingsley seems also to have arranged with Lord Cadogan
that his son should be made Clerk of St. Luke's, Chelsea, at
£200 a year, a sinecure appointment which the holder gave up
as soon as he was in a financial position to do so. Charles had
to scramble to read enough Divinity to enable him to present
himself three months later for ordination at Farnham Castle.
Fanny was still silent, as she was oppressed by the attitude her
family had taken up; and he found himself worrying a good deal
as to whether he had a vocation for the priesthood or was merely
being ordained as a means to matrimony. In other words,
'Was he desiring to be a deacon in order to serve God or that
he might marry his beloved?' He prayed that the examiners
might reject him if his motives were not pure; if he were
accepted he would take it as a sign that he had not 'sinned too
deeply for escape'. At Farnham he went through the ordeal
of yet another examination and then waited in silence for 'the
seals of admission to God's service'. After ordination he proceeded straight to Eversley rectory, where he stayed till he could
get lodgings elsewhere.

Mrs. Augustus Stapleton of Warbrook, one of his congregation, noted in her diary [1] that 'the new curate' read the lessons
for the first time on Sunday, July 3. On July 17, 'the new

[1] Stapleton MSS.

Drawing for 'Elizabeth of Hungary' by Charles Kingsley

curate' preached, on July 24 'the new curate took the whole service'. It is from Mrs. Stapleton too that we learn that Mr. Kingsley's brother, Henry, at this time a puny boy of twelve, was keeping the curate company. In August one of Charles's Cambridge friends, Peter Wood, received a joking letter inviting him to stay at Eversley.

> Peter!—whether in the glaring saloons of Almack's, or making love in the equestrian stateliness of the park, or the luxurious recumbency of the ottoman, whether breakfasting at one, or going to bed at three, thou art still Peter, the beloved of my youth, the staff of my academic days, the regret of my parochial retirement!
> Peter! I am alone. Around me are the everlasting hills and the everlasting bores of the country. . . . I am wasting my sweetness on the desert air. . . . Oh Peter, Peter, come down and see me! . . . Take pity on me! I am like a kitten in the wash-house with the lid on. Prevail on your friends about here to give me a day's trout fishing. . . . I am not discontented with my situation or regretful that I buried my first class in a country curacy like the girl who shut herself up in a band-box on her wedding night.

Peter Wood, who responded with alacrity to this appeal, found his friend in a thatched cottage fenced off from the green at Eversley Cross 'as happy as if he were in a palace'.

The straggling parish Charles Kingsley had to minister to consisted of three hamlets, Eversley, Eversley Street, and Eversley Cross, each grouped round a patch of common land. The hamlet group was encompassed by moorland and marsh-land, and self-sown fir trees grew everywhere, giving a rather wild aspect to the whole scene. The people of the parish were mainly heath-croppers, poachers by tradition, whose forefathers had shot the royal deer straying from Windsor Forest into their wilderness. Sir John Cope of Bramshill (a five-bottle man of seventy-six) was lord of the manor, patron of the living, and master of hounds.

The villagers seemed to Charles Kingsley extremely neglected, and to his surprise he found that no grown-up man or woman could read or write. The children were given occasional teaching by the parish clerk, but of religious instruction there was no trace. The new curate at once began to organise classes in what was known as 'the schoolroom', an apartment ten feet

D

square by seven feet high. Its stuffiness and heat when crowded with pupils was almost unbearable, but hardly more unbearable than the sick-visiting he also set himself to do. To play the part of a good parish priest and civilise Eversley would tax both his time and his courage.

Little pride could be taken in the village church. Fanny Kingsley tells us that when she first went there it was none too clean and pewed to the altar, as the Copes sat inside the chancel in a small ceilinged room. The altar, or rather table, was draped, she says, with a moth-eaten cloth, and beside it stood a broken chair. Inside the font had been placed a cracked kitchen basin to hold the water used at baptisms. Alms were collected in saucers of wood, but as the congregations were both frugal and sparse little money found its way into them. The last touch of desolation in her eyes was given by the sheep that cropped the neglected churchyard graves.

Realising that the only chance he had of making the church a factor in the life of Eversley people was to get to know his parishioners one by one, Charles Kingsley knocked at every cottage door and spoke to the inmates of his willingness to serve them. Their response was discouraging; they seemed to want little or nothing of him. The conditions of village life that struck him so forcibly as squalid were viewed with complacency by those who imposed them and indifference by those who endured them. The villagers rarely left home except for a fair and had no other kind of life with which to compare their own. Distrustful of innovations they were inclined to be suspicious of the stranger's zeal.

With Fanny always in mind, Kingsley at this time wrote some verses entitled *A Hope*.

> Twin stars, aloft in ether clear,
> Around each other roll alway,
> Within one common atmosphere
> Of their own mutual light and day.
>
> And myriad happy eyes are bent
> Upon their changeless love alway;
> As strengthened by their one intent,
> They pour the flood of life and day.

So we through this world's waning night
May, hand in hand, pursue our way;
Shed round us order, love, and light
And shine unto the perfect day.

How often in his cheerless rounds did the poet wonder if circumstances would ever permit of his marrying his Fanny. To a friend staying with him he said he feared he would have to spend the rest of his life reading old books or 'bumping his head against the ceiling like a caged bird'. 'How hard it is', he added, 'to go through life wishing for the goods of others. Look at the rectory! Oh, if I were there with a wife, how happy, happy . . .' and then he pulled himself up, remembering that he of all people must not allow himself to covet his neighbour's goods. He constantly dreamt of Fanny and would write to his mother, 'I dreamt last night that Mrs. Glyn knows all and that we met in her house happily'. Things were indeed changing, for Fanny was getting bolder. Cowley Powles looking in on his friend unexpectedly one autumnal day found Charles dementedly jumping up and down on a packed portmanteau. 'Whatever is the matter?' he asked and Kingsley replied excitedly, 'I am going to see *her* to-day!'

Fanny had at last announced her engagement and Mrs. Glyn, her sister, had summoned him to her home, Farnborough Park. The Grenfell family had now tardily agreed to recognise Charles Kingsley as Fanny's future husband. One of Fanny's sisters, Mrs. Bird, used to tell a story to illustrate what the family really thought of the bridegroom. 'Charles said to me in his impertinent way, "My dear, what is your objection to this marriage?"—and I answered, "My objection to this marriage is YOU".' She added, 'We thought him an oaf in manners, unorthodox in religion, and too young for our sister Fanny'.

Now that Fanny made no secret of her love things began to move in conformity with her planning. Her brother-in-law, Sydney Godolphin Osborne (who when his brother succeeded to the dukedom of Leeds, became Lord Sydney), was persuaded to interest himself in Charles's career. He was a tall, bearded, talkative man who, as S. G. O. on the *Times*,[1] had made himself

[1] *The Letters of S. G. O. on Public Affairs to 'The Times', 1844–88,* 2 vols., 1890.

the advocate for those unwilling or unable to speak for themselves.   On leaving Oxford he had, without either inclination or repugnance, become a parson; in fact he was in the Church of England rather than of it, for his real interest lay in surgery, medicine, and applied science.   He wrote on the wages of agricultural workers and earned the hostility of farmers for trying to get labourers properly housed.   Just at the time Charles Kingsley got to know him he was being threatened by Mr. Bankes, M.P. for the county of Dorset, with having to appear at the Bar of the House in consequence of a statement he had made on the starvation wages paid by Dorsetshire farmers and the deplorable conditions in which their employees were condemned to live.   When twitted by Mr. Bankes on his 'unhappy love of notoriety', he replied, 'I am not ashamed to own my desire that my name should be coupled with that of the agricultural labourer, I wish to make his cause as notorious as possible'.   His chief aim in life was to throw open the doors of opportunity to everyone by education.   Lord Melbourne called him 'a popularity-hunting parson,' but, as he wryly riposted, his was not the sort of popularity that led to deaneries or palaces.

Fortunately for us Carlyle knew Lord Sydney fairly well and wrote of him with extraordinary perspicacity.

> The strange Rev. Lord Sydney, the famous S. G. O. of the newspapers, and one of the strangest brother mortals I ever met; a most lean, tall and perpendicular man, face palpably aristocrat, but full of plebeian mobilities, free and easy rapidities, nice laughing little dark grey eyes, careless, honest, full of native ingenuity, sincerity, innocent vanity, incessant talk, anecdote, personal, distractedly speculative, oftenest purposely distracted, never altogether boring. To me his talk had one great property, it saved all task of talking on my part.   He was very intrinsically polite too and we did very well together.[1]

Sydney Godolphin Osborne was thirty-six at this time and rector of Durweston in Lord Portman's gift.   When he spoke to his patron about finding a living for his future brother-in-law he was promised the first that fell vacant, which might just

[1] J. A. Froude, *Carlyle in London*, vol. II. pp. 368-9.

possibly be Pimperne. Fanny was therefore advised by Sydney to persuade her lover to resign from Eversley and apply for the curacy of Pimperne near Blandford. Kingsley did as he was told, and on being released from duty at Eversley wrote, 'I am parting from this beloved place, hallowed to me by my prayers, my tears, my hopes, my first vows to God'. Fanny made the transfer acceptable by telling him that she was so certain of his being selected for the Portman living that there would be no risk in being married in the first days of the new year. On top of this good news came the directive to report at Pimperne in April.

In one of many notes to Fanny, Charles wrote:

> What a place will Pimperne be on summer nights, we might go and sit in the church sometimes at night, but I am not fond you know of going into churches to pray. We must go up into the Chase to pray, nothing but God's cloud between us and His Heaven.

They were married early in 1844, but neither Charles nor Fanny tells us where. Miss Mitford's gossip leads us to think it must have been a very quiet wedding, for in speaking of the crowd at Kingsley's funeral she says, 'the very people who would have scorned to attend his wedding were present at his burial'. Elaborating the theme she tells us, 'He won his sweet wife by charm of character . . . She was a girl of family, fashion, fortune, beauty, he a young curate without distinction of any sort, without even literary distinction for at the time he had not published.' To Miss Mitford it was a highly romantic story. 'He loved her, she loved him, and without any un-seemly elopement, they lived down and loved down a pretty strong family opposition and were married.' She might have added, 'and were happy ever after'. As a matter of fact they were married by special licence in Bath on January 10, 1844. The bride gave her domicile as 21 Queen Square, Bath, and the bridegroom declared himself as of Chelsea parish, London. No ages were recorded. The officiant was Sydney Godolphin Osborne and the witnesses were G. M. Grenfell and B. I. Gren-fell, presumably sisters of the bride. The only other witness was C. I. Warme.

As bridal offering to his wife Charles had, as we have seen, prepared a life of Elizabeth of Hungary. Inspired by Ambrose Phillips's square folio volumes he bought and had bound quires of vellum-like paper of the same dimensions on which to transcribe his own version of the saint's life. The most unexpected feature of this uncompleted manuscript is the way in which it has been illustrated by its author. There are pencil sketches of the flagellation of a female figure in a chapel, of the Landgrave looking down from his bed on his wife sleeping naked on the floor, pen drawings of ferns such as ceterach and hart's-tongue, and angels holding a suspended cross at the back of which a nude female figure stands on an anchor. Round the base of the cross are grouped devils with porcine and alligator characteristics. The most finished and elaborate of the illustrations is a picture of a naked girl staggering, cross on shoulder, up a jagged mountain track with evil entities jeering at her. Explanatory words accompanied the drawings, 'Baby, wherever in *popish* books you find the word holy, it alludes merely to mortification', a word which, like the term asceticism, excited Kingsley's imagination to frenzy.[1]

In the *English Notebooks* of Nathaniel Hawthorne there is a passage which may bear on these drawings or others like them. Hawthorne in conversation with W. G. Clark, tutor of Trinity College, Cambridge, began to discuss Charles Kingsley, whom he did not like and thought a 'dangerous man'.

> As well as I could gather [notes Hawthorne] he thinks there is some radical defect in Kingsley's moral nature; a lack of sincerity; and furthermore he believed him to be a sensualist (not, as far as I understood, that he practically sins in that way) in his disposition; in support of which view, he said that Kingsley had made drawings such as no pure man could have made or could allow himself to show or look at. This was the only fact that Mr. Clarke adduced.[2]

A word of comment is perhaps called for on the use of the word sensualist in this paragraph. Charles Kingsley always owned to being a sensuous but not a sensual man.

[1] This book, sold at Sothebys in 1926, is in the British Museum.
[2] *English Notebooks*, p. 189.

The introduction to the life of Elizabeth opened with these words:

> Fanny! my beloved, my own, my sister, my wife! Why do I write this book? Not only to wile away the weary present; not only to delight your eyes and ears in happier days; if it were not part of my appointed work I could not touch it. I have been too long idle, I must work—You are part of my labour field—my own peculiar soil, my garden shut up, my fountain sealed where I must not only rest and feed, but labour, labour ever—happy toil! Therefore I write for you, even when alone and far away, knowing that some day you will read and learn.[1]

In trying to show full sympathy with and understanding of Fanny's tenets Charles ran perilously near being equivocal about his own.

> You know what first turned my attention to the Oxford Tracts; but you do *not* know that my own heart, too, strangely yearned towards them from the first; that if they had not, I felt from secret warning struck at the root of our wedded bliss, I too had been ensnared! Love saved me! Tender Love! some men's afflic-tion, but my bliss, has been a guide to heaven! . . . Is human love unholy—inconsistent with the perfect worship of the Creator? Is marriage less honourable than virginity? Are the duties, the relations, the daily good of men, of earth or heaven? Is nature a holy type or a foul prison to our spirits? Is genius the reflex of God's mind or the self-will of man? These were the heart ques-tions and in this book I try to solve them. If I succeed, then we are safe! If not our honest home is Popery! Popery and celi-bacy! You felt it thus, baby, when you said, 'In that case Roman-ism *and* a nunnery must have been my end.' Bless you for those words. No woman worthy of my love could marry holding Popish or Tractarian doctrines, without degradation and a wounded conscience! Lord! Thou hast saved us! Thou, Thou alone!
>
> But I do not fear! God will look on my prayers, my fasts, my study, my watchings! and we are safe! He will root out from your understanding, as He has done from your heart, all which pre-disposed you to the sense-bound and thankless Manichaeism of Oxford, as He has done for me! He will give you the true faith,

[1] Add. MSS. B.M.

darling, by His Holy Spirit, and by my poor words, a reason to give to others, for the hope which is in you.

Where the honeymoon was spent we do not know. It must have been fairly prolonged as it was not till April that Charles set off alone for Pimperne. To begin with he lodged in Blandford and then transferred to Sydney Godolphin Osborne's comfortable house at Durweston with its large sequestered garden. There Fanny joined him. Three most lovely miles of Cranbourne Chase separated the parishes, so for Kingsley it meant a daily walk through a chalk forest, and he often said, 'How much I should like to preach a sermon on chalk downs and chalk streams; they are so *purely* beautiful.' In spite of the prospect of succeeding to the living in the autumn, he did not take to the place and always hankered after Eversley as his true destination. 'Here I am till my Lord and Master Jesus Christ sends for me to Eversley! How merciful of Him to let me labour here instead of sending me away to some place I do not know!' A few weeks after penning this ejaculatory prayer he was offered the longed-for post at Eversley.

His stay at Durweston was of high value to him, for his host was only too willing to impart the results of his clerical experience and observations to so intent a listener. From this nonstop talker Charles heard all about the sins of the owners of cottages, all about the reasons for bastardy and the general degradation of village life, and much about the opportunities given to clergymen of helping to set wrongs right. In addition to holding advanced social views, Sydney Osborne turned out to be extremely antipathetic to Rome and all ritualistic practices. Charles Kingsley, eleven years younger and very inexperienced, was disposed to be seriously influenced by his brother-in-law's outlook, indeed he was in a short while to adopt as his own most of the opinions held by his host and to resolve to be as persistent as Sydney in making known what was really wrong with England. The leaven began to work in him before he left Pimperne, for often in the pulpit he would look down on the underfed paupers in his congregation and feel depressed at 'having to talk to them about the joys of heaven'. His feelings were reinforced by the comments of his lugubrious clerk who told him that labourers went about with weights on their hearts and wound up by saying, 'They have no hope of change in this life and in the next they cannot be worse off'.

When by himself in the evenings he would go over the various points raised by S. G. O. He could not hope immediately to follow him closely as he had no standing in the world and would be looked down on by county M.P.'s and Cabinet Ministers. S. G. O. had the *Times* as his platform, and could without fear of consequences expose the vile conditions existing, for instance, in the Duchy of Cornwall—'the decaying glassless hovels set in cesspools, in which human beings were sheltered with no more regard, nay with less regard, to decency than farm beasts, and paid wages that keep them in a state of scarcely intermittent pauperism'. Charles Kingsley felt that he might never be in a position to address Lord John Russell, Prime Minister, by name or point out to him, as S. G. O. did not hesitate to do, that one section of society spent vast sums in banquets, balls, and operas while another section lived in degrading poverty. If he were to charge landowners, as Sydney did, with 'looking coldly on that patient race to whom they owe their wealth and for whom they provide no food but a potato', he would never get a hearing. Please God he may one day be shown how to break a lance on behalf of the downtrodden!

Among the screeds written to his wife at this time is one telling of the impression made on him by a visit to Salisbury Cathedral. It is characteristic of the way he squeezed a moral lesson out of everything he saw. To him the building represented

> one clear dark system of stern, elegant, soul-crushing asceticism·
> That glorious spire rises too huge for the rest of the Cathedral
> having split and crushed its supporters. Fit emblem of the result
> of curbing systems. The moment the tower escapes above the
> level of the roof it bursts into the wildest luxuriance, retaining the
> general character of the building below, but disguising it in a
> thousand fantastic excrescences—like the mind of man crushed by
> human systems and then suddenly asserting its own will in a burst
> of extravagance. . . . And then its self-willed fancies exhaust them-
> selves and it makes one final struggle upward in a vast simple
> pyramid like that spire; emblem of the return, the revulsion rather,

to 'pure' and naked spirituality.... Oh! that cathedral is an emblem unconscious to its builders of the whole history of Popery from the twelfth century to the days when Luther preached once more Christ crucified for us.[1]

His letter ended less didactically in praise of a trout stream, a theme far nearer his heart. He had spent a blissful day at Bemerton and had seen George Herbert's house, the church he served, and the very meadows where he had once fished. With something akin to reverence he had thrown flies on that memory-haunted stream and to his surprise had hooked two grayling, a fish new to him, 'smelling just like cucumbers'. The simpler pleasures, how incomparably enjoyable they were!

[1] *Charles Kingsley*, vol. I. p. 118.

Chapter 4

EVERSLEY PARISH

The Church of England is not a mere depository of doctrine.

DISRAELI

IN May 1844 Charles Kingsley, while staying with his parents in Chelsea and still uncertain of any appointment, heard the exciting news that the rector of Eversley had 'absconded'. A great deal lay behind this bald announcement, as we may gather from a letter written by the Bishop of Winchester to Mr. Augustus Stapleton some weeks earlier. In announcing that a charge of 'a most revolting nature having been laid before him against the Rector of the Parish of Eversley', he was dealing with the man immediately under the Church Discipline Act and had summoned him to give an account of his conduct.[1] The sinning rector, however, did not wait to be examined, but bolted abroad, and all the Bishop could do was to issue a monition ordering him to return within a prescribed period after the expiry of which the benefice would be declared void. That moment had now arrived, the benefice was vacant, and Mr. Stapleton suggested to the patron of the living that he could not do better than offer it to Mr. Charles Kingsley junior. This advice was accepted by Sir John Cope, who, after interviewing the young curate at Arthur's Club, bestowed the living on him right away, and told him to report to his bishop and arrange to take up work at Eversley as soon as possible. Quite overcome at getting what he had so long wanted, Charles on reaching home burst into tears, tears which he excused by saying he was 'quite worn out'. On the previous day, a Sunday, he had taken the whole duty at St. George's Hospital and had preached at both Chelsea churches.

As soon as they could arrange to despatch personal effects and comforts by van, the young couple moved into Eversley rectory, and set to work to make a few of the rooms habitable.

[1] Stapleton MSS.

Fortunately the summer was due and the full horrors of life in a damp house were not revealed to them till the autumn. Most of the garden consisted of a line of fishponds running from Glebe field to Church farm and they thought that if these were abolished the house would automatically become drier. Acting as his own engineer and gardener Charles Kingsley filled up the garden ponds and stocked those in the Glebe field with trout. For the time being this seemed a nice arrangement, though they were to find in the end that it did not solve the difficult problem of drainage. As no damages could be extracted from the absconding rector and as the patron of the living did not hold himself responsible for repairs or improvements, the Kingsleys were immediately faced with outgoings they could ill afford. To people less in love with each other it would have been a highly discouraging introduction to domestic life but they were too happy to take things of this kind much to heart. To begin with, they made and rolled lawns where the garden ponds had been, planted roses and geraniums, grew a few vegetables, and made their one sitting-room civilised by hanging Cowley Powles's 'exquisite Rafaelle' above the chimney-piece. It was a print of 'La Belle Jardinière' and, as they told the giver, 'an unfailing source of delight' to both of them.

The church, they found, badly wanted money spending on it, and for the purpose of immediate cleaning and repairs Sir John Cope was induced to contribute £100. It took Charles Kingsley some little time to appreciate just how badly the 'absconded' rector had let the parish down. He had held services at irregular intervals, and if afflicted with a cold or any other ailment would send his clerk to the church door at eleven o'clock on a Sunday morning to tell the few persons who turned up that there would be no service. From time to time he had been assisted by a curate who managed to carry on to his own satisfaction if the rector was absent, but who found him impossible to work with. Charles Kingsley's task was to put public worship on another footing and make his parishioners feel that church-going should play an important part in their lives. But in setting out to reorganise the services of the church and bring them into greater conformity with those to which he had been accustomed, Kingsley at once knocked up against obstruction. For instance, when he expressed his intention of instituting monthly communions, the church-wardens told him that they were in the habit of providing wine three times a year only on the customary sacrament days— Good Friday, Easter Sunday, and Christmas Day. Never in the memory of the oldest inhabitant or in the annals of the parish had any extra celebrations been held.

Though it is laid down in the Anglican prayer-book that morning prayer shall be read daily in churches, few clergymen at this date heeded the rubric in this respect. As for Sunday services they were carried through plainly and without symbol or gesture. It was usual to preach in a black gown, and though a surplice and scarf were worn during the prayers, psalms, lessons, and litany, the stole was looked upon as something of a fandangle. Hymn-books were unknown and such singing as took place was confined to the metrical version of the psalms printed at the end of the prayer-book. It was as like as not set going by a clerk with a tuning-fork or even a flute. At Evers-ley there was a miniature wind orchestra consisting of two oboes and a horn played by very old men.

Thomas Mozley,[1] Newman's rather outspoken brother-in-law, had, by the date Kingsley settled at Eversley, read morning prayer in an empty church every day for six years. By force of constant reiteration he had come to think the petitions 'incred-ibly wordy and tedious', and used to say that a man who persisted in private life in using two words for one and in repeating him-self continually would be avoided as a nuisance. On what ground could stupidities intolerable to man be thought the language fittest for God? The people of England had never, it seemed to him, taken to daily morning prayer, and personally he could not blame them for it.

Every clergyman was watched by lynx-eyed parishioners and every ritual movement he made was commented on. Mozley began by administering baptism in a way that was not altogether approved of. After he had taken his first christening a woman came up to him and said she had something she wished to tell him, 'something that didn't really matter but which set people smiling'. When Mozley asked what it was, she replied that

[1] See *Reminiscences, chiefly of Oriel and the Oxford Movement.*

they had noticed him putting his finger in the font before christening the child. No one had ever seen this done before and they would like to know why he did it. Mozley thought the question over and realised that he himself had never watched anyone baptizing a baby. Was he right to indulge 'in this little piece of hyper-ritualism?' Had he valid precedent for making the sign of the cross on the water or not? Other clergy told him that villagers did not like to see water in a font blessed. They appeared to fear its supernatural effect and to sniff 'Romish' tendencies in anything to do with cross-making. The Church of England having seemingly lost all internal principle of cohesion could appeal to but one powerful sentiment in her members— dread of the Papacy. For fear of transubstantiation sacraments had been allowed to dwindle to ceremonies, and from dread of ecclesiastical authority every man seems to have been encouraged to form his own creed. The contrast between the professed principles of the Church of England and her differing and some-times slipshod practices, struck many members of that body as unsatisfactory. Is it any wonder that those who cared about her future should have inaugurated the so-called Oxford Move-ment, which was designed to reinfuse the English church with the grandeur of Catholic tradition and a more spiritualised way of worship?

The stories told by clergymen holding livings in the dioceses of Oxford and Winchester record strange parochial experiences. Some of Charles Kingsley's best friends are among the narrators. Charles Kegan Paul, for instance, tells how as a very young man he was invited by Wilberforce, Bishop of Oxford, to take charge of the living of Bloxham near Banbury. He had been informed that the incumbent was old and almost past work, but was mildly surprised when he arrived on the scene to find the holder of the living was ninety and his curate over seventy. The services they had conducted for years past had become a byword in the neighbourhood and Bloxham congregations the witnesses of almost incredible incidents. It was the custom of the rector, as at Eversley, to hold a communion service on three days in the year, and on these occasions a clerk placed a black bottle containing the sacramental wine on the table that did duty as an altar. At one of these services the nonagenerian Mr. Bell on finding that the cork had not been drawn from the bottle of wine asked of his congregation, 'Has any lady or gentleman a corkscrew?' Since no lady or gentleman could oblige, the implement was fetched from the public-house opposite and the bottle safely uncorked.

Kegan Paul is also responsible for another story about a would-be communicant. At one Easter Sunday celebration a worthy old lace-maker, Mrs. Boffin, had presented herself at the altar. When the rector reached her he said, 'Mrs. Boffin, you here again? Why I gave it you on Friday and I'm not going to give it you again to-day. Go away!' Mrs. Boffin told Kegan Paul this story herself, and gave it as a reason for ceasing to be a communicant. The new curate could hardly believe what she said till he had ascertained from other of his parishioners that it was a perfectly true statement. Presently the two old clergymen packed up and quitted Bloxham, leaving the inexperienced Kegan Paul to reorganise a much-neglected parish. Cases of this kind, though perfectly authentic, were admittedly unusual and mainly due to lack of supervision. It should not, however, be lost sight of that we owe such records of irregularities to clergymen actually holding livings at the time they wrote. Owing to suspension of Convocation [1] there was little organisation within any diocese. No one worked harder for reform in the staff work of the Church of England than S. G. O. He wrote to the *Times* to show up how unsatisfactory were the relative positions of bishop and clergy, and as he always spoke from personal experience he is worth paying attention to. In describing a visitation he says:

We are summoned to a neighbouring town to meet the Bishop, we follow him to morning service, hear one of our brethren preach a controversial sermon; our names are called over, we stand within the communion rails within which the Bishop sits. He proceeds to read a long essay on church matters—we receive his blessing and disperse—till dinner. The poorer curates disappear—the Bishop is surrounded by Rural Deans. Waiter comes round for 8/- then Rural Deans for Clergy Widow Fund 10/-. Bishop's health is drunk, he is thanked for admirable charge. In the end the Bishop rises, bows to all and drives away in a neat London-made

[1] Revived, 1852.

brougham, chaplain inside, butler with mace case (he had acted as mace-bearer) outside.[1]

Bishops, according to Lord Sydney, were out of touch with the ordinary clergy and got all their information from arch-deacons. A bishop drove in a coach, had a house in London, a palace in his diocese, a seat in the House of Lords, and during the season preached charity sermons in the West End. Being such a very busy man he has no time for his clergy and they do not venture to call on him as 'he is too elevated, too *great*, and more often than not too worldly'. In addressing the editor of the *Times* on this subject Lord Sydney declared:

> We need Sir, more bishops of a very different worldly position. Let us have gig-bishops of £1500 a year who would visit the clergy—preach for them—discuss parochial affairs—all without fuss—call in at the schools—see the churchwardens.

Clergymen, he continues, rarely find a bishop friendly to them or disposed to be interested in what he calls this 'slop-work among curates', who, after an expensive education, are expected for a paltry hundred pounds to do the work of an absent vicar drawing six or eight hundred pounds a year. He is himself 'beset by letters from curates trying to live on salaries not as good as that of a whipper-in to hounds'.

From time to time Lord Sydney reported scandals originating in patronage and told how the Bishop of Sarum,

> on the recommendation of his legal adviser, Mr. Phillimore, instituted a man of eighty, many years past duty, with a large and most important benefice, it being notorious that the eighty-year-old nominee of the patron was only put in to enable the patron to sell the next presentation at a great advantage. The rector of Spills-bury, let me tell Mr. Phillimore, has never resided.

He also mentioned the parish of St. Ervan where the induction of what he called 'a paralytic Warming Pan' had taken place. The man was unable to read the Thirty-nine Articles and the

[1] *The Letters of S. G. O. to 'The Times,' 1844–88.*

Drawing for 'Elizabeth of Hungary' by Charles Kingsley

walk up the aisle, although supported, so exhausted him that he collapsed and died a few weeks later.

When we come to examine Charles Kingsley's work we shall see how much he was influenced by the open warfare carried on by Lord Sydney against the weaknesses of the Establishment. Almost at once he began to see himself in a parallel role, not because he desired to attack the inequalities of the Church as such, but in order to use his position as a clergyman to attack abuses in the social system which abuses, owing to his indifference to doctrinal issues and lack of sacerdotal feeling, affected him far more.

Fanny Kingsley was pleased at the friendship that grew up between her husband and her brother-in-law and at the interests they seemed to have in common. She could not foresee, however, what twists and turns Sydney's admonitions and advice would produce in Charles's mind and to what, from her point of view, regrettable activities they would spur him.

In the narrative published by Mrs. Kingsley references are to be found to the obligations incurred by subscription to the Thirty-nine Articles defining the Anglican profession of faith, and it is evident that Charles and Fanny took them seriously and literally. Some clergy did neither. We find one clerical critic alluding to them as articles of peace and worth about as much as articles of peace usually are, and another going so far as to say, 'I do not think anyone likes the Thirty-nine Articles'. The seventeenth, a rigmarole in any case, was considered by many to be very confusing.

The more we read of the opinions aired by the clergy in early Victorian days, the more rifts we discover. The Church catechism came in for a good deal of censure. 'The Church catechism', wrote Mozley, 'has been the sorest trial of my long life. From youth to age it is the wheel on which I have been racked and tortured.' It seems that as a child of eight he had had the catechism and 'Scripture proofs' drummed into him till he knew them by heart and had never troubled to examine them doctrinally before taking Orders. He had accepted what he had been taught, even to the literal inspiration of the Bible, and was very much shocked and startled when Robert Wilberforce

E

told him he did not believe in them at all.   Mozley was the kind
of clergyman who relied in his preaching on the simplicities of
the Sermon on the Mount and eschewed polemical discussion,
for which he had neither aptitude nor training.   Blinkered and
steady he pursued conscientiously the path in life he had chosen.

Charles Kingsley, though he never wore colours, never
dressed as a clergyman as he abhorred anything in the nature of
sacerdotalism.   If his curate were preaching, he would hurry
to the vestry, doff gown and surplice, and sit in the rectory pew
with his wife.   At the conclusion of the service he would turn
round in the pew to face the congregation and give the blessing
in his lay suit.   When John Martineau in after years asked him
to say grace at his table he replied, 'I will say it this once as *you*
have asked me, but *never* ask me again.   Every man is a priest
in his own house.'   He was always at pains not to offend
the susceptibilities of latent church-goers and yet anxious to fill
his church.   The difficulty over monthly communion was got
round when Mr. Stapleton offered to provide the necessary
wine, but he soon found out that it was not his efforts to provide
more frequent sacramental opportunities that were appreciated
by his flock so much as the straightforwardness of his often
topical sermons.   It was because of these and because of his
wonderful patience and kindness to the sick and the old that
people began coming to church, but among the slow suspicious
natives of Hampshire he could never hope for quick results, for
their trust was a plant of almost imperceptible growth.

As the railway to Reading was not at this time completed, the
Kingsleys, like most of their colleagues, led curiously isolated
lives.   Though Eversley was but thirty miles from London
they had no daily paper, no weekly one even, and for books had
to rely on those brought from Cambridge or borrowed from the
libraries of country houses.   It is not easy to set oneself in the
rural England of 1845 or to imagine the want of cohesion and
supervision with which dioceses were administered prior to
Bishop Wilberforce's efforts to resuscitate the authority of
Convocation in 1852.   Men were appointed to livings to work
on any lines that seemed good to them.   For the first seventeen
years at Eversley Kingsley carried on as best he could, and when,
at the end of this period, archdeacon and rural dean began to take

an interest in his manner of running the parish he protested to
the Bishop at their interference, complaining that it made him
feel he was no longer trusted.

Not long after the Kingsleys had settled at Eversley, Charles
learnt of the death of his eldest brother in the tropics.   The
news gave his father a bad shock, for it reached him as he was
sitting reading in Chelsea Public Library.   There he overheard
a man saying, 'What a dreadful business about the "Royalist".
Every officer on board dead and those who did not die of fever
eaten by cannibals!'   The old rector fainted away for Gerald,
his first-born, of whom he was so proud and who had served so
gallantly five years earlier on H.M.S. 'Pique' at the bombardment
of St. John d'Acre on the Syrian coast, was a lieutenant on the
gunboat.   A few days later he was informed by the Lords of
the Admiralty that every man serving on H.M.S. 'Royalist' in
the Gulf of Carpentaria had been felled by a death-dealing fever.
Charles Kingsley wrote of the tragedy in the following melancholy words:

> And there he lay, and the wretched crew in the little brig, roast-
> ing and pining day after day—never heard of or hearing from a
> living soul for a year and a half.   The Commander died, half the
> crew died—till in May no officer was left but Gerald, and on the
> 17th of September he died too. . . . Then one Parkinson the boat-
> swain, had to promote himself in order to keep the pennant flying,
> all the officers being dead, and so brought the brig home to Singa-
> pore . . . leaking, with her mast sprung, her crew half dead, a
> doomed vessel.

When Fanny Kingsley as a widow came to write the life of
her husband, she was careful to avoid praising or even mention-
ing members of his family with the intention it would seem of
focusing attention on the subject of her memoir.   Gerald is
not spoken of, Henry, who lived for six years at Eversley, is not
noticed, nor indeed are the rest, with the result that but one
Kinsgley existed in the public mind, and that the surname in a
bookseller's catalogue inevitably denoted Charles.

Fanny's first child, Rose, was born in February 1845 at the
rectory, and in the following May Charles was offered an
honorary stall in the collegiate church at Middleham by Dean

Wood, who was appointing his son, Peter, to another of the vacant canonries. This son was the Cambridge friend who had been so warmly welcomed at Eversley when Charles first took up his curacy there. The canonry had no duties connected with it, but was, so Fanny says, of 'sufficient historic interest to attract Mr. Kingsley's acceptance'. And from the building-up point of view, of which she never lost sight, even a sinecure stall had the distinct advantage of enabling one to call oneself 'Canon'.

Going up to Middleham to read himself in, Kingsley was at once hurried off sight-seeing by his host the Dean. He was conveyed to Coverdale, Wensleydale, Richmond, Bolton, 'famed for having been Mary Queen of Scots' prison', and Leyburn Scar, 'near which this evil woman was taken'. He picked forget-me-nots for Fanny from the high altar of Jervaulx and saxifrage from the refectory. As it was May he could enjoy delightful fishing excursions, made possible by the generosity of his new northern friends, who provided him with the right tackle and the 'finest of fine casts' which made his own 'look like tow-rope'. After ten perfect days he returned to the intensely monotonous life of Eversley. He was thankful to be back, for he loved monotony. What, after all, could be more monotonous than marriage, he used to ask, and what more entirely enjoyable? and where could one find a greater hymn in praise of monogamy than 'The Song of Songs'? It is always said that repetition is the language of love, and life pulsed as quietly at Eversley as bead-telling; each happy day brought to Charles its measure of satisfaction in parish work and marital joys.

He was apt to take great trouble over selecting candidates for confirmation and for six Sundays before the laying on of hands would preach on the creeds, the catechism, and the general teaching of the Church. To present oneself as a candidate was such an obvious way of pleasing the rector that the stablemen at Bramshill offered, although already confirmed, to be 'done all over again' if Mr. Kingsley liked. Mrs. Kingsley had little inclination for parish activities, and her husband was more than willing that she should leave the coal club, the shoe club, the lending library, and the maternity club to be run by him. Woman's place, as he was never tired of saying, was the home, and so long as Fanny generated such extraordinary domestic felicity and peace he was content.

Owing to his desire to prove that married life was essentially sanctified and essentially right he did all in his power to fight any tendency to asceticism in church teaching, and asserted without ceasing that Christianity was founded on family life and was intended to maintain family life. Any statements in writing or otherwise that tended to sap the foundation of these beliefs worried him without uplet, and for this reason he decided to reshape his narrative life of Elizabeth of Hungary, originally written for one person and to achieve one purpose, into a play to be published to the world. The story had emancipated Fanny from the errors of Manicheism and the revised version, cast in dramatic form as *The Saint's Tragedy*, would no doubt convert others. 'Dear Elizabeth', he said to his wife, 'shall appear as a poem if I wait seven years to finish her.'

Feelings of this kind impelled him when congratulating Cowley Powles on his approaching marriage to write in rhapsodic strain.

> Oh Salt Asphaltic lake of Polemics; Oh, teeming tropic sea of Eros! of love of man as man, of marriage, and lessons which the heart and home alone can teach—Heaven's glories—the face of Christ our Lord, for ever mirrored in their pure Eden depths. . . . May God bless you and her and admit you in His good time into the inner temple of the Garden of Eden, which surely still exists on earth, for those who have faith and purity enough to believe in their own high honours.[1]

The winter of 1845–6 went by in the utmost domestic felicity, and as husband and wife sat over the fire in the evenings they were apt to discuss the rather confusing trend of Church affairs. The desertions from the establishment, which included Newman, Faber, and many other well-known clergymen, worried Fanny a good deal, but Charles took the robust view that 'perversions' of the kind could only have the effect of weakening the High Church party and could have none but a strengthening result on the Broad Church. All the same he had to admit that it raised a

---

[1] *Charles Kingsley*, vol. I. pp. 137, 138.

feeling of unrest and uncertainty that we may see reflected in a
letter written by him at this time to Powles.

> Nobody trusts nobody. The clergy are split into innumerable
> parties, principally nomadic. . . . Pardon my jeremiad, but I am an
> owl in the desert, and it is too sad to see a huge and busy body of
> clergy, utterly unable to gain the confidence or spiritual guidance of
> the nation. . . . Popery and Puritanism seem to be fighting their
> battle over again in England.[1]

Influenza drove them to Shanklin in May 1846. They had
all been ill, and the house, in spite of fires in every room and
new stoves in passages, never seemed to dry out properly.
Fanny, now she had a child to think of, began to wonder
whether it should not be completely reconstructed or even
removed to another site. The cost of patching and installing
new sanitary appliances had been a great drain on their resources
and no help was forthcoming from their patron. Released
from clerical duties, Charles set himself at Shanklin to remodel
his 'Elizabeth'. He half thought of publishing the result serially,
but as he shaped the play came to think 'it would never do to
cut her into pieces and serve her up in a magazine'.

Sometimes he and Fanny would discuss the ways in which
Christ's living power was being exercised in the world they
lived in. Charles would say that it was the business of every
well-intentioned man to try and discern how He was influencing
events. The new trend in life was towards democracy, and as
it could not be arrested and might prove good, the best thing
would be to Christianise it. He wondered whether democracy
might not turn out to be the very pith and marrow of the New
Testament and Christ its prophet. To his thinking there was
something dangerous and diseased in the established forms of
religion, and if a great social upheaval supervened, such as the
Revolution in France, they might well be swept away like
rootless plants. How foolish people were in saying that just
because new churches were being built the Church of England
was entering on a fresh lease of life. He knew better than that,
for he could not but regard the apparent impetus imparted to
her by the Tractarians as the flaring of a candle before sputtering

[1] *Charles Kingsley*, vol. I. pp. 137, 138.

out. And it was the aristocrats who had written 'Mene, Mene' on her walls. To one man he said, 'The curse of our generation is that so few of us deeply believe anything . . . We must pray God to give us faith; faith in something that we can live for, and would die for.'

When he had completed turning 'Elizabeth' into *The Saint's Tragedy* he decided to consult four persons on whose honesty of judgement he could rely to give him an opinion as to whether it was worth printing. The four men were Dean Wellesley, F. D. Maurice, Derwent Coleridge, and Cowley Powles. All were in favour of publication. After reading the first scene in the second act, set in Elizabeth's bower, Maurice told him he thought it must give offence; on re-reading it he changed his mind, and warned Kingsley that he must make quite sure that people would understand what he was driving at, perhaps a preface should be written to explain the author's intention? Kingsley jumped at this idea and persuaded Maurice rather against his will to be the writer of it. His hedging, half-apologetic words may be read in any edition of *The Saint's Tragedy*. They are not worth quoting, but the gist of them was that the author, in his opinion, was too bold for the taste and temper of the age and had included lines and scenes that he from cowardice would have excluded. Kingsley in his own explanatory paragraphs insists that his sources are practically contemporary, as his principal authority, Dietrich of Appold, was born a few years before Elizabeth's death and had had speech with various aged persons who had known her. He takes this princess to be 'type of two great mental struggles of the Middle Age',

> first between that between Scriptural or unconscious, and Popish or conscious, purity: in a word between innocence and prudery; next of the struggle between healthy human affection, and the Manichean contempt with which a celibate clergy would have all men regard the name of husband, wife, and parent. To exhibit this latter falsehood in its miserable consequences . . . is the main object of my poem.

He does not mention the Virgin Mary because 'Dietrich of Appold makes no reference to her,' and says that he leaves it to

those who see in Mary 'a complete substitute for the Saviour,—
I had almost said for all Three Persons of the Trinity', to explain her non-appearance.   He claims to give a truer picture of
'the coarse and stormy Middle Age' than many other writers, and
in discarding the miraculous stories that have been woven into
the life of Elizabeth he claims to be serving truth.   It was the
hope of the author that every Englishman who read the play
would be roused to ask certain questions of himself as to the
comparative value of the two contradictory theories of life.   If
it deters one young man nibbling ignorantly at that root of
household purity, family life, which to the writer's mind consti-
tutes the distinctive superiority of Protestant over Popish
nations, his book will have done its work.   One is apt to
wonder whether he knew that in the Roman Catholic Church
marriage is a Sacrament, and family life by teaching and tradition
held to be sanctified.

The principal figures in *The Saint's Tragedy* are Lewis, Landgrave of Thuringia, betrothed as a child to Elizabeth, daughter of
the King of Hungary, the Saint herself, and Conrad of Marpurg,
papal commissioner for the suppression of heresy.   Lewis, after
talking with Conrad on the eve of his marriage, is half afraid
that his longing to make Elizabeth his wife may degrade the
girl he worships, in short that wedlock may be treason to
purity.   Dare he pluck the spotless rose of her maidenhood?
He knows she loves him, but is in two minds whether she can
serve God as a wife as well as she could as a nun.   Act II opens
with the bridal feast of Lewis and Elizabeth.   Minnesingers
carol within the walls of the castle,

> How gaily smile the bright heavens,
> The light winds whisper gay;
> For royal birth and knightly worth,
> Are knit to one to-day.

Strains of a different kind are sounded by the monks outside the
walls.

> A fastu et superbia
>   Domine libera nos.
> A carnis illectamentis
>   Domine libera nos.

In the next scene we are transported to Elizabeth's bower. Lewis is sleeping comfortably in the alcove and his bride lying naked on the floor: we learn that she has 'fled yon luxurious and unnerving down and widowed herself from Eden'. Why widowed? Because monks have told her 'love is of the flesh and wedlock something that it were shame for modest lips to speak of'. Lewis, on waking, asks the reason for 'this madness'. How can self-inflicted tortures please God? They talk and laugh and kiss for they are very much in love.

Conrad, in the third scene, is invited to counsel them both. He impresses them by his eloquence and Elizabeth begs him to become her director. Henceforward, though she fulfils her duty as wife and bears Lewis three children, she allows her body to be mortified by flagellation which deeply distresses both her husband and her tirewoman. On being told by her director of the poverty in the town below the castle she gives all away, foregoing food, clothing, and comfort. But it is not enough, Conrad insists on complete obedience, forbids her to give alms but permits her to wash lepers and lavish menial care on idiots. Dressed meanly she has to carry her new-born infant to a remote church to offer him to Christ. The castle reserves of wheat are soon exhausted, clothes and jewels gone; Lewis is directed to the Crusades and dies on the way of malaria. The widow, aged twenty-four, with her children is turned out by his heirs who find themselves ruined by Elizabeth's charities. She takes refuge with the Bishop of Bamberg, her uncle, who urges her to cease self-mortification and marry again, but she tells him that she is the bride of Christ and Christ alone. Conrad continues to order her about, her penances become more severe and in the end she dies—an emaciated figure on a bed of straw. Conrad then thanks God that he has been permitted to make at least one saint in his lifetime and at once puts up a case for her canonisation.

Never before had Kingsley composed five hundred lines of blank verse and to him it was a delightful and encouraging discovery to find he could write anything, even rather bad poetry. People familiar with the legend cannot feel that he was very profitably employed nor be grateful for having the girl saint with her lapful of roses caricatured by Kingsley as the half-witted victim of a sadistic monk, but the theme had had hold of him for more than six years and it was a great satisfaction and relief to him to have forced his obsessive thoughts into a dramatic mould.

The manuscript was submitted to the publisher Pickering with Maurice's recommendation and was refused. John Parker then announced that he was willing 'to run the risk' of printing it. Because of the Tractarian controversy and the heart-searchings that had resulted from Newman's secession it is said to have produced a sensation at Oxford. Cambridge and London passed it over with indifference.

Once it was in circulation, Kingsley had no misgivings about its value as propaganda. Fanny Kingsley admired it immensely now that she shared the views expressed in it. They were both surprised and rather pleased to learn that a song from the second act, ringing a little anachronistically in our ears, 'Oh! that we two were Maying', had been selected by Hullah to set to music and a few years later was being sung in every drawing-room in the land.

Chapter 5

CHAMPION OF THE CLOD-HOPPER

*The artistic temperament—whatever may be its disadvantages—
always ensures its possessor against two evil things, namely, the
fear of man and the love of money.*

E. T. FOWLER

A SON was born to the Kingsleys early in 1847, and they
named him Maurice after his godfather, F. D. Maurice, who
had become to Charles the ideal teacher and exemplar of
saintliness. In May parents and children went to the New
Forest for two months leaving Mr. and Mrs. Kingsley, senior,
in charge at Eversley. Charles took the duty at Pennington
Church near Lymington, and the whole family lodged at
Milford where he wrote *Airly Beacon*, one of his most popular
songs:

> Airly Beacon, Airly Beacon;
> Oh the pleasant sight to see
> Shires and towns from Airly Beacon
> While my love climbed up to me.

> Airly Beacon, Airly Beacon;
> Oh the happy hours we lay
> Deep in fern on Airly Beacon,
> Courting through the summer's day.

> Airly Beacon, Airly Beacon;
> Oh the weary haunt for me
> All alone on Airly Beacon,
> With his baby on my knee.

On his long rides through the forest he hammered out other
verses which we have as *The Red King*, *The Outlaw*, and *Oh!
she tripped over Ocknell Plain*. He also collected material for a
story tentatively named 'Darling, the History of a Wise
Woman'. This was never written, for as soon as he got home
it was driven out of his head by more urgent affairs.

Each time they returned from the south coast the defects of Eversley rectory seemed more intolerable to Fanny. Charles's father and mother having lived there for two months fully endorsed her decision that something must be done before winter even should Sir John Cope refuse to co-operate. So afraid was the patron of having his hand forced that he denied himself to Kingsley, saying he was too busy to see any callers and was not active enough to come and inspect the condition of the house. This gave both Kingsleys a distinct sense of grievance and hardened Charles's attitude towards landlords in general. The state of the rectory is described in letters as 'deplorably damp'. No repairs of a structural kind had been carried out within the memory of man, with the result that Kingsley when he took over the house found himself under the necessity of patching roof, stables, and offices. He had also had to replace the 'disgusting nuisances' he had found there with 'necessary conveniences', and to do a good deal of outside draining. Despite these improvements dry-rot was appearing in the woodwork, and books and clothes and prints mildewed under his eyes. Such reconditioning as he had done had involved him in much expense and now he had to face further outlay for the sake of Fanny and the children. 'Could not Sir John be made to help?' Fanny kept asking, but Sir John was obdurate and gave them to understand that whatever was good enough for his uncle, Sir Richard, when he had lived there without complaint was good enough for other rectors and their families.

Once again Kingsley called in the plumbers, carpenters, bricklayers, and drainers. They one and all told him that the rectory was badly sited; it was below the level of the adjacent graveyard with its foundations resting on blue clay. Fond as he had grown of the place he had ruefully to admit its grave disadvantages as a house. One of his predecessors had offered to rebuild the house on glebe land, but Sir John had flatly refused permission for any change of site. All that autumn such improvements as were practicable were proceeded with, and by Christmas Kingsley was faced with big bills which he had to find some way of meeting. A week or two after *The Saint's Tragedy* had been published he approached John Parker to find him 'regular employment for his pen', as 'bricklayers and carpenters in an old tumble-down house' have involved him in expenditure he cannot meet out of income. Hack-work of some kind is what he would like, 'he could furnish poetry of almost any pattern at a very moderate price per yard'. The result of this appeal was that Kingsley had an article entitled 'Why Should We Fear the Romish Priests?' accepted for the April number of *Fraser's Magazine*. It was followed up in May by the first of two articles on the National Gallery.

The chief result of Sir John Cope's curmudgeonly behaviour combined with the condition of the rectory, was to stimulate the rector's interest in housing and in the relations between landlord and tenant. Was it not monstrously unjust that he, in order to keep alive, must spend at least £1000 of Fanny's fortune in repairing and in part rebuilding a house of which he had no permanent control? This personal feeling of resentment generated acute compassion for the villagers whose cottages stood on undrained land and who were constantly the victims of what was known as 'low fever'. Looking out on his little world with eyes opened by S. G. O., Charles Kingsley began to view the sins and shortcomings of his parishioners as the inevitable outcome of their manner of existence. By intensive parish visiting he soon got to know the ins and outs of village life, and, sure of Sydney's sympathy, he suddenly determined to ventilate the grievances of his clod-hoppers in a new manner. A novel seemed to him the best way of doing this and his pent-up resentment found its outlet in *Yeast*.

Many of the homes he went into were no better than pigsties. Bedrooms without windows were stuffy at all times and in illness fetid. How often now did he find occasion to use his great auger to bore holes above the bedsteads of the sick to admit a little of 'God's fresh air'. And children brought up in these surroundings, what had they to look forward to? Those who were strong enough to survive infancy got no real education, for either they had to stay at home to mind the toddlers or at ten years old were driven out to earn a pittance in the fields. Landlord and farmer both began to assume for Kingsley a most malign character, and seemed to be conniving to keep the agricultural worker in a state of hopeless subordination.

The more Kingsley enquired into things the deeper grew his resentment. Hitherto while at Eversley he had walked in the blinkers, but now he could see without hindrance. What struck him very forcibly to begin with was that most of the potential rural amenities were sacrificed to game preserving. Village people were forbidden to wander through woods in the pleasant days of spring and summer, but were pressed into them as beaters in the sodden days of autumn. Poachers, when caught, were treated with great severity and sentenced cruelly when they appeared before a bench of landlords. Though root crops might be laid waste by hordes of hares, villagers were not allowed to protect their allotments against the ravages of ground game either by trapping or shooting. The whole lovely countryside with its resources for happy recreation seemed to be exclusively devoted to the pastimes of the well-to-do who creamed the enjoyments of sport and employed poor men to tie their flies, clean their guns, and groom their hunters. Some of them even expected a keeper to put up their rods, fasten on their casts and select their flies. To a man who could do these things for himself and liked doing them for himself, the rich began to assume the guise of parasites on the poor. Badly paid, cabined and bound down, the villagers really were not much better off than serfs.

How impossible it was to reconcile this state of affairs with the profession of Christianity indulged in by landlords and propertied persons! The position of a clergyman like himself could not be more invidious. Here he was, an educated man and capable, if need be, of giving voice to the many grievances of the villagers, fenced off from them by his very way of life, his big house, his good clothes, and his theoretical equality with the landlord. How was it possible for a parson who depended for his living on the good will of the squire ever to speak his mind either to his employer or to those to whom he was paid to minister? Napoleon, Kingsley remembered, had called the clergy the black-coated police; he winced to think of himself in such a role and determined that, cost what it might, he would do something or say something to change living conditions not only for his own flock, but for every flock in England. If Carlyle could make everyone read about the People's Charter by publishing a thick pamphlet called *Chartism*, surely he could do something to make people realise what the labourer's life was really like. He found himself drifting into sympathy with the Chartist agitators. After all, why should not the poor man have his say in affairs, his vote, like his so-called 'betters'? But was the profession of Chartism compatible with the profession of Christianity? This was a problem he must discuss with F. D. Maurice from whom he had already learnt so much about the meaning of the Church of England, and who, in his book *The Kingdom of Christ*, had revealed to him the coherent view of the Word of God by which he now conducted his life.

From henceforth Kingsley seems to draw nearer and nearer to Maurice, whom he addresses as 'My dear, my dearest Master'. In Cowley Powles's presence he told Fanny that 'he was the man of all men I have seen who approaches nearest to my conception of St. John, the Apostle of Love'. One day Kingsley and Maurice were looking at a reproduction of Leonardo's fresco of 'The Last Supper' and Maurice complained of the girlish, sentimental face given to St. John. 'But why?' asked Kingsley surprised. And his master replied: 'Why? Was not St. John the Apostle of Love? Then in such a world of hate and misery as this, do you not think he had more furrows in his cheeks than all the other apostles?' Kingsley looked hard at the heavily lined face of his friend, a face that suddenly revealed to him 'what it meant to this tender-hearted man to share the sorrows and infirmities of the world'.

Fourteen years older than Charles Kingsley, Frederick Maurice had, when at Cambridge with John Sterling, his future brother-in-law, founded the Apostles' Society to which Tennyson and Monckton Milnes later were to belong. Like Kingsley he had been attracted by the idea of a legal career, and while at the University had taken a first class in Civil Law. He was a Unitarian by upbringing and only baptized into the Church of England in 1831, the year he decided to read for Orders. With this purpose in view he went to Oxford and there happened to make friends with W. E. Gladstone, then President of the Union. After being ordained in 1834 he went through the mill of a country curacy at Bubbenhall near Leamington and then became chaplain at Guy's Hospital, where he lectured the students twice

a week on moral philosophy.   This post he held for ten years.
Freedom from parochial work enabled him to edit *The Education
Magazine* and write books.   Carlyle thought of him as a
'singular' young clergyman.   At the time of the agitation about
the Thirty-nine Articles he wrote a characteristic pamphlet to
prove that 'subscription was not a bondage, but a deliverance
from bondage'.   Sterling showed it to Carlyle who read it as the
earnest word of an earnest man, but his verdict (which Sterling
was spared the sight of) was summed up in the following jingle:

> Thirty-nine English Articles
> Ye wondrous little particles
> Did God shape His universe really by you?
> In that case I swear it
> And solemnly declare it
> This logic of Maurice's is true.

Maurice had held a professorship of English Literature at King's
College since 1840, and on resigning from Guy's Hospital in
1846 had been appointed Reader at Lincoln's Inn.   On Dr.
Jelf's special recommendation he was also made theological
lecturer at King's College.   Kingsley had got to know him
personally in 1844 when he rented Chelsea rectory for a few
months.

On being consulted, Maurice approved Kingsley's plan of
writing a propaganda novel to draw attention to the condition
of the agricultural labourer, so the rector set to work with a
will to try and bring home to people some of the grim facts of
village life.   He decided, for obvious reasons, to write anonymously, but in spite of this protective covering both composition
and publication caused him a great deal of anxiety.   The book
was written mainly at night when the house was quiet, and he
arranged with John Parker for it to come out serially in *Fraser's
Magazine*, a periodical subscribed for in most country houses.
The problem, of course, was to make each instalment effective as
propaganda and yet interesting enough to attract the eye of those
indifferent to social reform.   He was not breaking new ground,
for Disraeli in *Sybil*, published three years earlier, had also
described the life of persons on the land and had also dealt with
the sanitation of towns and the condition in which cathedrals

were kept. Pamphlets had been printed on the curse of the Factory System (1832) and on the employment of children (1840), but they had achieved no apparent results. It was left to Kingsley to throw landowners into convulsions. The first chapter of *Yeast*, aimed at the squires of England, contained a lively description of a meet of fox-hounds outside a covert, a scene dear to the author's heart, in which he showed himself the equal of Surtees, for he gave readers the feel as well as the aspect of weather and landscape. This wintry sketch is excellent:

> A silent, dim, distanceless rotting day in March on which the spiders, weather-bewitched, had agreed to cover every brake and briar with gossamer cradles and never a fly to be caught in them . . . a soulless, skyless, catarrhal day.

and so is this scene in the wood-ride:

> . . . red coats flashing like sparks of fire across the grey gap of mist at the ride's mouth: a whipper-in bringing up a belated hound, bursting into pathways, smashing and plunging with shut eyes through ash-saplings and hassock grass: a fat farmer sedulously pounding through the mud . . . until the line streamed out into the wide rushy pasture startling up peewits and curlew . . . then on to rolling grass lands spread out into flat black open fallows, crossed with grassy baulks with here and there a long melancholy line of tall elms while the high chalk ranges gleamed above the mist. . . .

Lancelot Smith, the rich young hero of the story, is mounted on a vicious horse which, in bucking, pitches him forward in the saddle and jerks a small book out of his pocket. It is picked up and handed to the Master of Hounds, who, after looking at its back, returns it to the owner. The title of the little volume is *The Devout Life* by St. Francis of Sales. In this rather naïve fashion are we made aware that Lancelot is interested in religion. As he slips the book into his pocket to the accompaniment of 'wandering hound music' there is a sudden hubbub and then a jubilant shriek, 'Stole away! Stole away! A toot of the horn, the dull thunder of many horsehoofs.' A check ensues, hounds lose scent, but pick it up again. Lancelot sights the tired fox, sighs regretfully and says to himself that the game

F

loses its charm when 'the mysterious delight of pursuing an invisible object which gives to hunting and fishing their unutterable, almost spiritual charm vanishes'.

As the hounds tear through a little graveyard and up the hill beyond, Lancelot's attention is riveted by a figure he sees emerging from the near-by chapel, which strikes him as 'queen-like'. Into the eyes of this 'St. Catharine among women' he gazes, and she, standing still, returns his gaze. Something has happened between them; it is a case of eye-wedlock. Before they have time to realise the miracle Lancelot's horse bolts up the hill. He sits loosely and the reins dangle in his hand. Men looking at him say he is 'tipsy and holding on by his spurs'. Taking charge of its rider the horse in an abortive jump at the Park palings falls: both roll over headlong on to the hard flint road. Lancelot is carried to Squire Lavington's house, Whitford, where he is carefully tended for fracture and shock. When he comes to his senses he finds that Squire Lavington is the father of the queen-like figure and of another daughter. Lancelot is nursed by men, for in those pre-Crimean days well-brought-up girls were not allowed so much as to see men in bed. Convalescence on a sofa, however, gives Lancelot and Argemone the chance they need to probe each other's minds. Argemone turns out to be rather *précieuse*, Tractarian in sympathy, and a stickler for dogma. Lancelot loathes dogma and is quite content to seek God in Nature. Argemone, though she thinks him very ugly, admires his mind and character immensely and discerns in him another Mirabeau—'a man with the longest of heads and the noblest of hearts'. She is not, however, completely at ease with him for he has the reputation of 'a profligate'.

The pair fall irretrievably in love, had indeed done so at the moment of their first encounter in the graveyard. Lancelot, to whom Argemone's mind is an open book, makes no attempt to court her in the conventional sense, for he realises that the only way to win the proud heiress of Whitford is to prove himself worthy of her. In this delayed action there is definite reference to Charles Kingsley's long-drawn wooing of Frances Grenfell. Certain passages in Mrs. Kingsley's private copy are marked as reminding her of episodes in the past.

But Lancelot spoke no word all the way home, and wandered till dawn in the woods around his cottage, kissing the hand which Argemone's palm had pressed.

'I see—I see it all, Argemone!   We love each other!   You are mine never to be parted!'   What was her womanhood, that it could stand against the energy of his manly will?   The almost coarse simplicity of his words silenced her with a delicious violence.

And lest we should miss the clue, Fanny, in her life of her husband, points out how closely Lancelot resembled him in character and mind.   At one moment she arranged that *Yeast*, which was by far her favourite book, should be buried with her, reminding her as it did of the intimate understanding that had characterised her intercourse with Charles from 'the first flashing moment of recognition'.   In the novel Argemone died of typhus contracted in visiting her father's cottagers.   In real life Fanny outlived Charles by sixteen years.

Two of the actors in the story are gamekeepers, one of them secretly in love with the squire's younger daughter and she with him.   Lancelot (who is Kingsley complete with stammer and all) makes a great friend of this young Cornishman, Tregarva by name, and talks with him about the beauties of Nature, the exquisite purity of the chalk streams in the neighbourhood, the bridal blossom of the fruit trees, and all the rich natural loveliness lavished on man for his delight.   Tregarva listens, but wonders what the use of all the beauty could be as it did not affect the life of those who lived among it.   Did it lessen the squalor of village life?   Did it cure the fevers and the agues?   Did it affect the penury and stale discontent?   Gravely he gives Lancelot to understand that though there be luxury and leisure at the Hall, wealth in the farm-houses, and good fellowship at the parsonage, there is abject misery in the cottage.   He leaves Lancelot speculating as to whether the root cause of all the ills Tregarva describes may not be game-preserving.

Tregarva in his spare time writes verses, and in reading them Lancelot gets the gamekeeper's slant on the preserving of game. One of his ballads entitled *A rough Rhyme on a rough Matter* finds its way into Squire Lavington's fly-book, put there by Tregarva's enemy—the other keeper.   It is twenty-one quatrains long, and the Squire becomes livid with rage after look-

ing at the opening verses.   Lancelot is ordered by him to read
the ballad aloud.   The first quatrains,

> The merry brown hares came leaping
> Over the crest of the hill,
> Where the clover and corn lay sleeping
> Under the moonlight still.
>
> Leaping late and leaping early
> Till under their bite and their tread
> The swedes and the wheat and the barley
> Lay cankered and trampled and dead.

give no inkling of the tragedy that is to develop in the course
of the ballad.   But a poacher's widow sits watching the hares,
and as she watches she thinks of her murdered husband and of
the dark plantation where they buried him.   She sings:

> I am long past wailing and whining
> I have wept too much in my life
> I've had twenty years of pining
> As an English labourer's wife
>
> A labourer in Christian England
> Where they cant of a Saviour's name
> And yet waste men's lives like vermin's
> For a few more brace of game.
>
> There's blood on your new foreign shrubs, squire;
> There's blood on your pointer's feet;
> There's blood on the game you sell, squire
> And there's blood on the game you eat!

The reading of these verses irritated the propertied readers of
Fraser's Magazine as much as they irritated Squire Lavington.
Indeed the gentry for whom Kingsley had written the book
found it so nauseating and subversive that they threatened to
cancel their subscriptions.   In spite of the fact that no one but
Parker knew that the book was by a clergyman, Kingsley was
intensely agitated and vexed by its reception and found it
mortifying to be requested by the editor of the periodical to
shorten it as it was affecting the circulation adversely.

The novel, as a novel, is formless, and its second theme roused as much resentment as its first. Lancelot has a Tractarian cousin who becomes a Catholic. The introduction of this figure gives Kingsley the opportunity to tilt at 'Mari-idolatry' and to descant on his other prejudices about the Roman faith. The priest who has converted the cousin (in whom some affected to see a 'sympathetic portrait' of Father Newman) is interviewed by Lancelot. He extols 'Our Lady on whose loving heart he now rests' and Lancelot impatiently exclaims that he is a man, not a child and does not wish to be mothered or petted. The priest then points silently to a crucifix whereupon Lancelot throws his head back, and in the words of George Fox says, 'I want a live Christ not a dead one. . . . I come to you full of manhood and you send me to a woman. I go to the Protestants full of desires to right the world—and they begin to talk of the next life and give this one up as lost.' Presently the cousin announces that he is about to enter a strict order devoted to the worship of the Blessed Virgin and hopes to emulate the devout Mary of Oignies who inflicted on her most holy person eleven hundred stripes in honour of that all-perfect maiden. Lancelot's soul revolts within him, he says nothing but thinks the more. 'Such a decision', he concludes, 'would have better pleased Kali the murder goddess of the Thugs!'

There is an account of a village fair attended by Tregarva and Lancelot, who as he walks along the plashy turnpike cannot help noticing how superior in clothes and health the quite young men look compared with the married men. Tregarva explains this easily, for a married man with wife and children to keep receives no higher wages than a lad. And he also explains that boys who have to go out earning at the age of nine or ten either feeding or following farm-horses are so tired when they get home that they tumble into bed only to be shaken up at half-past four in the morning to report at five for their slice of bread and dripping. 'Day in, day out they go to work and any mother will tell you that they are sometimes too tired to eat, too tired to take off the sweaty shirt they have been working in all day and never washing their skins once in seven years.' The fate of the girls was in a way worse than that of the boys. Tregarva's ballad had something to say about them.

Our daughters with base-born babies
Have wandered away in their shame;
If your misses had slept squire, where they did,
Your misses might do the same.

Can your lady patch hearts that are breaking
With handfuls of coal and rice,
Or by dealing out flannel and sheeting
A little below cost price?

What a responsibility lay on the parsons! Why could they not do more to right these obvious iniquities? Why could they not compel squires and farmers both to humaner ways? And Tregarva answering his questions says, 'Every poor man in the vale thinks that the parsons are afraid of the landlords.' Lancelot did not believe this and said it was the plain duty of the clergy to tell the landlords the plain ugly truth about their prosperity. Tregarva then pointed out that parsons one and all must keep the right side of their patrons, for how else could they get funds for schools or coal clubs or lying-in societies? If they spoke their minds to the overlords how could they hope to run a parish or keep it together?

In an Epilogue, Kingsley anticipates the criticism that his book is fragmentary and without method, but how could it be otherwise when tradition and stereotyped systems are breaking up under him like ice in a thaw? He is in a 'yeasty' state of mind and so is society at large. In discussing some of his characters he says of Squire Lavington on his death-bed that no minister of any denomination could require of him repentance for the state of the Whitford estate, seeing that that would have involved a recognition of those duties of property which the old gentleman to the last staunchly denied, and which are not supposed to be included in any Christian creed. And the result of this monstrous attitude to the poor of Whitford was that they became more profligate, pauperised, and reckless year by year, effects that economists put down to what they chose to call 'an overstocked labour market' or 'too rapid multiplication of the species'.

Kingsley raises a good number of other problems to which he finds no satisfactory solution. One of them concerns the empty cathedrals of England. Now that popular, unified religious life has vanished he dreams of their taking on a new life as winter gardens, concert halls, museums, debating chambers, or centres of civic life. One afternoon Lancelot visits St. Paul's Cathedral with a friend;

> The organ droned sadly in its iron cage to a few musical amateurs. Some nurserymaids and foreign sailors stared about within the spiked felons' dock which shut off the body of the cathedral, and tried in vain to hear what was going on inside the choir. As a wise author—a Protestant too—has lately said, 'the scanty service rattled in the vast building, like a dried kernel too small for its shell.' The place breathed imbecility and unreality, and sleepy life-in-death, while the nineteenth century went roaring its way outside.

'When will life return to this cathedral system?' asks Lancelot, and his companion replies, 'When was it ever a living system? When was it ever anything but a transitory makeshift, since the dissolution of the monasteries?' 'Why not away with it at once?' snaps Lancelot impatiently. His friend is sure that one day a use will be found for cathedrals again, and in the meanwhile they are being kept rainproof. Their life will wake the dead some day and Lancelot takes heart of grace when he hears the words the choir are singing: 'He hath put down the mighty from their seats and hath exalted the humble and meek'.

Chapter 6

EXPERIMENT WITH SOCIALISM

Censure is the tax a man pays to the public for being eminent.

SWIFT

IT was with a good deal of satisfaction that Charles Kingsley watched his adored master, Maurice, extending his appeal to the intelligentsia of the day. Lincoln's Inn Chapel was now crowded on Sunday afternoons with men eager to listen to the Reader's exposition of doctrines, which they often confessed they found it impossible to define. Most of the disciples resembled Kingsley in so far as they were deeply conscious of the preacher's power of diffusing an atmosphere of Christlikeness. The spell he cast over their minds made them take an alluringly fresh view of religion. Carlyle, as might be expected, was one of the exceptions, he remained totally unimpressed by Maurice's eloquence. He would praise the Reader's character and intentions and then dub him 'an entirely uninteresting man of genius' whose sermons were 'not only confused but confusing'. Another critical Scot, Mountstuart Grant Duff, who sat under Maurice some thirty or forty times, said he never carried away one clear idea or got the impression that the preacher had more than the faintest conception of what he himself meant, and Kegan Paul said he 'never could make head or tail of what the man was driving at'. Having originally imbibed his theology from Maurice's *Kingdom of Christ*, Charles Kingsley would tolerate no criticism of his idol, though even he had to admit that Maurice's teaching occasionally needed interpretation to the outer world. Soon he came to regard himself as the populariser of the doctrine and principles of the 'forthteller'.

It is only too easy to quote the opinions of contemporaries on Maurice, from Aubrey de Vere, who found listening to him like eating pea-soup with a fork, to Jowett, who after sitting through a university sermon shrugged his shoulders and said, 'Well, all I can make out is that to-day was yesterday and this world the same as the next.' Criticism of this sort could only come from people who had not got the feeling of the man nor entered into his powers of wide sympathy, selflessness and open-heartedness. They thought of him merely as a performer in the pulpit. But no matter what was said or thought there can be no doubt that Maurice wielded great influence and was taken very seriously indeed by many people. He had, on occasion, a tart, unexpected sense of humour. When lecturing a class of young men on the Old Testament, he came to the story of Jacob's questionable behaviour to Esau, and interjected 'After all, my brethren, this story illustrates the tendency of the non-sporting man in all ages to be a liar and a sneak'.

That Maurice did not present himself well to strangers was a little tiresome to his intimate friends. Ludlow thought it was due to his innate shyness and humility, and to a trick he had developed of speaking with bowed head and in low tones. 'What shall be done to the prophet who prophesieth into his waistcoat pocket?' Kingsley used to ask of him.

One member of the inner ring of disciples, John Ludlow, seems to have understood Maurice from the very first moment they met, and it was this young barrister who in his turn in-structed his master in the foreign doctrine of Socialism, in the end persuading him to believe that Christianity and Socialism were very closely allied and could be blended and made to serve as an antidote to Chartism. General Sir Frederick Maurice, when writing his father's biography, stated that John Ludlow was the real founder of the Christian Socialist movement. Neither the Reader nor his friends knew anything about the theory or practice of socialism, but were all indoctrinated by Ludlow who, having known Louis Blanc in Paris, had had peculiar opportunities for studying it. 'He got round Maurice', says F. J. Furnivall, an early recruit, 'and really led us.'

Ludlow, though sixteen years younger than Maurice, had seen more of life than the average English clergyman. As a child in France he had witnessed scenes in the revolution of 1830, and as a man was in Paris in February 1848 protecting his sisters who lived there. While qualifying for the English Bar in London he had worked for reforms in India, the country of his birth. He was the only man among the Mauricians who had first-hand experience of social upheavals and of socialist remedies for unrest, and he is the one person who tells us from the inside the story of the Christian Socialist movement in England.

A frequent visitor at Eversley, Ludlow tells us how one Sunday afternoon Charles, being in exceptionally good spirits, brought out in his characteristic stutter: 'N-now, J-John T-Townsend' (the name under which Ludlow used to write), 'I am g-going to c-commit a p-petty l-larceny, I am g-going to t-take a s-sermon of M-Maurice's and t-turn it into a l-language understanded of the people.' He did this so effectually that no one could possibly have accused him of plagiarism.

To the original group of founder friends Thomas Hughes was presently added. He was an enthusiastic admirer of Maurice and a tireless worker. The four men are summed up by Sir Norman Moore in this way.[1] 'In the Christian world I would have compared Ludlow and Maurice to holy abbots, Kingsley to an itinerant preaching friar, and Hughes to a lay brother of some attainment. Of the three Ludlow seemed to me the gravest, Maurice equally serious but less clear, Kingsley the least profound.' 'The Prophet' was held by Kingsley to be 'the truest man of his day', a rare person with strange insight and power, deeply spiritual and deeply humble. Though none of them went as far as Alfred Tennyson in calling him 'the greatest mind since Plato', they did think of him as towering spiritually by head and shoulders over everyone else. Tennyson had seen a good deal of Maurice when the Reader first left Guy's Hospital for Lincoln's Inn, for he lodged close to him, and wrote most of *The Princess* in Lincoln's Inn Fields. Maurice at that time was too busy with the founding of Queen's College to pay much attention to Socialism; it only became of paramount interest to him when the February revolution of 1848 exploded in Paris.

Ludlow had a sympathiser in London in Minter Morgan, one of Robert Owen's friends. For years this man had been proposing to socialise Christianity by organising a Church of England self-supporting village community and had caused the diorama of such a model village to be painted in one of the rooms in his house. It was lighted from behind and a footman

[1] C. E. Raven, *Christian Socialism*, p. 56.

unfurled it to display to visitors. When he made it known that he was willing to bequeath twenty thousand pounds to anyone who could work his scheme successfully, a certain number of people came to inspect the picture. Maurice, Ludlow, and Kingsley were all invited to see it, but, though they had Morgan's ideas explained to them, they made no bid for the endowment.

Besides the discussions for working men initiated at Cranbourne Tavern by the founders of the movement, Maurice was at home for Bible reading and talk once a week in his own house in Queen Square, Bloomsbury. Charles Kingsley was a fairly frequent attendant at these informal gatherings, at which the possibility of assimilating Chartism into Christian Socialism was often under consideration. On one occasion he found himself in a minority of one and said he felt 'as Lot must have done in the Cities of the Plain when he seemed to his sons-in-law as one that mocked'. Then and there he was nicknamed Parson Lot, a name that stuck to him and which he used afterwards in writing in *Politics for the People* and *The Christian Socialist*, the articles that were to make him and his opinions known through the length and breadth of England.

Early in April 1848 the rector of Eversley was summoned by the Council of King's College to receive instructions for the May term lectures at Queen's College. His visit to London coincided with the Chartist demonstration advertised to take place on Kennington Common, an occasion on which neither the Council nor anyone else was attending to business. Kingsley, when he called at Queen Square, learnt that Maurice was ill but had left a note for Kingsley to take to John Ludlow who was to be found at his chambers in Chancery Lane. Unlike most men that day Ludlow was working as usual when his clerk ushered in the excited young clergyman, who stammered out that he was anxious to prevent a collision between Chartists and troops. 'The poor fellows mean well,' he said, 'it would be horrible if there were bloodshed.' He was intending to go to Kennington Common to see what one man could do. Perhaps Ludlow would come too? Ludlow, though quite convinced that the meeting would come to nothing, agreed to do so.

The two men walked off together but they got no further than Waterloo Bridge where they were told the meeting had been cancelled and that the demonstrators had been dismissed by their fiery-headed leader, Feargus O'Connor, M.P. Even he had shrunk from exposing his followers to the pressure that might have been exerted by the 170,000 special constables enrolled by the Duke of Wellington to cope with the demonstrators. Kingsley and Ludlow, who had talked all the way from Chancery Lane, talked all the way back to Queen Square, and by the time they reached Maurice's doorstep had decided that the situation called for immediate action on their part.

The rest of the day was spent in discussing with Maurice what it might be feasible to do. They were agreed that no time must be lost in Christianising Socialism, but no one had any very clear idea of how this could be achieved. Maurice announced that his friend Charles Knight had offered to put his magazine at their disposal if they really had a formulated gospel to preach. One of them suggested tracts, another posters and a weekly news-sheet. Kingsley took fire over the idea of a poster and sat down to write it at once. Within forty-eight hours it was in print and was being pasted up all over London. Before the end of their meeting the friends had resolved to issue a penny periodical and to initiate debates on Christian Socialism at Cranbourne Tavern.

Here is the draft of Kingsley's poster, the first socialist manifesto ever issued by a clergyman of the Church of England.

Workmen of England!! You say you are wronged. Many of you are wronged and many beside yourselves know it—above all the working clergy know it. They go into your houses, they see the shameful filth and darkness in which you are forced to live crowded together; they see your children growing up in ignorance and temptation for want of fit education; they see intelligent and well-read men among you, shut out from a Freeman's just right of voting; they see too the noble patience and self-control with which you have as yet borne these evils, and God sees it.

You think the Charter will make you free—would to God it would. The Charter is not bad; *if the men who use it are not bad.* But will the Charter make you free? Will it free you from slavery to ten pound bribes? Slavery to beer and gin? Slavery to every spouter who flatters your self-conceit and stirs up bitterness and headlong rage in you? There will be no true freedom without virtue, no true science without religion, no true industry without the fear of God, and love of your fellow citizens. Workers of England be wise, and then you *must* be free, for you will be *fit* to be free

A WORKING PARSON

It was the best Kingsley could do for the moment, but it smacked of sermonising, seemed to make light of political activities, and did not tackle the chief difficulty, the conviction of the working men of England that the State Church, as well as the Law of the land panned out in practice as the agents and props of capitalism. Kingsley thought it might be possible to disabuse them of this idea by proving that organised religious bodies and courts of law alike functioned for their protection, and indeed were the only forms of protection the community could rely on as defences against the predatory selfishness that flourished, not among employers only, but in every walk of life. Christianity alone, he argued, could avert the terrible social convulsions looming ahead. Lawless conspiracy to preserve property and violent experiments to break down monopolies and privileges were equally to be feared. He argued in the same way during debates at Cranbourne Tavern. At one gathering, presided over by Maurice, workmen attacked both Church and clergy with venom. The awkward situation was eased when Kingsley, in one of his fits of irresistible impulse, stood up, threw back his head and stammered out, 'I am a Church of England parson—and a Chartist.' The audience at once showed friendly interest and even approval of the speech that followed this startling announcement. It is Tom Hughes who tells us how highly effective this declaration was among the working men present, and how it damaged him with the rest of the community including the Church of England and took years to live down.

In conclave at Queen Square it was decided to model the penny periodical to be issued by the Mauricians on Cobbett's *Political Register*. In it comments, from the religious angle, on all questions of the day were to be set forth in short pithy paragraphs. Ludlow was appointed editor with Kingsley as assistant. Both were humble-minded young men and willing to accept the arrangements laid down by Maurice. *Politics for the People* was to be a weekly and the first number was issued by John Parker early in May. Its chief concern was to consider the relation of the capitalist to the labourer and to examine what a government could or could not do to lessen unemployment and secure a living wage for all. The articles were to be unsigned or supported by a pen-name. 'I do hope the first number will go forth with God's blessing', wrote Maurice to Kingsley. 'We want poetry very much, and something on pictures, and could you not write a working country parson's letter about the right and wrong use of the Bible—I mean protesting against the notion of turning it into a book to keep the poor in order.' Thus almost casually was 'Parson Lot' invited to emerge into the limelight of publicity. With 'Parson Lot' was now associated his Cambridge friend, Charles Mansfield, a man to whom Ludlow became devoted and whom Thackeray declared to be the kind of man who must have the rudiments of wings under his waistcoat.

Mrs. Kingsley was frankly apprehensive about the effect on his career of Charles's new interests. He had a battle to go through with all her friends and relations, religious and worldly, who each and all from their own particular standpoint deprecated the line he took, which they thought likely to spoil his prospects in life. Kingsley, however, since he had the backing of his clerical brother-in-law, did not take such discouraging advice seriously.

The new magazine soon had a distinguished list of supporters including Professor Connington, Dr. Guy, A. H. Clough, David Masson, John Spedding, Sir Edward Strachey, Bishop Thirlwall, Alexander and Daniel Macmillan, and S. G. O. E. V. Neale, the only rich man supporting the movement, brought in his friend F. J. Furnivall (author of *Association as a Necessary Part of Christianity*) who later abandoned the religious basis of Socialism. To begin with, the editing of *Politics for the People* was extremely cautious. In the first number a prospectus addressed by Ludlow to the 'Gentlemen of England' and one by Kingsley to the 'Workmen of England' were printed. A letter from a Chartist praising those who had enrolled as special constables conveys the impression of having been inserted to give Ludlow and others the chance of denouncing any appeal to violence or in order to show that the general sense of the community was against violence. So hedging did the first number appear to Tom Hughes that he almost wondered 'what side of the fence Ludlow and Maurice were on'. It surprised him more than a little to hear that Maurice, not realising that clergy were barred, had tried to enrol as a special constable himself.

'Parson Lot' in his first letter dubbed himself a radical reformer whose only quarrel with the Charter was that it did not go far enough. It seemed to him a poor, bald, constitution-mongering cry compared with the French demand for the organisation of Labour. Though willing himself to die to make men free, it disgusted him to read paeans on 'divine liberty' and 'heaven-born fraternity'. There was nothing new, he wrote, in the Chartist demands, most of their doctrines were to be found in the 'Reformer's Guide to the New Testament'. No agitator should have recourse to the devil's weapons; all must remember that stirring up bad blood was the devil's work. Once again he told working men that if they were fit to be free God Himself would make them free. In a second letter he talked of the Bible as 'the true reformer's guide', the true voice of God against tyrants and humbugs. He assured them that the Bible demanded more for them than they demanded for themselves; it was 'the poor man's comfort and the rich man's warning'.

Articles by 'Will Willow-wren' (Charles Mansfield) dealing with 'the great Green-book of Nature' were set off by articles by 'Parson Lot' on the British Museum and National Gallery, 'truly equalizing places in the deepest and most spiritual sense'.

> The British Museum is my glory and my joy; because it is almost the only place which is free to English citizens as such—where the poor and the rich may meet together, and before those works of God's spirit, 'who is no respecter of persons' feel that 'the Lord is the maker of them all.' In the British Museum and the National Gallery alone the Englishman may say, 'Whatever my coat or my purse, I am an Englishman, and therefore have a right here. I can glory in these noble halls, as if they were my own house.' ... Would

that the Deans and Chapters who persist in making penny peep-shows of God's houses, built by public piety and benevolence—of St. Paul's and Westminster Abbey, which belong not to them at all, but to God and the people of England would go to the British Museum in Easter week and see there hundreds and thousands wandering past sculptures and paintings which would be ruined by a blow, past jewels and curiosities only protected by a pane of glass. if by that; and then see not a thing disfigured—much less stolen.

This extract must suffice to show what Kingsley's general attitude was, but before abandoning the subject it may be as well to look at what he has to say about his favourite pictures. The first is Titian's 'Bacchus and Ariadne', and the second a 'Holy Family' by Francia with St. Sebastian in the foreground, and the third, which he evidently likes best of all, the portrait of the Doge by John Bellini, 'an ideal portrait giving a *full* idea of a complete character'.

He is such a gentleman as I have seen among working men, and nine-shillings a week labourers often and often; his nobleness is in his heart—it is God's gift, therefore it shows in his noble-looking face. . . . He was a thoughtful man too; no one with such a forehead could have been a trifler; a kindly man too and honest—one that may have played merrily enough with his grandchildren, and put his hand in his pocket for many a widow and orphan. . . . His eyes almost show the marks of many noble tears. . . . His lips are very thin, he may have sneered many a time when he was younger, at the follies of the world.

And so on and on in unctuous beguiling of the working man, a kind of flattery which must have sickened the very people it was meant to please.

In June 1848 Kingsley read *The Purgatory of Suicides: A Prison Rhyme in Ten Books*, written by Thomas Cooper, the Chartist, while incarcerated in Stafford Gaol. It has close on ten thousand lines divided into stanzas and is dedicated to Carlyle. Kingsley wrote to congratulate the author on his 'brilliant poem'. He fears that Cooper may distrust him because he is a Church of England clergyman and asks:

Shall God make us brother poets as well as brother men and we refuse to fraternise? It has long been intolerable to me to be regarded as an object of distrust and aversion by thousands of my countrymen—just because I am a clergyman—just because I am a clergyman, the very office which ought to have testified above all others for liberty, equality, brotherhood, for time and eternity. . . . I would shed the last drop of my life-blood for the social and political emancipation of the people of England, as God is my witness; and here are the very men for whom I would die fancying me an aristocrat.

He asks to be allowed to call on Cooper, and in the end they make friends, and we find Cooper in his autobiography alluding to 'my good friend Charles Kingsley', who was in the long run to convert him to Christian Socialism. The first prayer Kingsley enjoined on him was, 'Lord if Thou dost exist, let me know that Thou dost exist'. His acceptance of Christianity deprived him of the confidence of all Chartists and landed him in destitution, but through Kingsley's efforts a purse was made up to save him from the workhouse.

As Ludlow was spending his spare time in investigating the conditions in which the sweated tailor lived and worked, Kingsley weighed in with an article for *Fraser's* entitled 'Cheap Clothes and Nasty', in which lay the germ of his next novel *Alton Locke*, a book which he tells us he felt guided from above to write. 'Only my own folly can spoil it and I pray against that daily.'

Early that summer the rector of Eversley received a letter from John Ludlow informing him that though recommended by Maurice he had been rejected by the Council of King's College for the post of assistant lecturer in divinity. The intimation of failure was a shock. 'The Council's conduct has not been over civil to Maurice', he commented, before expressing resignation to the will of God. After all he has enough to do what between parish work, preparing lectures for Queen's College and writing for *Politics for the People*. Ludlow tried to cheer him by telling him he would in time become the greatest novelist of the age.

The trials of the summer of 1848 proved altogether too much for the rector's equanimity. To begin with there was the stir *Yeast* in its serialised form was causing. The editor kept writing to say that in deference to public opinion he really must wind it up. Then there was the constant criticism of his

socialistic activities from the members of Fanny's family,
Fanny's own fears for the future, the bills for reconditioning the
rectory, and last of all his rejection by the Council of King's
College, a rebuff that made him feel suddenly that he could not
carry on with his lectures at Queen's College.   He lost magnetism so fast under these worries that he was obliged to retire to
Bournemouth to recover tone.   After a month by the sea, he
returned, only to collapse as before.   'Ill-health', says Mrs.
Kingsley, 'obliged him to resign his post at Queen's College',
but it was another name for nervous exhaustion.   By September
it was obvious that Kingsley could not face the winter's work at
Eversley, so a curate was engaged to look after the parish and in
October the family settled at Ilfracombe.   Charles felt himself
'thoroughly de-magnetised'.   Friend after friend visited him
and went away despondent at the condition in which they found
him sunk.   Riding, walking, conversation even were all an
effort and his only happiness lay in wandering along beaches
collecting seaweeds and shells.   It was not till the spring of
1849 that he felt well again.

Politics for the People came to an end after seventeen numbers
had been issued.[1]   In spite of the fact that no contributor was
paid, it ran up expenses that its promoters could not afford to
meet.   Maurice had had to defend 'Parson Lot' against Julius
Hare and many others who disliked his opinions.   To all he
said, 'Neither Kingsley nor Ludlow are conceited, though
young men often are.   They are the best possible mediators
between the working class and the upper and middle classes.'
But neither the upper nor the middle class agreed that this
was so.

[1] May–July 1848.

Chapter 7

HERESY HUNTING

Words are an amazing barrier to the reception of Truth.
SYDNEY SMITH

SOME weeks after *The Saint's Tragedy* had appeared, Charles Kingsley paid a visit to his old friend, Cowley Powles, at Exeter College, Oxford, and found himself 'a minor lion' as everyone seemed to have read his play and wanted to discuss it with him. While there he made acquaintance with Archdeacon Manning, 'a curious specimen to be walking about this nineteenth-century England, but he looks a *good* man'. He also met Arthur Clough, and Anthony Froude. The former he took to immediately, but the latter struck him as rather cold, polished, and remote. As a matter of fact it would seem that Kingsley's ebullience over the February revolution in France, which as we know he had heard about from Ludlow, and over Socialism, was so repellent to Froude that he involuntarily shrank back into his shell. In writing to Cowley Powles afterwards he said that he had no doubt Kingsley was a fine fellow and then went on:

I almost wish, however, he wouldn't talk Chartism and be always in such a stringent excitement about it all. He dreams of nothing but barricades and provisional governments and grand Smithfield bonfires where the landlords are all roasting in the fat of their own prize oxen. He is so musical and beautiful in poetry and so rough and harsh in prose, that he doesn't know in the least that it is because in the first the art is carrying him out of himself and making him forget, just for a little, that the age is entirely out of joint.

Froude at this time was engaged in writing *The Nemesis of Faith*, a successor to two jejune stories, *Shadows of the Clouds* and *The Lieutenant's Daughter*. The immediate effect of its publication, so far as the author was concerned, was disastrous, for the Fellows of Exeter condemned the novel as heretical and empowered William Sewell, the senior tutor of the College, to burn the book during a lecture in the College Hall. What made it particularly strange that Sewell should undertake such a job was that he himself had written a novel, *Hawkstone*, the chief interest of which lies in the tussle between English Catholics and Roman Catholic 'schismatics', but with the great difference that the hero, instead of losing faith in all religions, restores a ruined priory and installs in it a cultured, well-disciplined community of Anglicans. To make it perfectly clear that he utterly disapproved of Roman Catholicism, Sewell, towards the close, allows a Jesuit to be eaten by rats.

The Nemesis of Faith, which is to some extent autobiographical, has for hero Mark Sutherland, son of a country clergyman who is looking for a profession. He has taken a good degree and leans towards the Church, but is pained and shocked to find how worldly is the outlook of those in charge of it. All the talk is of livings not of the care of souls. Another deterrent is that before he can be made into a clergyman he must declare that he unfeignedly believes in all the canonical books of the Old Testament, a profession he cannot make since the God of the Old Testament seems to him a revengeful fiend and eternal punishment a most horrifying doctrine. How can he be expected to believe in a God who keeps a hell prison-house?

Presently a Bishop offers Mark's father a living for his son. Mark consults a Dean as to what he should do given the state of his mind. The Dean pooh-poohs his scruples and doubts and advises him to treat them like a passing sickness. A friend tenders the same counsel and Mark gives way, allows himself to be ordained deacon, and begins work on the outskirts of a large town. The gentry of the place do not take to him or his sermons, the church empties, and when the Bishop sends for him he has to own that he has already bitterly repented taking Orders. Given leave to travel for three years, he goes abroad and meets a Mr. and Mrs. Leonard who take a great fancy to him and invite him to share their house on Lake Como. Business claims take Mr. Leonard away from home and Mark falls in love with Mrs. Leonard and she with him. Mrs. Leonard would be quite willing to run away with Mark, but is anchored by a child whom she cannot abandon. Sailing one day on the lake, the two, deeply absorbed in each other, tell the child to

lie still in the bow. Suddenly the bows are flooded by a breaking swell and the child gets drenched, develops fever, and shortly
afterwards dies. Mark and Mrs. Leonard feel terribly guilty
and remorseful. Mark rushes away meaning to take poison,
but is stayed from doing so by an old College friend, an Anglican
clergyman turned Catholic priest, who persuades Mark to confess
his sin and become a Catholic too. Mrs. Leonard tells her
husband all that has happened during his absence and retires
into a convent where she dies.

Writing on New Year's day 1849 from Dartington rectory
Froude gave Kingsley to understand how unsettled he was in
mind. *The Nemesis of Faith* was about to be published.

> I wish to give up my Fellowship. I hate the Articles. I have
> said I hate chapel to the Rector himself. I must live somehow. . . .
> There are many matters I wish to talk over with you. I have a
> book advertised. You may have seen it. It is too utterly subject-
> ive to please you. . . . There is something in the thing I know; for I
> cut a hole in my heart and wrote with the blood. I wouldn't write
> such another at the cost of the same pain for anything, short of
> direct promotion into heaven.

In March Maurice wrote to Kingsley: 'I have done your
bidding and read Froude's book with what depth of interest
I need not tell you. It is very awful and I think may be a very
profitable book.' The sketch of Newmanism drawn in its
pages seemed to him 'admirable'.

John Ludlow, in reviewing the novel for *Fraser's Magazine*
as 'a real book', said that it truly reflected the mind of an author
who obviously was entirely unfitted to be teaching or leading
others. In his opinion it was a hopeless, negative sort of story,
not exactly immoral, but far better not published; indeed publication was a sin and should be repented of. How meaningless
it was to call a book in which the hero never believed in anything Faith Avenged! The *Morning Herald* and the *Standard*,
on learning that its author had been selected to fill a pedagogic
post in Van Diemen's Land,[1] denounced the work as blasphem-
ous and its perpetrator as an atheist unfit to teach anyone
anywhere. Extremely exasperated, Froude in a letter to the

[1] Headmaster of Hobart Town High School.

Standard protested that as his book was 'pure fiction' an apology was due to him. The *Standard* thereupon renewed its attack and described the cremation in Exeter College Hall. On the very day Froude's letter was published,[1] Dr. J. L. Richards was consulting 'My dear Principal' on the matter of removing Froude's name from the College roll, 'he having requested me by letter to do so'. This from the Rector's point of view was a welcome simplification of the situation, since it enabled him to avoid the scandal that might result from the action of those Fellows who would have liked to expel Froude from the College straight away. Like his brother, 'the dead Puseyite', he was 'an ultra-Newmanite' and had on that ground been invited by the Tractarian Fellows of Exeter to fill a Fellowship in their College. He had been refused testimonials by Dr. Hawkins, Provost of Oriel, and had finally, contrary to all rules, been admitted to Exeter without them. The case for retaining Froude was not very strong, but what a relief it was to know that the culprit was willing to assume the initiative himself! To the surprise of many people who were not in Dr. Richards's confidence, Froude made no trouble of signing the document of resignation when it was presented to him. After he had taken this step Froude was treated as an outcast, hardly anyone daring to speak to him. Clough in indignant sympathy resigned his Fellowship of Oriel 'tho',' as Arthur Stanley said, 'with less explosion than Froude'. Ten years later the atheist was requested to replace his name on the books of Exeter College!

As soon as Froude's father, the Archdeacon of Totnes, heard of his son's condemnation, he stopped all allowances and banished him from the rectory at Dartington. A hard man himself, he told his son in unequivocal terms that he would have nothing further to do with him. To lose one's home and one's living at the same time was a severe blow, but it was to a slight extent softened by Charles Kingsley who promptly invited the outcast to stay with him at Lynmouth.

The Archdeacon was a type of clergyman that no longer exists. He was very well off, had made the Grand Tour, and was famed for feats of horsemanship. Archaeologist, painter, and collector of pictures, on settling down as vicar of Dartington,

[1] March 7, 1849.

he enlarged the vicarage to the dimensions of a substantial country house. His only daughter married a younger son of Mr. Mallock of Cockington Hall, Torquay. Like other younger sons 'he had suffered himself to be put into the Church' in order to take over two family livings. He was as much of an individualist as his father-in-law, for his health never permitted him to perform divine service, and he committed his parishioners to the care of a curate and went to live in a house overlooking the Exe where he spent his time in creating terraces and landscape gardens.

Charles Kingsley received letters of protest against harbouring a heretic from both father and mother, indeed his parents showed quite peculiar distress over the situation. To their first letter he had replied by saying that their anxiety on his behalf was needless and that they were paining themselves more than was necessary. In reply to a second letter he was extremely deferential:

I cannot but believe that dangerous as my present position may seem, I am not tempting God; that he has by a train of circumstances pointed out the course which I ought to take, and that he will help me through it. Pray for me, that whether right or wrong now, I may be taught what is right, and pray for me that I may be kept unspotted.

Froude is no atheist, no man less so. He is now writing a work on God, in the most reverent spirit. Neither is he an infidel, not even a mere Unitarian, though he has very wrong views about our blessed Lord's divinity, while he admires and loves his character and the revelation that he believes was made through him. And on this point it is that I hope to do him good. But the more I see of him, the more I learn to love the true doctrines of the Gospel, because I see more and more that only in faith and love to the incarnate *God*, our Saviour, can the cleverest, as well as the simplest, find the peace of God that passeth understanding.

The sentiments in Froude's book are *not* his own: they are those of too many men. It is a spiritual tragedy, that book, which is most fearfully true; and he wrote to shew what must be the end of a man, who, too weak for action, destroyed his own moral sense by daring and morbid speculation. I think he was most mistaken in writing it.

But now having said all this, I must say, that whatever may seem to me my duty to Froude there can be no doubt of my duty to *you*. And *therefore I solemnly promise you either to get rid of Froude or leave Lynmouth immediately, and not to remain in* his company one day longer than the common courtesies of life require. *Can I say more?* [1]

On learning of the financial dilemma in which Froude found himself, several liberal-minded men, among them Monckton Milnes and Bunsen, showed their sympathy in a practical way by making up a purse to send him to a German University to study theology, but he definitely did not want to study theology and after some deliberation refused to accept the help that had been tactfully and anonymously proffered. He was now not only without means but without the prospect of employment since the Council of University College which had appointed him to a lectureship at Hobart Town, Tasmania (a post he had applied for the previous year), had by this time asked him to withdraw his application.

John Martineau describes Froude as 'the handsomest, most fascinating man I ever saw', and there is no doubt that he was a singularly distinguished looking person of great charm when he chose to exert it. When he arrived at Lynmouth he was warmly welcomed by Charles and Fanny. With Fanny was her sister, Charlotte, two years older than herself and since two years a convert to Roman Catholicism. At the time Miss Grenfell made Anthony Froude's acquaintance she had decided to enter a convent. But romance suddenly intervened and a courtship followed on the pattern of Fanny's except that it was less protracted. Froude, a year older than Kingsley, fell, as his host had done before him, deeply in love with a woman several years older than himself. After an ardent wooing he succeeded in persuading her to promise to abandon celibacy and marry him. Fanny was not altogether happy about the engagement and told Anthony that she was in two minds about congratulating her sister before she left Lynmouth. He at once wrote her a firm letter saying:

I warned you that I intended to take my own way in life doing (as I have always done) in all important matters just what I should

[1] Add. MSS., B.M.

think good, at whatever risk of consequences, and taking no other person's opinion when it crossed my own. Now in this matter I feel certain that the way to save Charlotte most pain is to *shorten* the struggle, and that will best be done by being short, peremptory, and decided in allowing no dictation and no interference. . . . Charlotte herself is really magnificent. Every letter shows me larger nobleness of heart. You cannot go back *now*, Mrs Kingsley.

Her professed faith, which horrified the Kingsleys as much as it did Froude, was laid aside without any apparent scruple and Charlotte during the happy ten years of her married life did not attend a Catholic service. Her baby, born at Taplow, was christened in the Church of England, and when she came to die, her body was laid to rest in Eversley churchyard with her brother-in-law reading the committal prayers.

Charlotte, like Fanny, had a small fortune of her own, but Froude as we have seen had been deprived of all income. He therefore felt bound to accept the first job that was offered him, which happened to be a private tutorship in the family of a Mr. Darbishire in Lancashire. In October 1849 as soon as their marriage had taken place, Mr. and Mrs. Froude went to Manchester and there made acquaintance with Miss Jewsbury, Miss Martineau, and Mrs. Gaskell—the literary lights of the north. Geraldine Jewsbury, a cheerful little creature, worshipping George Sand, was author of *Zoë or the Two Lives*, the first English novel in which the hero's career is conditioned by the victory of scepticism over belief. It had come out three years before *The Nemesis of Faith*, and as it dealt with much the same problems the two authors were immediately drawn to each other, forming a friendship that lasted for life. All lectureships and professions being closed to an ex-deacon, Froude by Miss Jewsbury's advice took up writing for a living. *The Cat's Pilgrimage* was composed in Manchester, and he worked hard at book-reviewing of which he made an immediate success.

Charlotte Froude was not altogether happy in the intellectual bourgeois circle that welcomed her husband's company so warmly, in truth she felt so out of her natural element that she persuaded him to take a little house at the foot of Snowdon, Plas Gwynant, where they could enjoy a state of unsocial and simple happiness. Visitors occasionally broke in on their solitude *à deux*—angler Charles Kingsley and Froude's great friend Arthur Clough were with them almost as soon as they had settled in.

Kingsley talked incessantly on fishing excursions and would tell Clough that it had pleased God to show him and Maurice things He had concealed from Carlyle. Clough took such confidences with a grain of salt, and so did Froude. Later on when Maurice in his turn was expelled from his chair at King's College for heretical teaching Froude wrote his mind to Clough, 'As thinkers, Maurice, and still more the Mauricians, appear to me the most hopelessly imbecile that any section of the world have been driven to believe in'.

We must now return to the main stream of our narrative to find Charles Kingsley, with 'magnetic tone completely restored' by Devonshire breezes, attending a meeting called by Chartists on Land Colonisation. This meeting was followed up by a great gathering of Tailors which he also attended. There he learnt that a union of women-shoemakers was about to be formed and that he was becoming widely known among provincial Chartists through his *Village Sermons*. He saw a good many people, breakfasted with Bunsen, 'such a divine looking man and so kind! Met F. Newman at dinner last night and breakfast with him tomorrow. I had a long interesting talk with Froude.' He called on Carlyle and 'dear Charles Mansfield', but the account of this visit to London is so peppered with Mrs. Kingsley's asterisks as to present an incoherent narrative. We are told, however, that he went to hear Maurice preach in Lincoln's Inn Chapel, and came away thinking that 'he looked like some great awful Giorgione portrait, but oh so worn, and the face worked so at certain passages in the sermon'. We learn that he visited the slum district known as Jacob's Island, for he wrote to his wife of his experiences.

I was yesterday with George, Walsh and Mansfield over the cholera districts of Bermondsey and oh God! what I saw! people having no water to drink—hundreds of them but the water of the common sewer which stagnated full of . . . dead fish, cats and dogs under the windows.

At the time the cholera was raging Walsh saw them throwing

the rice water evacuations into the ditch and then dipping out the water and drinking it!!!

Fanny at the time was staying with her sister Caroline Warre whose husband was an M.P. Charles begged her to show him his letter and entreat him to read the account of the slum in the *Morning Chronicle* of the previous week.

Try every nerve to get a model lodging house *there* [in Bermondsey]. . . . And mind you these people are not dirty debauched Irish, but honest hard-working artizans. It is most pathetic, as Walsh says it literally makes him cry to see the poor souls' struggle for cleanliness—to see how they scrub and polish their little scrap of pavement and then to go through the house and see 'society' leaving at the back poisons and filth such as would drive a lady mad, I think in 24 hours / with disgust / Oh that I had the tongue of St. James to plead for these poor fellows to tell what I saw myself—to stir up some rich man to go and rescue them from the tyranny of the small shop-keeping landlords who get their rents out of the flesh and blood of these men.

P.S.—£20 sent to us just to start a water-cart and send it round at once, at once, for the people are still in these horrors, would pay for itself. I can find men who will work this thing. Walsh, Mansfield, Ludlow and the Campbells will go and serve the water with their own hands rather than let it go on. Pray, pray, try and stir him and God will reward you!

This slum visit drove Kingsley half-demented, for no one seemed to be doing anything or think it their business to attempt to do anything in spite of the hair-raising communications sent to the press by Dr. Lynch, a London Commissioner of Sewers. Not knowing what to be at, Kingsley sat down to write an up-to-date article on the subject for the May number of the *North British Review*. Why on earth, he wondered, should well-to-do persons waste time and money in creating a plaything model parish like that of St. Barnabas, Pimlico, where there were three rich people to one poor, while whole square miles in other parts of London were suffering from the poison of complete neglect. Did no one trouble to read Dr. Lynch's reports? Had he not stated that 'in Farringdon ward seven and eight people were crowded into a room seven feet long and six feet high, under which ran a cess-pool which had not been cleaned out for thirty years'? Had he not also told the public plain facts about the graveyards in London? of the bodies buried in them that were dissipated in the air that was breathed by the living? of the churchyard of St. Andrew's, Holborn, raised to forty-six feet above the level of the street owing to layer upon layer of human bodies?

Kingsley flew around, upbraiding Ludlow for trusting to legislative measures for improvement, concocting a new sanitary league with Charles Mansfield, gingering up S. G. O. to write fiercely to the *Times*, and Tom Taylor to ventilate the scandal in *Punch*, bustling off to Oxford to see the Bishop and others in authority, and seeking interviews with Lord John Russell and Lord Carlisle. On all alike he urged that a public meeting of protest must be organised as soon as possible, there was no time to waste for women and children were dying daily.

Oh that one-tenth of the money that has been spent in increasing, by mistaken benevolence the cruelties of the slave trade had been spent in buying up these nests of typhus, consumption and cholera and rebuilding them into habitations, I do not say for civilised Englishmen—that would be too much but for hogs even.

The Bermondsey case is only the *experimentum crucis* of a vast question, 'And shall men do what they like with thier own?' Mind if I begin and find it work, I should try for compulsory legislation for all landlords.

And then he went back furiously to write *Alton Locke* and infuse the story with the passion generated by recent experience. He succeeded in making it the one novel of the Victorian era that no one interested in social conditions can afford to neglect.

The story of the book is roughly that Alton, son of a cockney named Locke and educated by a puritanical mother, becomes imbued, when apprenticed to a 'sweating' tailor, with Chartist ideas. His instinctive love of poetry leads him to friendship with an old Scottish bookseller, Saunders Mackaye. Many people said that this very much alive figure must have been modelled on Carlyle and maybe the sage thought so himself for after reading the first chapters in manuscript he wrote to Kingsley, 'Your book is definable as crude . . . the impression is a fervid creation still left half-chaotic. But', he added slyly, 'Saunders Mackaye is nearly perfect. I greatly wonder how you did contrive to manage him, his very dialect is as if a native had done it.'

One of Alton's songs (composed by Kingsley as he wandered about Dartmoor) breathes of revolution and shows how deeply its author had been affected by brooding over conditions in Bermondsey and elsewhere.

> Weep, weep, weep, and weep,
> For pauper, dolt, and slave!
> Hark! from wasted moor and fen,
> Feverous alley, stifling den,
> Swells the wail of Saxon men—
>   Work! or the grave!

> Down, down, down and down
> With idler, knave and tyrant!
> Why for sluggards cark and moil?
> He that will not live by toil
> Has no right to English soil!
>   God's word's our warrant!

> Up, up, up and up!
> Face your game and play it!
> The night is past, behold the sun!
> The idols fall, the lie is done!
> The Judge is set, the doom begun!
>   Who shall stay it?

In succession to Saunders Mackaye, a Dean discovers Locke's poetical gift. The Dean has a beautiful daughter, Lillian, with whom Alton falls hopelessly in love. She and her cousin, Eleanor Staunton, persuade him to emasculate his revolutionary verses before publication, a weakness he lives to regret bitterly. Gibed at by Chartist comrades, he volunteers for a mission that involves him in a riot and is sentenced to three years' imprisonment. On release he learns that Lillian is about to marry his prosperous cousin. The cousin is shortly afterwards stricken by typhus from wearing a 'sweated' overcoat. Alton then visits the typhus district, and is led by Downes, a 'sweated' tailor, to his workshop, a lean-to with boarded walls dimly illuminated by the rush-light he carries in his hand. Through the chinks in the flooring a sewer reflecting the flame is just visible. Downes tears a half-finished gentleman's coat off three corpses lying on the bare floor—those of his wife and children who had all died of typhus. When he demands money for gin, Alton accuses him of accursed tippling and just as he is saying, 'If you had been a water-drinker like myself', he is suddenly interrupted with, 'Curse you and your water-drinking. If you had had no water to drink or wash with but that—that—that—pointing to the foul ditch below—if you had emptied the slops with one hand and filled your kettle with the other.' At this moment two policemen arrive and Downes stumbles drunkenly from the rickety balcony into the tidal ditch. Alton Locke describes the ghastly scene, the double row of miserable house-backs lining the sides of the ditch—the rambling jetties, balconies, rotting piles, the bubbles of poisonous gas floating on the oily water, the lumps of offal, the carcases of dogs, all emitting an unwholesome stench,—it is the very mouth of hell. When finished the overcoat that covered the corpses is sent to a gentleman in the West End, is handled by his valet and worn by the purchaser: both die of typhus. Alton Locke falls sick too, and is nursed by Eleanor Staunton who instructs him in Christianity. He then starts for America but dies on the way.

Fanny, on whom the copying of this novel devolved, suffered a great deal from the 'state of nervous prostration to which the writing of the book had reduced him'. Repeatedly did she entreat him never to write another novel.

As a result of his Bermondsey experience a passion for sanitary reform overmastered Kingsley. His interest in social improvement now became centred in it and it alone, for he argued that since the root of all that is good in man lies in the purity and vigour of his domestic affections, a condition of affairs in which the health and stability of the family are constantly imperilled connotes the sapping of the very foundations of society. During the next few years we shall find Kingsley giving more and more of himself to this type of reform. It was the one and only crusade that now seemed to him intensely and incontrovertibly worth while and from every point of view right.

When the rector took up his work again at Eversley he was fortified in this opinion by the condition in which he found the parish, for with the onset of summer a low fever had broken out. This epidemic involved him in much sick visiting. Everyone was nervous lest the fever should turn out to be the harbinger of cholera. To allay the increasing apprehension that a miasma of infection was brooding over the whole of England and might at any moment envelop Eversley, Kingsley preached three sermons entitled, *Who Causes Pestilence?* These were later published. The whole situation depressed him terribly; he simply could not stand up to the sick calls or maintain the role of heartening up his people. He felt his magnetism oozing away rapidly, and by mid-July his health had so deteriorated under the strain that he was once more ordered away by his doctor.

We need hardly say that he made tracks for Devonshire, this time to the house of the Rev. J. Drosier at Coldbrook on Dartmoor, the home of the man who was coaching his brother Henry for Oxford. He spent three days there and was pleased to receive an excellent account of Henry's work. As usual on a holiday Charles Kingsley was armed with the works of Rabelais, and wrote to his wife to say what great pleasure he was again deriving from their re-perusal. 'Were he seven times as unspeakably filthy as he is, I consider his works as priceless in wisdom and often in true evangelic godliness.'[1] 'Having learnt deep things from Rabelais', he proposes to take an intensive course of Ruskin, not nearly so congenial an author, but still a teacher of considerable importance.

Long excursions on foot to fish moorland trout streams reinvigorated him and stimulated an acute interest in the early British remains near Coldbrook. These consisted of a town with a circular wall ringing a group of circular granite huts set among the peat bogs that testified to its having been, once upon a time, a forest site. On another ramble he stumbled on 'two

[1] *Charles Kingsley*, vol. I, p. 211.

splendid Druid circles'. How full the moor was of wonderful, life-giving surprises! Believing as he did in 'a wounded bird going back to his nest', he was convinced that no place re-magnetised one so quickly as the county of one's birth. Did Englishmen as a rule feel this way, he asked of Fanny, or was he exceptional in being 'the one man who suffered from *heimweh* as nostalgically as the expatriate Swiss or Highlander?' His spirits automatically rose. Once again he felt like singing.

I cannot tell what you say, green leaves,
I cannot tell what you say:
But I know that there is a spirit in you
And a word in you this day.

I cannot tell what you say, rosy rocks,
I cannot tell what you say:
But I know that there is a spirit in you
And a word in you this day.

I cannot tell what you say, brown streams,
I cannot tell what you say:
But I know that in you too a spirit doth live
And a word doth speak this day.

THE WORLD'S ANSWER

Oh green is the colour of faith and truth,
And rose the colour of love and youth,
And brown of the fruitful clay.
Sweet Earth is faithful, and fruitful, and young,
And her bridal day shall come ere long
And you shall know what the rocks and the streams
And the whispering woodlands say.

When he again returned to his parish, Percy Smith, a Balliol man, became his curate. Smith was a great friend of Kegan Paul, whom he invited to Eversley despite the fact that he had no spare room and had to put him up at the public-house. Paul really wanted to consult Kingsley about taking Orders, and in the course of several long talks the rector enabled his disciple 'to dismiss all faith whatever in the popular doctrine of eternal punishment and the whole class of dogmas that tend to confuse God and the Devil'. The better to instruct him Kingsley had him to stay at the rectory, and succeeded in persuading his guest to adopt his views and become a clergyman, a part Paul sustained for a few years only before reverting to the status of layman and finally joining the Church of Rome. One evening Percy Smith and Kegan Paul dined at the rectory. When dinner was over, Kingsley took them both into his study and began to orate on mesmerism, folk-lore, legends, the properties of plants, the disposition of animals, and the characteristics of gypsies. Paul describes him as 'talking with twenty parson power and as totally unlike the conventional clergyman'. He notes that he was extremely restless, could not sit quiet at meals, and paced up and down the grass plot outside his study window while concocting the next sentence or paragraph of what he was about to write. When it had reached its proper shape he would rush indoors and stand at a rough desk, projecting like a shelf from the wall, to scribble it down.

Alton Locke being finished, it was offered to John Parker, who was too timid to accept it for publication. Carlyle, however, came to the rescue, recommending the book to Chapman and Hall as 'a new explosion or salvo of red-hot shell against the Devil's dung-heap'.

The novel drew heavy fire from the critics, and Kingsley thought it incumbent on him to explain that he had prayed hard over the message the book was intended to convey, and that he had been most scrupulous about trying to say 'the right thing in the right way'. A little more precisely he says:

> The moral of my book is that the working man who tries to get on, to desert his class and rise above it, enters into a lie and leaves God's path for his own. . . . I believe that when you put workmen into human dwellings and give them a Christian education, so far from wishing discontentedly to rise out of their class, or to level others to it, exactly the opposite takes place. They become sensible of the dignity of work.

The author felt he could speak with authority in these matters, having been brought up in familiar intercourse with the poor in town and country and being 'the son of a mother who was a second Mrs. Fry in spirit and act'. But his explanation revealed that in spite of his passion for sanitation and frenzied desire to improve the living conditions of the people, he was no democrat at heart, but as strong a believer in the social as he was in the ecclesiastical hierarchy.

Chapter 8

A DECLARED CHARTIST

It is the slovenliness of men and women which for the most part makes their lives so unsatisfactory.

JOHN MORLEY

OWING to long absences from Eversley and the obligation Kingsley was under to provide a curate to take his duty, it became more urgent for him than ever to try and supplement his fixed stipend. Taking pupils seemed to offer a solution, but in spite of the touting done by Maurice and others none were forthcoming in 1849, though in January 1850 a delicate schoolboy, rising sixteen, John Martineau, arrived to be coached for the University. He describes in a very lively way the life he led as an inmate of the rectory at Eversley. Charles Kingsley was at the time in his thirty-first year and at the height of his powers. The schoolboy took to him warmly and companioned him on all his walks. 'Nothing', Martineau says, 'could be more exquisitely delightful than a walk with him about his parish. No bird, beast or insect passed unnoticed, he caught every sound, every breath, every sign.' But for all his manliness, his pupil observed in him 'a deep vein of *woman* which showed itself in nervous sensitiveness and intensity of sympathy'. His only recreation lay in throwing a fly on the stream that bordered his parish. He seemed to work few hours in the day and that without system or regularity, but with so intense an application as to put a great strain on his vital powers.

At this time Charles Kingsley did not take in or read any daily newspaper and drew all his information about current affairs from the *Spectator*. It was his habit to get up at five in the morning to work quietly at writing. At 8.45 A.M. he read morning prayers before the assembled household. Prayers were followed by a substantial meat breakfast and then everyone settled down to work till 1 P.M. After lunch they walked till 5 o'clock and then dined. More work was done between seven and nine, then came evening prayers, then bed.

It surprised John Martineau and rather pleased him to observe that his tutor never laughed, 'just like me', as he told his mother. The boy found his stammering very unpleasant, and his kindness most winning. It excited him very much when a gang of burglars began operating in the neighbourhood, for sometimes a servant would come in after dusk and say that he heard footsteps in the garden and out they all would rush with pistols to give chase. The fate of a neighbouring clergyman, Mr. Hollest, who had been killed after firing on thieves from his front door at Frimley, made the strictest precautions necessary. In August a second and older pupil by the name of Lees arrived at the rectory to read for Orders. Lees took his full share in protecting the house and sat up in turn with the rest, pistol in hand. One Sunday John Martineau stayed at home with Mrs. Kingsley to guard the house during afternoon service. Mr. Kingsley was in a highly nervous state that day and could hardly get through the prescribed prayers. Suddenly he rose from his knees, left Percy Smith to carry on with the service, and bolted off to hunt through the stables where he thought he had seen a man lurking earlier in the afternoon. On the day Fanny Kingsley went to Maidenhead to see Charlotte Froude and her new-born baby she was careful to buy burglar alarm bells at Reading on her way back. Kingsley and Lees set out on horseback to meet her, armed as usual with their pistols as she could not hope to reach Eversley till seven. At this time the rector, on Speaker Shaw-Lefevre's advice, summoned what Martineau called 'a bluebottle', which did not scare the thieves, for two or three evenings later on hearing suspicious sounds, Kingsley ran out of the back door and fired at a man some fifteen yards off, but 'unfortunately', to use John Martineau's words, 'his pistol was loaded with slugs not bullets'. Next morning three policemen came over from Winchester and on examining the door found it damaged with a jemmy. Presently the crime wave died down as unexpectedly as it had arisen.

One day Kingsley described to his pupil what he had seen of the rioting in Bristol in 1831, as a schoolboy.

'That sight,' he said turning suddenly to me, 'made me a Radical.' 'Whose fault is it,' I ventured to ask, 'that such things can be?' 'Mine,' he said, 'and yours.'

'I understood partly then, I have understood better since, what his Radicalism was.'

The Froudes came to stay at the rectory in October 1850. Before they arrived Mrs. Kingsley told John Martineau a good deal about her brother-in-law, what a miserable childhood he had had, and how, though sickly, he had been sent to rough it at Westminster School, where he had been utterly wretched. Oxford he had loved, and after winning his Exeter fellowship had been able to live in College in comfort. She told John that *Shadows in the Clouds* by Zeta was really by Froude, that it was a book that had 'made people very angry', and that Anthony then had become 'reckless' and had written *The Nemesis of Faith*.

The rector still called himself a Radical, though he detested the Manchester school and had little use for constitutions and political machinery. These seemed to him of little import compared with the explosive force of the enthusiasm he had worked into *Yeast* and *Alton Locke*. It has often been said that Kingsley contributed little or nothing in the way of remedy for the evils exposed in these novels, but we must remember that he had a horror of doctrinaire glibness and cut-and-dried cures for social imbroglios. As a staunch believer in individual effort and right-mindedness he was prone to think that if only a man were God-fearing, he could trust God to put things right.

Kingsley had almost the same dislike of dogmatic theology as of dogmatic socialism. For instance, the recital of the Athanasian Creed had always presented great difficulties to him; he had his own private reservations about its meaning, and he did not wish his flock to think that he accepted the face value of its damnatory clauses. He therefore decided to explain the Creed carefully to his congregation in a thoughtfully prepared sermon. There was at this time no hymn-singing to cover movements in and out of the chancel and so the rector went to the vestry in silence, preparatory to preaching, to take off his surplice and reappear in a black gown. Minute after minute passed and he did not return. Presently the clerk came and whispered in Mrs. Kingsley's ear that Mr. Kingsley wanted to see her in the churchyard. There he was sitting on a tombstone, the picture of despair. 'Fanny, what shall I do?' was all he could say. He had forgotten to bring his sermon to the

church.   Fanny promptly decided that so much time having
been wasted a shorter homily must somehow be extracted from
his study, not an easy thing to do as every member of the
household was in church, the rectory locked up, and the key in
the pocket of a servant.   But in the end the key was fetched by
Fanny, who ran to the house and brought back an old address as
substitute for that on the Athanasian Creed, which was preached
the following Sunday.

One of the excitements of 1850 was the launching of *The
Christian Socialist* under the editorship of John Ludlow.   Sub-
titled *The Journal of Association*, it was intended to advocate
reform by peaceful methods, to diffuse principles of co-operation,
the practical application of Christianity to the purposes of trade
and industry, and to induce working men and women to form
co-operative associations among themselves.   Ludlow, on account of his study of the *associations ouvrières* in Paris, was asked
by his colleagues to draft a bill for legalising the future position
of similar associations in England.   In the same year Lord Derby's
Conservative Government facilitated the passing of a private
measure recognising the legal existence of such Associations,
thereby enabling promoters to put their finances on a sound
footing.   Kingsley, who sat on the Council for the Promotion
of Associations, gave a series of lectures in support of the movement.

The programme of the *Christian Socialist* was drawn up by
'Parson Lot', who undertook in its columns to reply to points
raised against Christian teaching.   The subjects he suggested
should be dealt with were:

    (I) Politics according to the Kingdom of God.
    (II) Art and Amusements for the People.
    (III) Opening of Universities to the People and Education in
           general.
    (IV) Attacks on Straussism and Infidelity.
    (V) Sanitary Reform.
    (VI) Association.   (Agitation on Partnership Laws: Stores and
           Distribution: Agricultural Schemes.)

He offered to supply a series of papers on what he termed
'Bible Politics', the object of which was to prove how false was

the belief that the Bible supported priestcraft, superstition, and tyranny. Actually Kingsley led off with a contribution of which Ludlow highly disapproved:

> I want to send you the first of three letters on the Frimley murder, and our present reign of terror, showing that Christian organisation of labour might have prevented it all and an increase of police is a mere ruinous driving inward of the disease.

His second contribution, *The Nun's Pool*, already rejected by Maurice for *Politics for the People* as 'entirely unsuitable', Ludlow liked no better than when he had first looked over it. It was printed, however, through the weeks July 5–August 20, for the editor was in a quandary and did not know what to do about 'Parson Lot's' articles and stories. Mrs. Kingsley includes in her book a long dissertation on teetotalism suppressed by Ludlow. Kingsley may have been in what he used to call a Pantagruelist mood, for he expressed the strongest disapproval of teetotalism and said that he viewed the movement with 'extreme dread'.

> Oh my teetotal brothers, in God's name, as one who has studied long and deeply the history of ancient asceticisms I entreat you to pause and beware. . . . So did the early monks abstain from marriage. The rise of mediaeval celibacy was exactly analogous to the rise of modern teetotalism. . . . I assert the identity of the two cases. The old monks and early fathers proved from logic, reason, Scripture, science and everything else that marriage was horrible, beastly, ruinous—the parent of every evil and misery on earth. They had serious doubts as to whether married persons could be finally saved. They discovered that Eve was a virgin in Paradise, and that marriage in Genesis does not mean marriage, just as the teetotalers have that Our Lord did not drink fermented liquors and that wine in the Gospels does not mean wine. . . . I will not be a bigot and a manichee, but only, as far as I can, a christian man. Because I am determined not to be a monk and not to be a teetotaler.

Ludlow, though he opined that a man must be ill to write such rubbish, was handicapped in telling Kingsley what he really thought for fear of 'paralysing' his contributor's pen. But he did manage to stop the series 'Bible Politics', a wise move as the point had been reached when the Parson had to treat of the extermination of the Canaanites 'which certainly would have horrified the whole kiss-the-devil school'. Kingsley had been so useful to Ludlow in converting his pupil Lees to Christian Socialism that he was anxious not to ruffle him more than necessary. Lees, it seems, was ready to lend Ludlow £100 to carry on with, and had offered to buy up the river slum known as Jacob's Island with a view to rebuilding.

When *Yeast* was published in volume form in May 1851, it attracted a good deal of notice and criticism, for the most part hostile. As a book it could never make a really popular appeal, being too little of a novel and too much of a political pamphlet or tract for the times.

One of the scenes described in the book had also been described by Dickens, an apparently common and consistently shocking scene that most of the inhabitants of London preferred to ignore. It is laid in the street outside a workhouse door, and men and women are seeking admission to an already crowded 'House'. The rain is pouring down and they have no other hope of shelter. When Dickens saw a similar scene, he emptied his purse among the outcasts and they melted away.

The *Guardian* side-tracked all serious discussion of *Yeast* by trouncing the author personally for writing the book at all. What did he mean by setting out to preach religious earnestness and high morality, while he was really destroying both!

> We are utterly at issue with him in an opinion which is implied throughout the volume that a certain amount of youthful profligacy does no real permanent harm to the character for a useful and even religious life, and that the existence of the passions are a proof that they are to be gratified.

The reviewer quarrelled with the author for making the hero a 'healthy animalist' who has 'gone through that course of profligacy which is considered necessary to develop the nature and impart breadth and manliness to the intellect of the apostles of the latest and most philosophical phases of Christianity'. This criticism seems carping and stupid to-day as it is only with difficulty that any allusion to vice or bad conduct can be found in the book. The review had the effect of infuriating Kingsley and he replied to the attack in the words of Father Valerian the Capuchin *Mentiris impudentissime*.[1]

Maurice expressed warm sympathy with Kingsley. It really was monstrous that an anonymous reviewer should charge a clergyman with being an advocate of profligacy. The *Guardian* supported its reviewer and refused to retract the charges made, but Kingsley was to some extent consoled for this by receiving private letters of gratitude and appreciation. One asterisked correspondent wrote that after reading *Yeast* he felt as if he had emerged from a mephitic cavern into the open day, another thanked him for portraying a sceptic seeking after God. It pleased him extremely that George Meredith wrote to say he had read the novel with *delight* and *admiration*. 'Education I have derived from it. It was the very book I was in need of.'

The Great Exhibition of 1851, which opened just at the time *Yeast* appeared, appealed in rather a strange way to Kingsley. Dickens disliked what he called the 'duffery of it all' very much and went to the seaside to be out of the eternal chatter it provoked. Kingsley's reaction was to burst into tears on entering the building. It was like 'going into a sacred place', for was it not dedicated to universal brotherhood and therefore universal peace? Among the foreign visitors to the Crystal Palace was Frederica Bremer who through reading Charles Kingsley's two novels had conceived a great admiration for him. Though a venerated and almost legendary figure in Sweden, abroad she is little known either for her social work or for her very dull books. Soon after arrival she hurried down to stay at Eversley, where she proved to be a gentle and congenial guest. Towards Charles she said she felt as a sister to a young brother. She told him that the greatness of the old Viking lay in his wanting to conquer the whole world for himself, whereas the mission of the spiritual Viking was a far higher one, that of conquering the world for God. In giving Kingsley her book, *Fridthof's Saga*, she inscribed it 'To the Viking of the New Age, Charles Kingsley, this story of the Vikings of the Old, from a daughter of the Vikings, his friend and admirer Frederika Bremer'.

Four days after the Exhibition opened, Kingsley preached at

[1] *Lettres provinciales XV.*

St. Margaret's, Westminster, on the unbelief of the day.   After admitting that something of the form and tradition of earlier times still linger in our ceremonies, when, for instance, we join in prayer asking God in whom we do not really believe to bless our Great Exhibition, he continues:

> We do not believe my friends—that it was God who taught men to conceive, build and arrange this great exhibition, and our notion of God's blessing it, seems to be God's absence from it; a hope and a trust that God will leave it and us alone, and not *visit* it and us in it or interfere by any 'special providences', by storms, or lightning, or sickness, or panic, or conspiracy; a sort of dim feeling that we could manage it all perfectly well without God, but that as He existed and has some power over natural phenomena, which is not very exactly defined, we must notice His existence over and above our work, lest He should become angry and *visit* us.

During the course of the Exhibition it was arranged that visitors to London should have the opportunity of listening to famous preachers on Sundays.   One of the series arranged was for working men at St. John's Church, Fitzroy Square, where the speakers were selected by Maurice.   Tom Hughes (though not a parson) was to be one of them, and so, of course, was Charles Kingsley, who rarely preached outside his own parish, but who, owing to his reputation as a socialist, was certain to draw a large congregation at St. John's.   The subject of the series was the message of Christ to the labouring man.   Taking for his text, 'The Spirit of the Lord is upon me because he hath anointed me to preach the Gospel to the poor', Kingsley began by asserting,

> that the business for which God sends a Christian priest to a Christian nation is to preach liberty, equality, and brotherhood in the fullest, deepest, widest, simplest meaning of these three terms. . . . I say those words express the very pith and marrow of a priest's business.   I say that they preach liberty, equality and brotherhood to the poor and the rich for ever and ever. . . . Woe unto you who are full for ye have received your consolation already. . . . Woe unto you that make a few rich to make many poor.   Woe unto you that make merchandise out of the needs of your brethren.   Woe

unto you for God the Father of all is against you, God the Son, the
poor man of Nazareth, is against you—God the Holy Spirit, who
cannot lie, is against you.

And what my friends is the message of the Lord's Supper?
What more distinct sign and pledge that all men are equal?
Wherever in the world there may be inequality, it ceases there.
One table, one reverential posture, one bread, one wine, for high
and low, for wise and foolish.

The real sting of the sermon did not lie in Kingsley's profession
of liberty, equality, and fraternity, but in his attack on landed
property. The preacher referred to one of the wisest institu-
tions of Moses by which at the expiration of a certain period all
land which had been sold was returned to its original possessor.
In Judaea there could be no permanent alienation of the soil but
only a lease of it from the time of sale to the next year of Jubilee.
Kingsley regarded this as an unparalleled contrivance for pre-
venting the accumulation of large estates and the reduction of
the people into the state of serfs and day-labourers. To him
it was a proof, if proof were needed, of the inspired wisdom of
Moses.

The sermon was listened to with close attention by the working men present, who were all convinced before hearing it that
the Church of England was the mainstay of the existing order of
society and the opponent of all change. But just as Kingsley
had ended and was about to give the blessing, he was dramatic-
ally silenced by the sonorous voice of the vicar, Mr. Drew, who
rising to his feet declared it to be his painful duty to state that
much that Mr. Kingsley had said was extremely imprudent and
much untrue. 'I may say also that it is altogether different from
what I had been led to expect.' This excited the congregation,
hissing was heard, and people began to surge forward. A
scene might have resulted had not Kingsley, with head deeply
bowed, descended the pulpit stairs and walked straight into the
vestry.

Returning late that evening to Eversley too excited to go to
bed, he spent the hours of darkness pacing up and down the
lawn. By breakfast time he had produced a poem, *The Three
Fishers*, and read it aloud to Fanny. An attack on him in the
morning papers was followed by a letter from Dr. Blomfield,

Bishop of London, expressing displeasure at the report he had received on the sermon and forbidding Charles Kingsley to preach in his diocese. A letter also arrived from Maurice, apologising for 'the strange and monstrous behaviour of Mr. Drew'.

At a meeting of working men on Kennington Common on the same evening a vote of sympathy was passed with acclamation, and it was suggested that the preacher should form a free church on the lines indicated in his sermon. Meanwhile Kingsley decided to have the sermon printed and to send a copy to Bishop Blomfield, who, after reading it, invited the author to come and see him at London House. At this meeting, which turned out to be unexpectedly friendly, prohibition to preach in the metropolis was withdrawn and a fortnight later the rector of Eversley preached the self-same sermon at St. Luke's, Chelsea. What between the sniping carried on against him by *Edinburgh* and *Quarterly Reviews* and the displeasing publicity he had achieved with his sermon, Kingsley felt the need to get away into a calmer and less fretting atmosphere. He chose to throw himself into the fifth century for his next novel and began work on *Hypatia*. At the end of July he was thankful to accept his parents' invitation to go with them to Germany. Charles had never been abroad before, nor had Henry who was one of the party.

A demure and observant girl of thirteen in mushroom hat and mackintosh also boarded the packet-boat at St. Katherine's Wharf on that sleety summer morning. It was Anne Thackeray, who was going with her father and sister to Germany. The decks were wet and slippery, but despite this an English family party was already established on them. The family consisted of an elderly gentleman in a dark suit and a lady sheltering as best she might from the drizzle and the smuts spewed out by the boat's funnel. It was the Kingsley family, consisting of the rector of Chelsea and his wife and two sons. Mr. Charles Kingsley and his brother were wearing brown felt hats with very high and pointed crowns and very broad brims. Mr. Thackeray too had bought himself an admired grey wide-awake for the journey which now, compared with the hat of the Kingsley brothers, looked to the Thackeray children quite commonplace. The two families fraternised until the roughness of the sea made polite intercourse impossible.

It was a stormy crossing [says Anne Thackeray], the waves were curling unpleasantly round the boat; I sat by Mrs. Kingsley, miserable, uncomfortable, and watching in a dazed and hypnotised sort of way the rim of Charles Kingsley's wide-awake as it rose and fell against the horrible horizon. He stood before us holding on to some ropes, and the horizon rose and fell, and the steamer pitched and tossed, and it seemed as if Time stood still.

The bad weather developed into a storm, a jib was carried away and a hundred women were sick on the cabin floor all night. At last they reached their haven, Antwerp. From there the two families travelled together by Rhine steamer to Cologne and Anne Thackeray decided that Charles Kingsley was 'a fine, honest, go-ahead fellow who charges a subject heartily, impetuously, with the greatest courage and simplicity, but with narrow eyes, (his eyes are extraordinarily brave, blue and honest) and with little knowledge of the world, I think, but he is superior to us worldlings in many ways, and I wish I had some of his honest pluck', sentiments more consonant with Mr. Thackeray's conversation perhaps than with the thoughts of an adolescent.

In Cologne cathedral Charles greatly admired the Kaulbach windows, and the great Lochner triptych of the Adoration of the Magi in the choir made him cry like a child, the head of the Virgin was of a loveliness that touched him deeply.

After settling their parents for their cure at Ems the brothers started on a walking-tour. It pleased Charles very much to find what an athlete Henry had trained himself to be during his term at Oxford. In a single year he had transformed his body into something well filled out and muscular. His school-friend, Edwin Arnold, watching the improvement in his physique had wagered him one day that he could not row a mile, run a mile, and trot a mile within fifteen minutes, yet he accomplished this remarkable feat. In a way Henry resembled Charles, but it was only a family resemblance, for he was very short and had a tight-lipped mouth with heavy lines running from nose to chin. There was about a foot of difference in their heights.

Henry Kingsley had matriculated at Worcester College, Oxford, in March 1850. After keeping all his terms at King's College School he had in 1847 transferred to the College itself to study Literature and Science. He had already begun to show a marked facility in writing and John Parker encouraged it by inviting him to meet Thackeray at dinner. Henry was too shy to speak, but after watching the great man intently he came to the conclusion that 'the man who had written the most remarkable tale—*Vanity Fair*, had the most remarkable face he had ever seen'.

Friends made by Henry at Oxford usually found themselves involved in money-lending transactions as Charles must have known only too well. Cordy Jeaffreson backed a bill for £80 because tradesmen were worrying Henry so much that he could not work. The £80 did not suffice to pay all his debts and Cordy Jeaffreson thought he would lose his money, but when a great-aunt of Henry died leaving him £300, he was able to repay it, and buy a ticket for Australia where he hoped to make his fortune.

The brothers went to Bingen by steamer, crossed the river and wandered down the right bank from St. Goar to Lurlei, where Charles scrambled up to the Lorelei's seat and picked a little bouquet for Fanny, whom he tells he is able to walk without fatigue, and to write poetry. The climate is bracing, the views beautiful; he can well understand people preferring the Rhineland to England. Enchanted by the wild-flowers and the butterflies, the rare oak-ferns clustering round the oak-scrub roots, the great blue campanulas, the white admirals, the fritillaries, he writes ecstatically of the great purple emperors flitting down to drink in the road puddles and 'flashing off their velvet wings a blue as of that empyrean which is dark by excess of light'. Charles and Henry sat happily in the sunshine to watch bright-eyed lizards hunt flies, while green locusts with red wings and grey locusts with blue wings buzzed, and pitched, and leapt about them. When the two set out for a tramp through the Eifel Gebirge letters ceased to be delivered at Eversley rectory and Fanny wrote to her mother-in-law for news. Mrs. Kingsley assured her that all was more than well with Charles, 'he is in very rude health and enjoying everything to the full extent of his powers moral and physical'. She thought he was momentarily cast down to learn that his letters were not reaching Fanny as punctually as they were posted. Each of the brothers carried two stone of luggage but were never tired. During his tramps Charles composed *The Ugly Princess*, and *The baby sings not on its mother's breast*, *The world goes up and the world goes down*, *Ask if I love thee*, *Oh thou hadst been a wife for Shakespeare's self*, copied them out in the evenings and posted them to Fanny.

During the tour Henry became confidential about his life at Oxford and his connection with the 'Fez' club which he had founded with Edwin Arnold. It was a society of fifty members, all haters of women, all pledged to pass their lives in celibacy and to diffuse the principles of misogyny in every section of English life. Cordy Jeaffreson was their doorkeeper. At their luxurious breakfasts everyone wore a fez and insignia on the masonic pattern and smoked oriental tobacco from oriental pipes. Each man was allowed to rise and address the company provided he could tell some story against 'the sex which would serve to confirm members in their conviction that women must be held in subjection as weak-minded and incorrigibly frivolous creatures'. Charles could laugh at all this and hope that one day Henry might be as lucky matrimonially as he was himself.

In *Two Years Ago* Kingsley made use of some of his Rhine walks and adventures, and in reflecting on Ehrenbreitstein asked himself whether any conqueror would tread its slopes again and call this 'Broad Stone of Honour' his? As he looked on the landscape he saw to his left fields of clover and corn while through the orchard to his right he could see a knoll of chestnut and acacia trees, tall poplar, feathery larch, and strange stonework gleaming grey beneath their stems.

Bank over bank of earth and stone, cleft by deep embrasures from which the great guns grin across the rich gardens, studded with standard fruit trees, which clothe the glacis to its topmost edge. And there below him lie the vineyards: every rock ledge and narrow path of soil tossing its golden tendrils to the sun, grey with ripening clusters, rich with noble wine: but what is that wall which winds among them, up and down creeping and sneaking over every ledge and knoll of vantage ground, pierced with eyelet-holes, backed by strange stairs and galleries of stone; till it rises close before him to meet the low round tower full in his path, from whose deep casemates, as from dark scowling eye-holes, the ugly cannon eyes stare up the glen.

It was in this mood that he wrote what Fanny thought a most significant poem which she calls *The Eagle*.

> I heard an eagle crying all alone
> Above the vineyards through the summer night,
> Among the skeletons of robber towers:
> Because the ancient eyrie of his race
> Was trenched and walled by busy-handed men;
> All his forest-chase and woodland wild,
> Wherefrom he fed his young with hare and roe,
> Were trim with grapes which swelled from hour to hour,
> And tossed their golden tendrils to the sun
> For joy at their own riches:—So, I thought,
> The great devourers of the earth shall sit,
> Idle and impotent, they know not why,
> Down-staring from their barren height of state
> On nations grown too wise to slay and slave,
> The puppets of the few; while peaceful lore
> And fellow-help make glad the heart of earth,
> With wonders which they fear and hate, as he,
> The Eagle hates the vineyard slopes below.

Kingsley's mind, so curious an instrument in some ways, will express its admiration for Gerolstein and then go on to reflect 'Germany is a wonderful country and though its population are not members of the Church of England, is full of as noble, simple, shrewd and kindly hearts as man could wish to see'.

Just before the walkers reached Treves they were put under arrest as their fishing-rods were suspected of being *todt-instrumenten* of a new kind. Clapped into prison they found themselves lying on 'a bare floor among fleas and felons'. The Germans had now become 'barbarians' who, taking their huge brown wide-awakes for Italian hats, had got it into their addle-pates that the hikers were emissaries of Mazzini, distributing political tracts. Next day on release they found their parents had arrived in Treves. Charles's chief feeling on visiting the remains of classical occupation was that he was standing over 'the skeleton of the giant iniquity—Old Rome'.

And as I stood last night in that amphitheatre, amid the wild beasts' dens and thought of the Christian martyrdoms and the Frank prisoners, and all the hellish scenes of agony and cruelty that place had witnessed, I seemed to hear the very voice of the archangel whom St. John heard in Patmos, crying, Babylon the Great is fallen! but no more like the sound of a trumpet, but only in the still whisper of the night-breeze, and through the sleeping vineyards, and the great still smile of God out of the broad blue heaven.

At Bonn he was enchanted with the Museum, praised the minerals and fossils, and all the wonderful new fish, crabs, and insects from the Solenhofen slate. 'I was in ecstasies', he wrote to his wife.

The outing 'was so great a success' that Charles Kingsley could go back to Eversley in good heart to find the energy he had stored up enabled him to dispense with a curate. Work connected with the *Christian Socialist* took him occasionally to London, where he made use of Chelsea rectory to the extent of sometimes giving a dinner there in his father's absence. One night his party consisted of John Parker, his publisher, McDougall, a missionary from Borneo, and Tom Hughes. The last-named had received a rhymed invitation cast in the form of an intoned litany:

And every man is too much inclined to behave himself as a beast
In spite of our glorious humanity which requires neither God
     nor priest
Yet is daily praised and plastered by a thousand fools at least
Request Mr. Hughes' presence at their jawshop in the East
Which don't they wish they may get it ; for he goes out tonight
     to feast
At the Rev. C. Kingsley's rectory, Chelsea, where he'll get his
     gullet greased
With the best of Barto Valle's port, and will have his joys
     increased
By meeting his old college chum McDougall the Borneo priest.

This invitation was written in what Tom Hughes calls 'one of his Rabelaisian fits' that came upon him frequently, when in the company of intimates. In these moods Charles Kingsley was like 'a great, full-grown Newfoundland yearling dog out for an airing, plunging in and out of water and rushing round shaking himself over everyone's clothes and all in rollicking good humour'.

Breaking then into less stately measure, Kingsley continued

> So come you thief, and drop your brief,
> At six o'clock without relief;
> And if you won't may you come to grief,
> Says Parson Lot the Socialist Chief
> Who signs his mark at the foot of the leaf.

On the evening in question Kingsley had been talking business with John Parker. Hughes joined them in the Strand office and they all walked out into the dense fog. At Hyde Park Corner Kingsley said, 'Isn't this like life? A deep yellow fog all around with a dim light here and there shining through. You grope your way on from one lamp to another and you go up wrong streets and back again, but you get home at last—there's always light enough for that!' Then suddenly addressing Hughes, Kingsley said, 'Tom, do you want to live to be old?' Hughes said he had no thoughts on the subject. Kingsley went on, 'I dread it more than I can say. To feel one's powers going and to end in snuff and stink. Look at the last days of Scott and Wordsworth! . . . For an eager, fiery nature like mine, with fierce passions eating one's life out, it won't do. If I live twenty years' (he lived twenty-five) 'I know what will happen to me. The back of my brain will soften and I shall most likely go blind.'

The only other person at dinner, McDougall, was a black-bearded man of unusual physical and mental power. John Martineau, who met him with Tom Hughes, thought him 'very jolly'. He was a qualified surgeon and a missionary in Borneo, and was later to become Bishop of Labuan.

Charles Kingsley was in great spirits that evening and stood in his favourite attitude, left arm clasping right elbow behind his back, to harangue them all. He talked of Froude's *History*, of trout fishing, of the Great Exhibition, and tilted against the 'high art' which had been the ruin of Germany—high arts and sciences. Goethe had been the ruin of Germany, a great fog coming down on the German people and wrapping them up. We were dead and the French were dead, till the French had their revolution of '48 and that brought us to life. He encouraged McDougall to tell them about Borneo, its people, its honey-bears and plants. Then he explained how he did his writing. 'I can't think, even on scientific subjects, except in dramatic form. It is what Tom said to Harry and what Harry answered him. I never put pen to paper till I have two or three pages in my head and see them as if they were printed. Then I write them off and take a turn in the garden.' Presently McDougall asked how he was to get back to the West End. As the fog was still very thick Kingsley and Hughes piloted him into the King's Road, where a passing link-boy was engaged to see him home.

Chapter 9

NEW INTERESTS

To live is to change, and to be perfect is to have changed often.

J. H. NEWMAN

THE year 1852 was a critical one for Kingsley and in an unexplained manner seems to have made a rather different man of him. The impulse to devote himself to social reform was weakening, and John Martineau tells us [1] that 'his convictions became more in accord with the natural tendency of his mind' and that 'he gradually modified or abandoned his democratic opinions thereby calling down on himself the reproach of inconsistency from those who considered he had deserted them'.

As a matter of fact Kingsley felt that he could slip out of the movement quite honourably as most of the grievances and injustices he had fought against were in process of being adjusted and he was not anxious to agitate for agitation's sake. Ludlow had reassured him about the future by declaring that the legal steps being taken for the statutory protection of trade associations were adequate. It was time for 'Parson Lot' to fade out and the *Christian Socialist* to be wound up. We may see in reading John Ludlow's *Essays* that he believed in evolution, not revolution, and was not made impatient by the passage of time. His influence over Kingsley was considerable. The rector's appeals for advice had always been met with pacifying words and Ludlow was able to convince him that the net result of their past efforts had been to advertise the cause of associations of working men, and that once these unions had been legally recognised the Council formed to promote them should come to an end. After three years they had won their point of securing legislative sanction for a movement that had once been decried by the press as 'revolutionary nonsense'. Kingsley accepted Ludlow's view and agreed that 'Parson Lot' must disappear.

[1] *Life of John Martineau,* by Violet Martineau, p. 307.

He could not, however, resist writing a poem *On the Death of a Certain Journal*. It was in six quatrains, of which this is the last:

> So die, thou child of stormy dawn,
> Thou winter flower, forlorn of nurse:
> Chilled early by the bigot's curse,
> The pedant's frown, the worldling's yawn.

Maurice, when he came to stay at Eversley, talked in much the same strain as Ludlow. Their joint campaign had been very much worth while, for had they not ventilated the subject until it became respectable, drawn the fire of the press, and stimulated investigations by the Bishop of London and by a House of Commons Committee? They had won their fight, there could be no doubt about it, and yet, Maurice would argue the slogan 'Christian Socialism' should not be lightly dropped, but should still be used by them as an indication of continuing sympathy with the worker. Kingsley, who was secretly pleased at being rid of the whole commitment, did not agree at all with this view, and but for his deep affection for Maurice would have quarrelled if not broken with him on this point. Fanny would probably have liked Charles to have done so; for it had become exasperating to them both to be constantly attacked by the press and by the personnel of the Church of England. Fanny was not stupid, and she realised that so long as her Charles remained closely linked with Maurice trouble was unavoidable. Nagging Conservatives like John Wilson Croker never ceased to sneer at 'those clergymen of the Church of England who preached undisguised Jacobinism and Jacquerie under the label of Christian Socialism'. Some gossips went so far as to wonder how it was that Maurice should still be allowed to teach Divinity at King's College. There were two schools of thought about all this, for we find Dr. Jelf, Principal of King's College, telling Maurice plainly that unless he disavowed Charles Kingsley he would be identified with him, and that Kingsley was identified with Holyoake, and Holyoake with Tom Paine. By now Fanny Kingsley knew, for many people had told her, that Charles had made his original mistake in inviting Maurice to write an introduction to *The Saint's Tragedy*. The situation bewildered her, since it was not only critics of the Right who sniped at Christian Socialism but also those of the Left.   There was Holyoake, editor of the *Reasoner*, warning workmen against the insidious campaign initiated by the clergy to nobble and emasculate pure Socialism, while the *Guardian* from another angle attacked Mr. Kingsley for being associated with several notorious infidels and with having contributed to the social-communist organ, the *Leader*. Would it not be advisable, it enquired, for Mr. Kingsley either to admit or deny his connection with this periodical?   Was Mr. Maurice perhaps backing him?   And should not the Council of King's College allay public apprehension without delay? Maurice tried to defend Kingsley by announcing that he had never written for the *Leader*, but as his own position had been insidiously undermined he could for the time being do no more.

Fanny Kingsley in her biography conceals the fact that both she and her husband suffered acutely under the persecution they were subjected to, but she was woman of the world enough to realise that nothing could put an end to this but promotion. Charles's talent for doing what from a worldly point of view was the wrong thing seemed to make her efforts to interest influential people in his future abortive.   In the opinion of most of her friends and relations he had no future.

The publication of Maurice's *Theological Essays* at this time proved a disaster both for the author and his friend.   Dr. Jelf was suddenly required by his Council of Governors to give a considered opinion as to whether the *Essays* disseminated teaching inconsistent with the holding of a Chair of Divinity.   He reported that he found nothing unorthodox in Maurice's book and only wished he could say as much of Charles Kingsley, 'a reckless, dangerous writer and in a high degree inflammatory', whom the Council had very wisely prevented some years earlier from assisting Maurice with his Divinity class.   The rector of Eversley was appalled at the language used about him.

In spite of Dr. Jelf's whitewashing report, Maurice soon realised that someone connected with the College must be working to bring about his dismissal.   This contingency he anticipated by asking the Council either to acquit him fully of heretical charges or deprive him of his Chair.   A Committee of Enquiry was promptly set up, and on his book, his teaching and his sermons he was condemned. His lectures were immediately suspended as detrimental to the reputation of the College, and he was summoned to have judgement officially pronounced upon him. Professor Trench, on this occasion, went out of his way to thank him for having been the main instrument in securing from the Crown the first Charter for female education.

Maurice's unsoundness was accounted to lie in his conviction that time and eternity co-exist in us. He used to say how difficult it was to recognise the eternal state under temporal conditions and not to lose touch with eternity in time. Dr. Jelf, on being asked to comment on this point, declared that he himself had never for a moment thought of eternity as anything but the future contrasted with the present. But Maurice believed that as we live and move and have our being in God, the spiritual part of man lives out of time, has spiritual relations, and enjoys or suffers a spiritual inheritance. In this respect he was said to have departed from 'the Orthodox Faith'. Members of the Honourable Society of Lincoln's Inn and those who attended the chapel there formally expressed their deep sympathy over their Reader's dismissal from King's College.

> We cannot forbear observing that the materials for a charge against you had to be sought in your sermons here and in your volume of Essays—also sermons—and that no such material could be found in your teaching at the College.

Carlyle, though he had no thoughts on the matter himself and took no interest in it whatever, had something to say to Arthur Helps about Maurice and eternal damnation. He could not help thinking that in the unlikely event of Maurice being turned out of the Church of England, it might do him good. His wry humour then got the better of him, and he added: 'The poor old Church of England believes in no damnation except ruin at the bankers'.

Tennyson's warm feeling for Maurice manifested itself in a poem embodying an invitation to Farringford.

> Come, when no graver cares employ,
> Godfather come and see your boy:
> Your presence will be sun in winter,
> Making the little one leap for joy.

For, being of that honest few,
Who give the Fiend himself his due,
Should eighty thousand college councils
Thunder 'Anathema' friend at you;

Should all the church men foam in spite
At you, so careful of the right,
Yet one lay hearth would give you welcome
(Take it and come) to the Isle of Wight.

During the period covered by these controversies Kingsley insured himself against a breakdown by continuing work on the novel he had planned before going abroad. His idea in writing it was 'to set forth Christianity as the only really democratic creed and philosophy as the only really aristocratic creed'. Rather fortunately its construction entailed a good deal of close reading. His main sources were the *Letters of Synesius* and Gibbon's *History of the Decline and Fall of the Roman Empire*. He used Alexandria as background and stage. Kegan Paul was at Eversley during the summer of 1851 while *Hypatia* was being written, and it impressed him to see what pains Charles Kingsley took to be correct in the smallest details.

On his way back to London Kegan Paul travelled with Miss Mitford, who had not yet made acquaintance with the famous rector. She said that she had driven past Eversley churchyard and had seen the rector conducting a funeral service and that he looked as she would have expected, 'like a pale student'. Her companion replied that Kingsley was as unlike 'a pale student' as anyone that ever lived, his physical frame being powerful and wiry, his complexion dark, and his eye bright and piercing. It was clear that the man Miss Mitford had seen in the churchyard was the curate. When she did get to know Kingsley she took to him at once. 'I have never met a man of letters the least like him', she wrote. 'Mr. Kingsley is not only a high bred gentleman but has the most charming admixture of softness and gentleness, with spirit, manliness and frankness and a cordiality and courtesy that would win any heart.' Charles Kingsley liked Miss Mitford immensely and wrote a sonnet 'To the Authoress of *Our Village*' in which he praises her writing.

The style severe, yet graceful, trained aright
To classic depths of clearness and repaid
By thanks and honour from the wise and staid;
By pleasant skill to blame and yet delight,
And hold communion with the eloquent throng
Of those who shaped and toned our speech and song
All these are yours.

A curious portrayal of Kingsley by Justin McCarthy stands out as a foil to that of Miss Mitford.

Rather tall, very angular, surprisingly awkward, with thin staggering legs, a hatchet face adorned with scraggy whiskers, a faculty for falling into the most ungainly attitudes and making the most hideous contortions of visage and frame; with a rough provincial accent and an uncouth way of speaking which would be set down for caricature on the boards of a theatre. Since Brougham's day nothing so ungainly and eccentric had been displayed upon an English platform. Needless to say Charles Kingsley had not the eloquence of Brougham, but he had a robust way of plain speaking which soon struck home to the heart of a meeting. Even those, who began by laughing or heartily disliking what he stood for, were won over by his sincerity.

Hypatia is one of the many books that are easier to read in early than in later life. A scene that sparkles with kaleidoscopic interest to the mind of a schoolgirl seems decades later a confused, overcrowded canvas of exceptional artificiality of treatment. So fluctuating are standards of accomplishment in different generations that what is impassioning at one moment in human history becomes intolerably boring at another. A few of the Scott romances are cases in point. Kingsley had the pleasure of receiving warm eulogies on the book from Sir Charles Wood, the Speaker, Mr. Shaw-Lefevre, and Dr. Keate. Elizabeth Sewell was made very unhappy by the unsociable picture of Christianity it disclosed, but at the same time thought it 'a marvel'. Miss Mitford admired his courage in tackling the subject and compared the novel with Lockhart's *Valerius* and Ware's *Palmyra*.

It is full of vigour and power. . . . Mr. Kingsley takes Cyril and Augustine down from their pedestals and lowers them into human

beings.   He animates that whole mob of Alexandria, animates and
individualises Greek, Roman, Egyptian, Goth and Jew.   He puts
life into the very sands of the desert.   But there are some strange
things and I half dread what the Bishops may say, though he is so
excellent as a parish priest and so much beloved in his parish.   I
hope they will take his vivid descriptions of scenes which doubtless
occurred, as parts of a picture; they will if they have sense.   It is
certainly a work of great power.

Some people were put off by the preface, which opens thus:

A picture of life in the fifth century must needs contain much
which will be painful to any reader, and which the young and
innocent will do well to leave altogether unread.   It has to represent a very hideous, though a very great age; one of those critical
and cardinal eras in the history of the human race, in which virtues
and vices manifest themselves side by side—even at times in the
same person—with the most startling openness and power.   One
who writes of such an era labours under a troublesome disadvantage.   He dare not tell how evil people were; he will not be believed
if he tell how good they were.   In the present case that disadvantage is doubled; for while the sins of the Church, however heinous,
were still such as admit of being expressed in words, the sins of the
heathen world against which she fought, were utterly indescribable;
and the Christian apologist is thus compelled, for the sake of
decency, to state the Church's case far more weakly than the facts
deserve.

The story opens with the visit of Philammon, a young
Christian monk from the desert, to Alexandria.   He comes
there full of curiosity and is swept off his feet by the novelty
of the sensations he experiences.   Fascinated by the beauty of
the Neoplatonist philosopher, Hypatia, he attends her lectures
and since the temperance and sanity of her doctrine compares so
favourably with the violence and fanaticism of Alexandrian
monks, is seduced from his faith.   The rackety turbulence of
the life of the city is depicted with a good deal of power.
Orestes, the governor, has to control with his legionaries not
only the intruding Goths, but the arrogant patriarch Cyril and
the aggressive Church he rules.   Beside virtuous Hypatia there
is a contrasting type, the hetaira Pelagia, whom Elizabeth Sewell

found far the more sympathetic of the two. After seeing Hypatia torn to pieces by a mob of furious Christians, Philammon returns despondently to the Thebaïd in the desert. Tennyson after reading the novel with great attention objected to the use of the word 'naked'. He did not mind Pelagia being stripped, but he could not bear that the virtuous Hypatia should be subjected to a similar ignominy.

Kingsley was ready to give authorities for all his characters and incidents as well as conversations and dissertations. 'He sometimes', Miss Mitford tells us, 'would turn over a whole volume of Synesius to search for a single detail and this in spite of the fact that by temperament he was artistic and impulsive.' The book, though laboured, was perfectly authentic. The historical Hypatia was the daughter of the mathematician Theon, and met her death in the manner described by Kingsley. Ludlow wrote to the author suggesting that the book was dull and the talk long-winded, whereupon Kingsley replied:

> As for the monks, 'pon my honour they are slow fellows—but then they were so horribly slow in reality. . . . Pambo's palaver is a crib from someone word for word. And his instances are historical ones. Moreover you must remember that Arsenius was no mere monk, but a polished gentleman and court intriguer.

The Queen read *Hypatia* with enjoyment and let it be known that she greatly preferred it to Mr. Kingsley's other works. Froude thought it infinitely better and more artistic than anything Kingsley had done. The press renewed its attack; but it comforted Charles to know that Mrs. Gaskell was being quite as sharply set upon for her domestic novel *Ruth*.

After a few numbers of *Hypatia* had appeared in *Fraser's Magazine* Parker got scared as to its suitability for general reading and told the author that the story was not adding to *Fraser's* reputation. Nettled, Kingsley assured Parker that, far from being 'personally tabooed', he found 'no falling off in the exceedingly good society of all sorts in which I have lived from my youth'.

Truth to tell, Parker was apprehensive about the future of publishing, for towards the end of 1852, the livelihood of those connected with the book trade was menaced by an American novel which, having swept its country of origin, threatened to swamp publishing enterprise in England. No one for the time being could be persuaded to ask for any work but *Uncle Tom's Cabin*. An account by Thomas Mozley of a dinner-party given by Rivington the publisher reveals to us how serious was the trade depression caused by the eruption of this novel. Mozley, having wept tears over it himself, attended the 'grewsome' feast, and looking at the faces of the novelists, essayists, and historians gathered round the dinner-table saw that they registered deepest gloom, for their works remained unsold and no publisher was venturing to float a new work. 'Mrs. Beecher Stowe', he said, 'had entered the garden of Eden and had reduced it to a wilderness.'

Having acquired the trick of stepping out of the present, Kingsley applied himself to the task of writing a Socratic Dialogue which he entitled *Phaethon* or *Loose Thoughts for Loose Thinkers*. This takes the form of a discussion between the author and a country gentleman on the theme that the intellect can, by seeking, find God, and in place of the God-concept hallowed by the Church, can set up his own discovery or creation. It is a warning, says Miss Mitford, not to let the love of nature degenerate into an exclusive worship to the neglect of the Creator, an injunction to seek the faith of the Low Church without its narrowness. 'Perhaps I like this pamphlet the better because I so entirely like the author.'

Though to us the dialogue may seem a dull performance it found its circle of readers. One correspondent, after saying she had read it through with pleasure, added that she was slightly shocked by its impropriety. Her comment, one supposes, could only have applied to the 'man-midwifery' analogy, but it was the kind of criticism that irritated Kingsley intensely, and he replied with outraged dignity:

I am surprised and pained that anyone should have found anything improper in a passage which has never been complained of by the many virtuous and pure-minded persons, ladies as well as gentlemen, to whom *Phaethon* was submitted both before and after publication. You must excuse me but when Mrs. Kingsley and my own mother are not conscious of any impropriety, *I* am bound in honour to see none. But even if there were, the illustration is I believe necessary to the argument, exactly in Platonic style, put into Socratic dialogue, but into the mouth of an Englishman, and finally the book is published at Cambridge for students and not for young ladies. And while students are in the habit of having the Latin and Greek classics put into their hands, I do not fear that *Phaethon* will much increase their stock of unsavoury images. You do not complain of a medical book for teaching of matters unfit for the schoolroom, why then of a theological one?

Confessedly, Kingsley was dead tired of defending himself against the pin-pricks and hostile criticism of which he was the constant target, and it was a great relief to him when the press and public opinion concentrated on the indictment of Sir James Brooke, ruler of Sarawak, for maltreatment of natives. Kingsley became absorbed in the evidence and was fired with the desire to support the Rajah in any future campaign against the Dyaks. This enthusiasm has to be taken seriously as it gave the death-blow to his interest in Christian Socialism. His friend, 'the missionary priest from Borneo' (who had stayed several times at the rectory), had imbued him with the belief that Brooke was a Christian hero and no pirate king. It excited Kingsley extremely to discuss what measures should be taken to exterminate the head-hunting Dyaks. McDougall had sailed aboard the 'Royalist', a cutter used by the Rajah to penetrate to the river villages of the Dyaks. Kingsley asked the missionary if it might not be a good idea to make the Rajah a present of a steamer so that he might get about more quickly. If only enough people could be interested in the subject the money for the steamer would soon be forthcoming. Sir James was at the moment standing his trial in London for his anti-Dyak expeditions and the press was very hostile to him. This made no difference to Kingsley, who had a very small opinion of the sense of newspaper men; he had known them wrong on nearly every important matter. Whatever anyone might say:

> Destroying the pirate fleet, *was* loving his neighbour as himself, and taking the blood-money, not to spend on himself, but to use it in civilising the wretched people whom these pirates have been butchering for centuries, *was* right.

Ludlow was a little impatient over Kingsley's new notions and begged him to continue to concentrate on working-men's interests. In reply Kingsley gave him to understand that he did not intend to think of such matters for the time being and was more than ready to 'pick a crow' with Ludlow over Rajah Brooke, for his spirit is stirred within him by the way the press was keeping up its attack on Brooke for 'the Borneo business'. In considerable excitement he wrote:

I say at once that I think he has been utterly right and righteous. If I had been in his place I would have done the same. If it is to do again I hope he will have the courage to do it again. The truest benevolence is occasional severity. It *is* expedient that one man die for the people. One tribe exterminated, if need be, to save a whole continent. Sacrifice of human life? Prove that it is *human* life. It is *beast* life. These Dyaks have put on the image of the beast and must take the consequences. 'Value of Life?' Oh Ludlow read history; look at the world and see whether God values mere physical existence. . . . Physical death is no evil. It may be a blessing to the survivors. Else why pestilence, famine, Cromwell and Perrot in Ireland, Charlemagne hanging 4000 Saxons over the Weser bridge; did not God bless these terribly righteous judgements? Do you believe in the Old Testament? Surely then say what does that destruction of the Canaanites mean? If it was right, Rajah Brooke was right. If he be wrong then Moses, Joshua, David were wrong. No! I say. Because Christ's kingdom is a kingdom of peace; because the meek alone shall inherit the earth, therefore you Malays and Dyaks of Sarawak, you also are enemies to peace . . . you are beasts, all the more dangerous because you have a semi-human cunning. . . . Honour to a man who dares act manfully on the broad sense of right as Rajah Brooke is doing.

Ludlow, in his turn, refused to be interested in Brooke or Borneo and went on toiling at the schemes nearest to his heart. The two men managed to keep up a serious correspondence for a while, but to Kingsley Ludlow had become 'censorious' and 'infallible in his own eyes'. 'Poor Ludlow', he wrote to Tom Hughes, 'when will he learn "Judge not that you be not judged"?' The rector was busy writing to people about the Rajah's 'shameful trial'. Told by Henry Drummond that a remarkable demonstration was about to take place in Sarawak, he informed one correspondent that 'the whole population *en masse* was applying to become members of Brooke's religion'.

Mountstuart Grant Duff, who first met the Kingsleys at a house-party at Newnham Paddox, noted in his diary at this time that Charles Kingsley enjoyed giving an imitation of Carlyle's conversation with Emerson during his stay in England. Emerson's persistent optimism had irritated the sage who tried to cure him of it by taking him to the lowest parts of London and showing him what was going on there. This done, he turned to him saying:

'"And noo man, d'ye believe in the devil noo?"'

'"Oh no," he replied, "all these people seem to me only part of great machines and on the whole I think they are doing their work very satisfactorily."

'Then,' continued the sage, 'I took him to the House of Commons where they put us under the Gallery. Then I showed him ae chiel getting up after another and leeing and leeing. And then I turned to him and said, "And noo man d'ye believe in the deevil noo?" He made me however just the same answer as before and I gave him up in despair.'

Both Tennyson and Robert Browning were guests this year at the rectory, but Fanny Kingsley is uncommunicative about them and passes in silence over the departure of her brother-in-law, Henry, for the gold-fields of Australia. He seems to have slipped away quietly from Oxford without sitting for a degree.

The death of Sir John Cope in 1852 gave the Kingsleys reason to hope that improvements in the rectory might be carried out. Sir John had for long believed that his family would become extinct with his death, and it was Charles Kingsley who told him that he had made acquaintance with an Irish minor canon of Westminster who believed himself to be directly descended from Sir Anthony Cope, first baronet. This information was confirmed subsequently by Ulster King at Arms. Sir William, however, proved not at all anxious to spend money in reconditioning the rectory and even showed himself unsympathetic about the repair of dwellings on the estate. We find Kingsley urging him to pull down certain cottages subject to flooding, the occupants of which were in constant ill-health, and calling Sir William's attention (at the request of the Local Sanitary Council) to a list of 'nuisances in cottages of yours in Eversley tything'. Sir William does nothing but express apprehension lest Kingsley's literary avocations should affect his parish work, whereupon the rector humbly replies: 'I only write in the forenoon. I admit all persons on parish business instantly at whatever cost of interruption. . . . I hope you will always mention at once any seeming neglect or mistake.'

Chapter 10

MARINE BIOLOGY AND THE CRIMEAN WAR

Praise is the best diet for us after all.

SYDNEY SMITH

ALL through the autumn of 1853 Fanny worried over Charles's state of mind; and worry, combined with the atrocious conditions under which she was compelled to live, ended by making her ill.   In December the doctors were insisting that she must be got away from Eversley.   Shortly before Christmas they both went to stay with the German Minister, Chevalier de Bunsen, at Prussia House, Carlton House Terrace. It was a refreshing change from 'the solemn, gloomy life', Kegan Paul tells us, that Fanny led at the rectory.   She greatly enjoyed the company of her host for they had a mutual interest in German theology and could discuss it by the hour.   She was also glad to meet his guests at meals and to have a chance of getting some new clothes preparatory to her flight from Eversley.

As the south rather than the north coast of Devon had been advised by her doctors, Charles wrote to ask Anthony Froude, ensconced at Babbacombe, to find them accommodation at Torquay which at the moment was the most fashionable seaside resort in England, 'a gay watering-place', Kingsley called it, 'with London shops and London carriages'.   A mild climate and a superficial resemblance to the Riviera were the attractions that drew county families from their vast cold houses and dank, avenued parks to bask for a while in winter sunshine and enjoy excellent company and food.   Before the opening of the railroad to Exeter had made this sheltered bay accessible to invalids and pleasure-seekers, it had been loved by poets and writers like Elizabeth Barrett and Charlotte Yonge, but from 1845 the place was overtaken by a wave of development and by 1853 many new houses had been built whose very names served to indicate the kind of persons who were to live in them.   Villas known as The Grove, The Grange, Oatlands, Apsley, Osborne, vied with other villas known as Borghese, Maggiore, Lebanon, Bella

Vista, and, in a class by itself for size, the residence of Baroness Burdett Coutts, Ehrenburg. A weekly newspaper, the *Torquay Directory*, published the names of arrivals with their addresses, and advertised concerts, balls, lectures, and sales for charity. As we skim the lists of visitors we see that the heavyweights of county life such as the Bathursts, Grevilles, Careys, Percys, Buccleuchs, were balanced by an international element which included Prince and Princess George of Oldenburg, the Duchesse de Chartres, the Comte de Paris, or Countess Welken from Berlin. Queens occasionally, and distinguished foreigners frequently, moored their yachts in the bay and condescended to disport themselves in the Royal Assembly Rooms or give their names as patrons of bazaars. A rich and eccentric Mr. Bevan, self-constituted arbiter of taste, ruled society, and under his direction etiquette and amusement were organised till the town of Torquay rivalled in sophistication Brighton under the Regency.

The solidity of the Victorian world, with its strict protocol and stricter prejudices, its conventions, its slow-moving equipages, its wigged coachmen and powdered lackeys, its hedged-in-ness and the unhurried tempo at which it moved magnificently through existence, can hardly be recaptured to-day because of the extreme tenuity and fragility of the records it has left behind, —a few diaries, some bundles of letters, and principal source of reconstruction, the novel of contemporary life. The whole scene gives the effect of a mirage; we cannot believe in its upholstery, its rigidity of code, its essential stuffiness that often among the less affluent became dreariness of an extreme kind.

By this self-important, self-righteous world with its insistence on conformity Charles Kingsley was rather naturally regarded as an outsider. Those who had read his novels knew he had struck at the foundation of its order and means of livelihood, and those who had not were content to call him a radical and leave him to his own devices. All the inmates of the Torquay villas were in the habit of going to church twice on Sundays and of listening to a sermon at each service. The clergy, already deeply prejudiced against a rector holding and preaching Chartist doctrine, decided that their pulpits and chancels must be closed to his dangerous influence. They held it impossible to countenance his surpliced presence in their churches, a view in which their pew-holders supported them. Into this unsympathetic *milieu* Charles Kingsley was now in all innocence projected. As wives and husbands in Victorian days were never asked out separately it is improbable that the ban was lifted in favour of Fanny or that she saw much if indeed anything of her former acquaintances, whose attitude would have been that since she had married such an uncouth individual she must take the consequences.

The Froudes had taken rooms for the migrants at one of the most recommended lodging-houses, Livermead, a comfortable, solid building of reddish stone close to the shore. They arrived there a few days after Christmas, as we may see in letters written by Kingsley on January 2 from Torquay. The relief to both Charles and Fanny of escaping from Eversley was immense; at last they could enjoy a healthy life free from the pricks of persecution. How great, by contrast with their happy expectations, was their horror to learn, shortly after arrival, of the attitude the churches were adopting. Fanny, generally so discreet and brave about their misfortunes, let herself go on the subject of the unchristian behaviour of the clergy who seemed at times to be enemies rather than colleagues. She had hoped, for she was a great admirer of her husband's sermons, that at Torquay he would get his chance of being heard by the right people, make a great name for himself as a preacher, and possibly touch the heart of some bestower of patronage. Torquay was so obviously a place of opportunity. Could it be that it held no opportunity for Charles? And was there no limit to the area in which he might be subjected to clerical proscription?

Though at first terribly cast down, Fanny found that her husband soon revived in the 'life-giving' air of Devonshire, and that his remarkable capacity for hurling himself whole-heartedly into new interests now came to his rescue and enabled him to banish from his mind all thoughts of ecclesiastical duties and fervently to take up the study of marine biology. Fortunately he had already made friends with a Baptist minister, Philip Gosse, who was at the time living in London and later came to Torquay. To him Kingsley despatched hampers of seaweeds and shells, for Gosse was an expert on the subject that now filled his mind, and was delighted to analyse and report on the specimens submitted. A local schoolmaster, William Pengelly, made himself known to Charles as a great admirer of his books and found that they had a great common interest in geology. Pengelly had been one of the first persons to explore Kent's Cavern, and to sort the bones of the prehistoric animals preserved in it, than which nothing could have thrilled Kingsley more. They took to making excursions together, burrowing among rocks and tunnelling into cliffs in order to solve geognostic problems of strata. Indoors Kingsley spent many hours classifying polypi and observing the behaviour of small crustaceans. When Max Müller came to Livermead, Fanny put a good face on life by telling him that 'the pleasure Charles derived from specimens picked up on the shore made him far more contented and good-spirited than the composing of sermons or the writing of novels'. In describing the situation in which Charles found himself at Torquay, Fanny writes: [1]

> At this time, and for some years to come, the clergy of all parties in the Church stood aloof from him as a suspected person. The attacks of the religious press, perhaps happily for him, had so alarmed the clergy of Torquay, High Church and Evangelical, that all pulpit doors were closed against the author of *Alton Locke*, *Yeast*, and *Hypatia*, and he spent quiet peaceful Sundays with his wife and children for the first time for many years. . . . It was a resting time, and the temporary cessation from sermon writing and parish work was very grateful to him, 'a combination of circumstances having during the last year', he wrote to a friend, 'so utterly exhausted me, physically and intellectually, that I must lie very quiet for a time, and I look forward with some dread even to the research necessary to make my Edinburgh lectures what they ought to be'.

The acquisition of a vivarium, an invention of his friend Gosse, afforded him special delight. He was often to be found chuckling at the inimitable fun to be extracted from watching the behaviour of the soldier crab. Gosse, it transpired, had even more ample sources of fun at his disposal; for he kept two soldier crabs in the same vivarium which never ceased fighting

---

[1] *Charles Kingsley*, vol. I, p. 404.

for the same empty whelk shell. Their antics and strategy were, as the minister said, 'quite terribly amusing'. Another friend who shared these tastes was Charles Mansfield, who came to Livermead for some weeks to make expeditions and help classify specimens collected.

The coasts of Devon and Cornwall were at this time still unravished, pools by the sea were still paved with submarine gardens where fairy blossoms of exquisite beauty might be inspected. They existed in their integrity partly because the aristocracy took no interest in the shore and partly because of the ignorance or indifference of the middle-class holiday-makers, whose notion of pleasure was bunching together on the sand or walking, dressed in their best clothes, up and down denes, piers, or promenades overlooking the ocean. Kingsley and Gosse by writing books that popularised the foreshore raised up an army of naturalists, and they were not the only offenders in this respect, for George Lewis and George Eliot, when resting in north Devon, paddled and pulled sea-weeds and gathered marine creatures and shells to carry to a foot-bath in their lodgings, activities that enabled George Lewis to write a quick-seller, *Sea-side Studies*, giving further encouragement to amateur beachcombers. Edmund Gosse, who records a later visit of Charles Kingsley to Torquay, is able to tell us something of Kingsley's headlong enthusiasm in the pursuit of his hobby. When he was a little boy he believed that his father was considered very unsociable by his neighbours, but the rector of Eversley, he says, paid no heed to his father's reputation and would blow into their house unannounced. One day he came at a time when Mr. Gosse was examining some would-be communicants in his drawing-room. The maid announced the visitor, whereupon the minister said in a loud voice, 'Tell Mr. Kingsley that I am engaged in studying Scripture with certain of the Lord's children.' Under the watching eyes of little Edmund the tall figure of the author of *Hypatia* careered up and down the lawn, very impatient and restless, till the moment came when the scripture class was released and he could pounce on the minister with a torrent of questions. Sometimes Mr. Gosse and his child were taken out trawling by Kingsley. Little Edmund was at first inclined to be frightened by the aspect of the hawk's beak that served Kingsley for nose and the queer rattling voice, but soon came to look on him as a cheerful presence and a relief from his father's utter seriousness. A frequent member of the trawling party was George Kingsley, the doctor, who shared to the full his brother's taste for marine biology. Many of his Torquay experiences were made use of by Charles Kingsley in the cruise of the 'Waterwitch' in *Two Years Ago*.

George Kingsley, about whom we know little except from his letters, was at this time twenty-eight years old. Like his brothers he had been educated at King's College, but unlike them had graduated in Paris before going to Edinburgh to take his degree in medicine. After helping to fight a cholera epidemic in Scotland he gratified his passion for travel by becoming companion-physician to members of the English aristocracy and going at one time to Spain with Lady Herbert of Lea and her fifteen-year-old son—the future Lord Pembroke of *The Earl and the Doctor* fame. George Kingsley was an admirable letter-writer and his correspondents, who were mostly women (the Duchess of Rutland and Lady Welby were among them), loved his understanding and sympathy and the general and genuine homage he paid their sex. Mary Gladstone wrote of him that he 'had a deadly power of fascinating women', and that she knew 'three of his tragic victims'. 'He always gave me the creeps', she added. We need not perhaps pay much attention to her verdict, for when she met Charles Kingsley she summed him up as 'a bumptious brute' in manner. With nearly everyone but Mary Gladstone, George Kingsley seems to have been popular enough. Maybe some of his correspondents thought him a little dangerous as he was not a professing Christian though several pious ladies tried to turn him into one. His influence over Charles made him seem particularly dangerous to his sister-in-law, who suspected him of encouraging his brother in his erratic opinions. From the few letters that have been preserved we may get an impression of the doctor's mentality and character and of the nature of his scepticism. In a letter to Lady Welby he says:

My want of faith does not prevent my advancing in a lean and hungry and wolf-like manner—but still advancing. I don't think

I get more hard or brutal or less inclined to help lame dogs over the innumerable stiles of this life from want of believing certain historical—what shall I call them? . . . As for future reward, we have nothing to do with it. It is the affair of God alone and what is right he will do. He is never angry—my God—he is never petulant and vexed like that miserable Jewish Jehovah.

Again in another letter he writes:

There is a thread running through all so-called Christianity which is hateful to me. I do not believe it (Christianity) is true, and not believing it to be true I must detest it.

Despite his unorthodoxy Charles admired George immensely as a strong, independent and humane man and when describing Tom Thurnall, the arrogant doctor in *Two Years Ago*, used him as a model. Fanny, of course, has nothing to say about him in her book.

The Kingsley children, while at Torquay, were taught to love and understand natural objects, and it was for them and with them that their father began to put together *Glaucus or the Wonders of the Sea-shore*, the first book of its kind for young people. This slender volume, outcome of many walks and much observation, was first printed sectionally in the *North British Review*. In *Glaucus* there is a dramatic account of that most flaccid of creatures, the long sea-worm, 'an animal as foul and monstrous to the eye as hydra, Gorgon or chimera'. In pointing it out to his family Kingsley said, 'It looks nothing more than a black shiny knotted lump, and yet, when taken up, is like slimy tape and seems capable of infinite extension'. The children were spellbound at the way he vitalised the seemingly inanimate thing.

Is it alive? It hangs helpless and motionless—a mere velvet string across the hand . . . you cannot tell where it begins or ends; it may be a dead strip of seaweed or even a tarred string. So thinks the little fish who plays over and over it, till he touches at last what is too surely a head. In an instant a bell-shaped sucker has fastened to its side. In another instant, from one lip, a concave double proboscis, just like a tapir's, has clasped him like a finger; and now begins the struggle, but in vain. He is being played with such a fishing line as the skill of a Wilson or a Stoddart could never invent;

a living line with an elasticity beyond that of the most delicate fly-rod, which follows every lunge shortening and lengthening. . . . The victim is tired now; and slowly yet dexterously the blind assailant is feeling and shifting along his side, till he reaches one end of him; and there the black lips expand, and slowly and surely the curved finger begins packing him end foremost down into his gullet, where he sinks inch by inch, till the swelling which marks his place is lost among the coils, and he is probably macerated to a pulp long before he has reached the opposite extremity of his cave of doom.   Once safe down, the black murderer slowly contracts into a knotted heap and lies, like a boa with a stag inside him, motionless and blest.

How far tauter and more graphic than anything the rector had hitherto put into lecture or novel is this wonderful account of a sea-worm catching its dinner! *Glaucus* shows what a far greater writer Charles Kingsley might have been had he not expended his powers on sermons, addresses to working men, and the rest of the obligations his profession and temperament drove him to undertake.

The red-legged cockle of Torquay became in his mind as exciting and interesting as the sea-worm.   Strolling along the shore with the children, he one day pointed his stick at some scarlet fingers protruding from the huge mahogany cockles at his feet and exclaimed, 'Why these must be the Mediterranean species, the very shell-fish of which great Cuvier did not disdain to make elaborate drawings!'   Every day fresh specimens were brought in to the vivarium so that Kingsley might adoringly watch, by artificial light, the unfolding of sea-flowers, and the fluttering motion of the fairy gills of slugs.   Life at Livermead literally revolved round these interests.   To the Froudes, to Powles, to all who came and went, he descanted on the wonders he was discovering.   How could anyone doubt the mysteries of grace who had studied the mysteries of nature?   And yet there was the unhappy Gosse for ever trying, and trying vainly, to reconcile science with religion as though there were some fundamental opposition between them!

The Froudes often came over from Babbacombe to spend the day at Torquay and it was to Charlotte that *Glaucus* was eventually dedicated.   One day Froude mentioned to Kingsley that he had been asked to review the new edition of Hakluyt's *Voyages*, a book that existed in such small numbers as to be unobtainable by the common man. The old folio edition was, of course, rare, and the 1811 edition, a five-volume quarto, had been limited to 270 copies and was intended only for libraries and collectors. To the great mass of readers the *Voyages* were entirely unknown despite the fact that the book might truthfully be called the prose epic of the English nation. Charles Kingsley labelled it 'the epic of the English commoner,' for the feats it recounted were performed by seamen from the banks of Avon, Dart, Plym, and Thames who, with no impulse but that 'that was beating in their own royal hearts, went out across the unknown seas fighting, discovering, colonising, graving out the channels, paving them at last with their bones, through which the commerce and enterprise of England has flowed out all over the world'. The genius, energy, and force of England had always been drawn seaward and Davises, Drakes, Joneses, Smiths, had sometimes had their adventures chronicled by a courtly pen, such as that of Raleigh.

Anthony told his brother-in-law that only one of the volumes, Raleigh's *Conquest of Guiana*, was tolerably edited. Whatever interest might have been evoked by the old narratives had been squeezed out of them in long laboured introductions and appendices that filled up valuable space and often smothered the original story. In no wise put off by what Anthony said Charles jumped at the chance of borrowing the work and enjoying Hakluyt at leisure. The stories proved moving and exciting; they made him for the first time conscious of the 'hugeness of English heroism', and obsessed him with the desire to go and do likewise. To read the Bible and kill the Spaniards, what an ideal vocation was the Englishman's of Queen Elizabeth's time! Most of the social ideas that had once filled Kingsley's mind and heart now seemed dull and stuffy and were of a sudden exorcised. Away went Liberalism, Democracy, and the rest as he began to out-Carlyle Carlyle in the worship of force of every kind.

What more glorious task could he think of than to make these Tudor adventurers familiar to the young Englishmen of his day, and retell the story of Queen Bess, that wonderful woman who kept her eye on all private undertakings, blessed the privately owned ships that drove the Spaniards from the sea and the private planters of American colonies, and in the interests of her subjects wrote letters to every potentate in the world? Despotic, peremptory, taking a living interest in her men's enterprises, waving a kerchief to Frobisher as his ship slipped down the Thames and holding the personal devotion of all English hearts! Was it not possible, Charles stopped to wonder, that Queen Victoria might be able to play the same great role?

How thrilling were the links in the grand story! The sword of Spain forged in the gold mines of Peru; the ships of Spain carrying gold to Europe only to be intercepted on the high seas, and intercepted by whom? why by the English privateer! The battles of England had been fought by these champions of the Reformation at their own risk and cost, and it was but fair that they should repay themselves with Spanish plunder. 'Indomitable, God-fearing men whose life was a great liturgy', said Anthony Froude, and his brother-in-law endorsed the verdict.

Charles Kingsley pored and pored over Froude's copy of Hakluyt at Torquay and by the time they left Livermead for Combe Court Hotel, Babbacombe, he had already written several chapters of *Westward Ho!* which he intended to dedicate to Rajah Brooke, in whom he saw the embodiment of a modern Elizabethan. He had sat down to work at the novel in a great flurry, for when a new idea struck him he could never wait to think it over, but crushed and pounded it into a book at once. The first chapter of *Westward Ho!* was being composed in February 1854 just as the Russians received the ultimatum from the British Government that opened the Crimean War. To Kingsley the days he was actually living through were also a source of great excitement. He gloated over the despatch of 10,000 picked men to Malta as well as over the 'six times larger' force that was being embarked by the French! Every detail of the fighting interested him. When in March 1854 he learnt that a British squadron under Charles Napier had destroyed Bomarsund in the Aaland Islands and Sveaborg in Finland, he rejoiced in the naval successes though they made him critical of those who were conducting the war. He gave vent to his feelings, as he so often did, to Tom Hughes.

So Sveaborg is extinct! Why not before? and will it be followed up by Cronstadt? My notion is that the Ministry will be half sorry for such easy and brilliant success because it will enable the nation (1) to ask why did you not do it before? and (2) to insist on a great deal more being done. If we can destroy the supposed impregnable Sveaborg without losing a man, we have a right to ask that a few more impregnable places may be taken even at the loss of a few lives; but I have yet to learn that the war is in earnest. . . . I always knew that the Puseyites for superstitious reasons about 'The Crescent and the Cross' disliked the war. . . . Be sure that there is a strong Russian feeling among the Puseyites, just because they hanker after the Greek Church *faute de Rome*.[1]

And when Tom Hughes wrote in the autumn to ask him for a ballad about the war he replied:

As for a ballad—oh! my dear lad, there is no use fiddling while Rome is burning. I have nothing to sing about these glorious fellows, except, 'God save the Queen and them.' I tell you the whole thing stuns me, so I cannot sit down to make fiddle rhyme with diddle about it—or blundered with hundred like Alfred Tennyson. He is no Tyrtaeus, though he has a glimpse of what Tyrtaeus ought to be. But I have not even that and am going rabbit shooting tomorrow instead.

In Fanny Kingsley's de-personalised story of her husband's life the following characteristic words have at this point been excised:

Would that the Rabbits were Russians, tin-pot on head and musket in hand! Oh! for one hour's skirmishing in those Inkerman ravines and five minutes with butt and bayonet as a *bonne bouche* to finish off with![2]

Just as he had got himself thoroughly steeped in *Westward Ho!* Kingsley had to interrupt his work to go to Edinburgh where the Philosophical Institute had invited him to discourse to them on 'Alexandria and her Schools'. He had replied by saying that though willing to give the lectures asked for, he was bound to give offence and traverse the views of Martineau, Emerson, and other Neoplatonists. No objections being raised,

[1] Add. MSS. B.M.   [2] Add. MSS. B.M.

and money not so plentiful that he could afford to disregard any chance of making it, he had to go. The expedition made him horribly nervous and he had a bad fit of crying in his hotel bedroom before the first lecture. But it gave him considerable pleasure to dine with an M.P. and his wife, both warm admirers of *Yeast* and *Alton Locke* whose names Fanny Kingsley saw fit to asterisk.

From Edinburgh he wrote in playful mood to his little girl, Rose:

> Miss Rose must thank God for giving her such a lovely mum with beautiful black hair and bright eyes and soft lips to kiss Miss Rose and darling, darling, feet for Daddy and Miss Rose to kiss.

Fanny used this letter in her book but squeezed all the playfulness out of it by printing:

> How happy Miss Rose must be with her dear mother. She must say, 'Thank God for giving me such a darling mother'.

On his way back from Scotland to Babbacombe Charles Kingsley had to go to Eversley to install a new curate. The place seemed to him miserably depressing without the family— 'almost like a grave'. In London he had long conversations with Charles Darwin and Philip Gosse, mainly on matters geological, met many acquaintances and heard a great deal of talk about the war in the Crimea. How he hated to think that it should be going on and he not in the thick of it! When the *Times* made S. G. O., who was going out to Pera as chaplain, its special correspondent, it was almost more than he could bear and he awaited Sydney's return from his six weeks' assignment with impatience. Sydney was able to tell him grand news about the pluck of English regiments at the Alma, but added that more troops were urgently needed and should, if the utterly incapable Lord Raglan were recalled, be despatched immediately as the French were piling up regiments, 'far better found regiments than our own'. Accounts of the hospital lines at Scutari, 'three miles of hungry men in foul beds', and of conversations with Miss Nightingale over 'missing stores' hardly roused Charles's interest, for to his mind the unwounded soldiers were the only important ones and they must be encouraged and praised. The heroism and the endurance of the fighting men should be stressed and advertised if only to assist recruiting

With this conviction in mind he wrote *Brave Words for Brave Soldiers* in which he boldly announced, 'The Lord Jesus Christ is not only the Prince of Peace; He is the Prince of War too'. The address was published anonymously and sent off in thousands to the army in the field.

Vernon Lushington in a letter to John Martineau wrote:

> I suppose you have read *Brave Words* published by Macmillan. No doubt, I think, Kingsley is the author. But whoever it is it is curious to see how Maurice is the prime mover and suggester of the thoughts. That text quoted and applied. 'I saw a man on a white horse' etc, is the text of the last sermon in the *Doctrine of Sacrifice*, a most notable production in every way, and that description of the Devil as the accusing Spirit is borrowed elsewhere from the same book.[1]

The Kingsleys moved in July 1854 to North Down House at Bideford which they rented for a year. It was a convenient locality in which to examine the harbours from which the ships set sail for the Caribbean and had the great merit in Charles's eyes of not being a resort of fashion. He described its setting in *Westward Ho!*:

> The little white town of Bideford, which slopes upward from its broad tide-river, paved with yellow sands, and many-arched old bridge where salmon wait for autumn floods, towards the pleasant upland on the west. Above the town the hills close in, cushioned with deep oak woods through which juts here and there a crag of fern-fringed slate; below they lower and open more and more in soft rounded knolls, and fertile squares of red and green till they sink into the wide expanse of hazy, flat, rich salt marshes and rolling sandhills where Torridge joins her sister Taw, and both together flow quietly toward the broad surges of the bar, and the everlasting thunder of the Atlantic swell. Pleasantly the old town stands there, beneath its soft Italian sky fanned day and night by the fresh ocean breezes. . . .

From Bideford he wrote to Maurice:

> I am shut up like any Jeremiah with my Elizabethan books. The novel is half done and a most ruthless, bloodthirsty book it is.

[1] Add. MSS. B.M.

Ludlow will be horribly shocked at the homage paid to Judge Lynch. I have a deal of the wolf-vein in me in spite of fifteen hundred years of civilisation.

Kingsley often called *Westward Ho!* a 'sanguinary' book, and there is no doubt that the parts he most savoured were the massacre of the Spaniards at Smerwick, the boarding of the Spanish galleon, the putting to the sword of its crew, and the fight for the gold convoy. He told Tom Hughes that the war had 'literally wrung the book' out of him, and that he found himself consumed by the desire to inspire the young Englishmen of his own day to become as adventure-minded as their forebears. The novel, a quarter of a million words long, was written at high pressure in seven months. It presents in its hero, Amyas Leigh, an idealised Charles Kingsley leading the life he would best have liked to live. It had enabled him to give vent to his feelings on the privilege of fighting and, if need be, dying for England's sake. As he told all his friends, it had done him a power of good writing it.

Macmillan was delighted with *Westward Ho!* and paid Kingsley £400 for the first edition, more than he had ever earned before. Mudie, he was told, had ordered 350 copies, and a large number had been sent to the army in the Crimea. It began to look as if the author's financial difficulties were at an end. By a great many people *Westward Ho!* was regarded not only as a good stirring story of adventure, but definitely as recruiting propaganda. The press was amiable and in some cases enthusiastic. A few critics compared it with that other famous and far less realistic Elizabethan novel, *Kenilworth*, a few more picked little holes in its structure,—he had not written of Barnstaple correctly, or of such-and-such a Devon family, and the accuracy of his quotations was questioned. To all critics the author modestly replied, 'I have taken it all from Hakluyt save what has been imagined by myself and that must be regarded as fiction.'

If Kingsley had died at this time at the age of five and thirty we should all think of him as a man of great promise cut off in his prime, but twenty more years of life added nothing to his literary reputation. In *Westward Ho!* he had reached the pinnacle of his achievement.

After the elation of great success came a drop into a trough of agonising doubt. Associating with Elizabethan sailors had made the author think of himself as 'a poor, queasy, hysterical, half-baked sort of a fellow'. Was he falling away from good causes and becoming a mere 'artist in words'? Had he been seduced by love of fame into neglect of his proper business of preaching and parish work? Writing was but a money-getting business after all, though the patriotic aspect of his work might perhaps be counted to him for righteousness. While waiting for a new afflatus, Kingsley found that the only philanthropic interest he still cherished was the cause of Sanitary Reform. On its behalf, he joined in a deputation to the Prime Minister, for, as he said, *some* clergymen must take a lead' and as far as he knew no one of his cloth pretended to the faintest interest in the subject.

I had an opportunity [he wrote to his wife] of telling Lord Palmerston a great deal which I trust may save many lives. Remember now it is a question of blood-guiltiness—that is all. But I am not going to London any more about sanitary matters. The utter inability of the Health of Towns Act to cleanse this or any other neighbouring parish made me consider what I have done as a parochial duty.

Summoned to give evidence 'before the House of Commons' on Sanitary matters and the insufficient pay of Parish Medical Officers, he particularly stressed the fact that on their meagre salaries no doctor could afford or be expected to give two of the most important but most expensive medicines—quinine and cod-liver oil. After eleven years in a parish he could testify that the pay of the parish doctor was much too low.

Sanitary Reform was now for Kingsley losing its humanitarian character and taking on a martial aspect. In writing to congratulate the author of a Cholera Report published in the *Times* he said:

It is a sad thing that 'food for powder' requires to be of the best quality; but so it is, and unless the physical deterioration of the lower class is stopt by bold sanitary reform, such as you have been working out, we shall soon have rifles, but no men to shoulder them; at least to use the butts of them when required. If we are to furnish any more drafts of men who will equal the heroes of Inkerman, we must open our eyes and first keep them alive when they are infants, and next, give them such an atmosphere to grow up in, that they shall become men and not rickety monkeys.

The rather truculent spirit imparted by Lord Palmerston to his government made Charles Kingsley glad to think himself a supporter of his foreign policy and a contributor, if only in small measure, to the prosecution of what every sensible man must think a righteous war. How sagacious too had the Prime Minister shown himself in refusing to permit the proclamation of a national fast-day against the cholera! Why should we put the blame for our stupidities on God?

Though a jingo spirit had been generated in certain sections of English life, the righteousness of the Crimean War was far from being universally recognised. W. H. Mallock tells of meeting Swinburne at this time in Jowett's rooms at Oxford. They were left alone together by their host, and Swinburne paced the room gesticulating as he talked. 'The most beautiful lines that Tennyson ever wrote,' he exclaimed, 'were those from *Maud*',

> That like a silent lightning under the stars
> She seem'd to divide in a dream from a band of the blest.

'Yes,' he went on, 'and what did the dream-Maud tell her lover when she had got him? That the salvation of the world depended on the Crimean War and the prosecution of Lord Palmerston's policy.' She

> . . . spoke of a hope for the world in the coming wars—
> 'And in that hope, dear soul, let trouble have rest,
> Knowing I tarry for thee,' and pointed to Mars
> As he glow'd like a ruddy shield on the Lion's breast.
>
> .   .   .   .   .   .
>
> And it was but a dream, yet it lighten'd my despair
> When I thought that a war would arise in defence of the right.

Maud makes strange reading to-day, though it gives the feeling of a moment in our history when high-minded people preferred the idea of death on the battlefield to the ignominious-ness of life in a peaceful society devoted to the worship of wealth. Ridiculous as it appeared to Swinburne, Tennyson genuinely felt, as he 'hail'd the banner of battle unfurl'd', that the country had woken to higher aims and had

> lost for a little her lust of gold
> And love of a peace that was full of wrongs and shames
> Horrible, hateful, monstrous, not to be told.

Whole-heartedly did Kingsley bless Tennyson for putting into words his own inarticulate feelings on the matter:

> It is better to fight for the good than to rail at the ill;
> I have felt with my native land, I am one with my kind,
> I embrace the purpose of God, and the doom assign'd.

Public interests and foreign wars did not, however, absorb all Kingsley's energy, for he and Fanny were unceasingly fighting their private battle on sanitation. Ever since the death of Sir John Cope they had bombarded his heir, the Rev. Sir William Cope, with letters calling attention to the unwholesome conditions under which he was constraining them to live. The correspondence left nothing to the imagination. It dealt with the radical necessity of rebuilding the rectory on another site and recapitulated the protests of a former rector, Mr. Debarry, who had offered to rebuild the house on the glebe at his own expense, but had been foiled in his wish by Sir John Cope. The condition of the structure had not improved since Mr. Debarry's day, and Kingsley now told his patron that it was frankly impossible for him to keep his wife and family at Eversley during the winter and that were it not for his awkward financial position he would seek leave to exchange the living for a healthier one. He even troubled to point out that rebuilding would increase the value of Sir William's property, and that Queen Anne's Bounty would lend the living the sum of £1000 to be repaid over a period of thirty years at £35 per annum plus 4 per cent interest. Sir William should also know that he has himself spent £1000 out of his own pocket in patching and replacing 'conveniences'. Most people would call it sewing new cloth on an old garment, but he had not failed in his duty to church property. There is nothing for it but to rebuild.

As to site the house lies in so very low and damp a situation on the level of the water-course which drains the whole of Coomless bog and exposed even after the hottest days of summer to such severe cold mists and night frosts that all my efforts to make it warm and dry have been hitherto unavailing. The water freezes in the bedrooms, books and clothes mildew and prints are spoilt on the walls in spite of constant fires and stoves upstairs and down and the cold of the house is for nine months of the year unparalleled. Even at the end of the last August Mr. Lempriere's servants actually gave him notice alleging that the cold made the offices uninhabitable.

In addition to all this we read that there was often extensive flooding of the kitchen and that dry-rot was spreading fast. Kingsley had asked Mr. Habershon, an architect, to draw up plans for a new rectory and submitted them to Sir William for his comments. It transpires in the course of the correspondence that Sir William has never been over the rectory. In spite of all reports on its actual condition he chooses to consider it 'a very pretty house, roomy and convenient' and cannot possibly consent to Mr. Kingsley's rebuilding it unless the proposed house is identical with the old. On looking at Habershon's plans he thinks them 'inconvenient and uncomfortable'. In the long last he falls back on 'Sir John's sound argument based on truth . . . the house is a good house as it stands, has been sufficient for many many rectors and indeed for yourself for many years . . . you do not feel for me or else you would hardly put me to the disagreeable duty of refusing your request of which as patron I cannot approve'.

In his letters Kingsley was always deferential and polite, but as he got no concessions out of Sir William is it any wonder that he and Fanny began to cast about them for some way out of the cruel hardship and threat to life implicit in permanent residence at Eversley? If only they could get preferment! Due to return to duty after an absence of two years they did not move back into the rectory but rented a house on high ground just outside their parish, Farley Court, and hoped for speedy promotion. Fanny was of opinion that Lord Palmerston should show his gratitude to the author of *Westward Ho!* in some tangible form and, as soon as peace was concluded, tried through her brother and other members of both Houses of Parliament to get her husband's name on to the Prime Minister's list for

clerical advancement.   Every appointment in her day and for
many a day after was a matter of finding the right strings and
pulling them.

Meanwhile Charles Kingsley, who had been consulting Richard
Monckton Milnes as to the best way of 'helping Thomas Cooper
the Chartist, in his extreme poverty', had been so impressed by
Monckton Milnes's kindness and generosity that he now at
Fanny's instigation tried to enlist his influence with the Government on the matter of his own preferment.   Inditing a letter
from Chelsea rectory he put forward his request.

MY DEAR MR. MILNES,
       I could not find the impudence, or you the time, last night for
the following matter.

I am trying, and with good hope of success, for the canonry at
Westminster, vacant by the death of Bishop Moule.

I know that Lord Palmerston is not ill-disposed towards me and
that Mr. William Cowper and others will help me, *unless* Maurice
is thought of (and Heaven forbid that I should put myself in
competition with him!)   Whether Lord Shaftesbury is as well-
inclined to me is a very different question.   But considering the
work which my wife's family have done for the Whigs this fifty
years, not to mention a little work which I may have done myself,
I do not think it so very preposterous a hope on my part, that I may
get one of those places which were originally meant for literary
parsons.

If you would help me in the matter, you would confer a very
deep obligation.   I am told that you have very great influence, and
that the Government are under obligations to you.   That you are
the most good-natured of men I know as well as anyone.   But if
you think me impertinent in any way, you have only to put this
letter in the fire, and forget all about it, while I shall remain as ever

Yours most faithfully,

C. KINGSLEY.[1]

It is evident from other letters that Pascoe Grenfell, Thomas
Hughes, and various M.P.s were also trying to help Kingsley.
Writing to his 'dear Tom' from Farley Court Charles Kingsley
says:

[1] Houghton MSS., June 11, 1856.

You are the brick I always knew you, so I shall say no more. . . .
Try Mr. Cowper by all means—I don't know him well enough to
ask anything of him and don't like to seem to have done so and
therefore to prevent his thinking that we are making a cat's paw of
him, as belonging to *our* party (or Lord Palmerston's thinking the
same or choosing to pretend that he thinks it) I would make no
secret to him of Mr. Grenfell's being on the same quest in my
behalf.

Of course all interest which Lord Goderich can use I should be
glad enough of.   Indeed though I should not have asked him to
propose me as first mover, I should have had no scruple now that
Mr. Grenfell has proposed me to have asked him myself to second
me.

Mr. Marshall is a good card.   Robert Lowe don't try—I know
the white man well and he is not one to whom I should ever wish to
be under an obligation.

Ball I know not.   They say he is a dissenter.   If so and you try
him, you may let him know that I am for admitting Dissenters to
the Universities and widening tests of every kind.   I will, when I
get power, back any such movements.   God bless you.[1]

It is disappointing to have to record that no more results
were achieved by this manœuvring than had been forthcoming
from Kingsley's correspondence with Sir William Cope.   For
the winter of 1855–6, therefore, Fanny felt justified in installing
herself at Farley Court, from which refuge Charles carried on
his parish work.

[1] Add. MSS. B.M.

Chapter 11

GREEK MYTHS AND FISHING

Angling is like poetry, men are to be born so.

IZAAK WALTON

FARLEY COURT in the parish of Swallowfield proved a very congenial house to Fanny Kingsley. Standing on a hill it was a comfortable contrast to the mildewed rectory. How much she wished it could become their home! Charles found it easy to write there, and quickly got ready for press *The Heroes*, a version of Greek myths for children. The impulse to rewrite these stories came from a reading of *Tanglewood Tales*, wherein Hawthorne had presented some of the old legends in what seemed to Kingsley a 'distressingly vulgar' way. In introducing the tales to his children he wrote, 'I love these old Hellens heartily'.

> Come hither children, at this blessed Christmas time, when all God's creatures should rejoice together, and bless Him who redeemed them. Come and see old friends of mine, whom I knew long ere you were born. They are come to visit us at Christmas, out of the world where all live to God; and to tell you some of the old fairy tales which they loved when they were young like you. . . . Next to the old romances which were written in the Christian middle age, there are no fairy tales like these Greek ones for beauty, wisdom, and truth, and for making children love noble deeds, and trust in God to help them through.

Compared with Kingsley's clear-cut narrative, Hawthorne's rendering seems chattily romanticised, but then as the American author himself said, he aimed 'at a tone in some degree Gothic' instead of the classical coldness 'which was to him as repellent as the touch of marble'.

The finding of the Gray Sisters by Perseus provides an example of the stylistic difference between the two authors. Kingsley's version runs:

> There at last he found the three Gray Sisters by the shore of the freezing sea, nodding upon a white log of driftwood beneath the

cold white winter moon; and they chaunted a low song together 'Why the old times were better than the new.'

Hawthorne introduces a whiff of farce into the scene by naming the sisters Scarecrow, Nightmare, and Shakejoint, and by letting Perseus address them as 'My dear, good, admirable old ladies', whereas Kingsley with greater dignity allows him to call them 'Venerable mothers'.

Again Kingsley describes the three Gorgons 'sleeping as huge as elephants', whereas Hawthorne says:

behold, there were the terrible Gorgons! They lay fast asleep, soothed by the thunder of the sea; for it required a tumult that would have deafened everybody else to lull such fierce creatures into slumber.

It is one of the Gorgons, Medusa, that Perseus has to slay. The hero has been warned not to look at her face but only at the reflection in his shining shield, and Kingsley says:

As he looked, from among her tresses the vipers' heads awoke, and peeped up with their bright dry eyes, and showed their fangs and hissed.

While Hawthorne, less terse and less vivid, writes:

In its surface [the shield] he could safely look at the reflection of the Gorgon's face. And there it was—that terrible countenance, —mirrored in the brightness of the shield, with the moonlight falling over it, and displaying all its horror. The snakes, whose venomous natures could not altogether sleep, kept twisting themselves over the forehead.

Invited to criticise the manuscript, John Ludlow, said that Kingsley should have told the stories 'as if from himself', but the author replied that as he would not have been able in that way to give the children the Greek spirit he had deliberately adopted a sort of ballad approach and tried to make his prose as metrical as possible. The little book, illustrated by the author with coloured outline drawings looking like tracings, was welcomed by thousands of parents and sold extremely well. Just as *Tanglewood Tales* had been the first real story-book for children published in the United States, so was *The Heroes* the first English children's book that was not written primarily to inculcate good morals.

Having enjoyed this diversion from the more serious business of novel-writing Kingsley sketched out *Two Years Ago*, a book that gave him great happiness to write. In an introductory note he explained that two years earlier England had had a cholera epidemic and was engaged in the Crimean War.

> Two years ago was the time for work; for men to do with all their might whatsoever their hands found to do. But now the storm has lulled once more; the air has cleared awhile, and we can talk calmly over all the wonders of that sudden strange and sad 'Two Years Ago.'

The book embodied a good deal of desultory personal experience. The first chapter takes us back another sixteen years, and introduces Edward Thurnall, M.D., his son Tom, and the doctor's assistant, John Briggs, who is about to leave to seek his fortune. Eighteen, Tom, whose two elder brothers are already doctors, after a visit to Paris joins the staff of St. Mumpsimus's Hospital in London where he becomes a popular house-surgeon. After a time he goes as anatomical professor to a South American Republic, finds it in a state of revolution, roams on to the Rocky Mountains, Spanish West Indies, Tahiti, Singapore, and returns home after four years to tell of further travels in Cairo, Constantinople, and the Kirghiz steppes. His eldest brother, John, dies, and his second brother, William, practises medicine in Manchester. Tom, the rover, bolts off again, this time to the Antipodes. While mining in South Australia a letter reaches him to say that his brother William is also dead, and that his father has lost all his money and is going blind.

The second chapter opens in the 'good old West country' at a fishing port, which though called Aberalva is recognisably Clovelly. Dark-eyed, dark-haired Grace Harvey, the schoolmistress, said to spend whole nights in prayer, rules the place and has far more influence than the papistical parson, Frank Headley. Headley had served in a fashionable London church with brotherhoods and sisterhoods attached to it, had then overworked in Bethnal Green and now has come to Aberalva (where nine-tenths of the people are dissenters) for a rest.   Aberalva is described from quay and red-sailed boats to lug-worms and pebbly beach.   Fair to look at, and tricked out with high fuchsias and colour-washed houses, it is foul within.   A great storm occurs and in the course of it a ship drifts shorewards wherefrom Tom Thurnall is thrown unconscious on the beach. He is rescued by Grace Harvey.   When he comes to he finds that his belt, full of savings in gold, has disappeared, and he concludes that Grace Harvey must be the thief.   Settling in Aberalva he fights a cholera epidemic and preaches sanitation.   In the end he goes to the Crimea as does Grace Harvey whom he eventually marries.   As foil to manly arrogant Tom Thurnall John Briggs turns up again as Elsley Vavasour.   He has a reputation as a poet, is married to an heiress, and is scared of meeting anyone who has known him as a dispenser.   In the end he worries himself to an early grave.   It will be observed that all the old Kingsley interests crop up in this book from wreck to cholera epidemic, from lectures on sanitation to the differences between Anglicans and Dissenters.   Every experience Kingsley could think of was packed into this book which is as shapeless and higgledy-piggledy in conception as it is in execution, but still he found it fun to write up the family shipwreck, to compose an idealised portrait of his brother George, and to tell of the love of a shy curate for a rich and high-born lady. Rather irrelevantly he explained the motive of the book to Maurice by saying, 'It is a side-stroke at the Tartarus doctrine which is never out of my mind'.   Kingsley hated the notion of hell and seems in some vague manner to have thought the Church of England ought to accept the existence of an intermediate state.   'It must be carefully taught,' he said, 'as otherwise people might mistake it for the Romish doctrine of purgatory.'

The sudden death of his Cambridge friend, Charles Mansfield, was a great personal grief to Kingsley.   Mansfield was in the way of becoming one of the first research chemists of his time, a possible successor to Faraday.   In 1849 he had published *Benzol: its Nature and Utility*, and his great achievement—which resulted in the foundation of the aniline industry—was the

extraction of benzol from coal tar.   For a while he had worked
with the Christian Socialists, had even driven a water-cart in
Bermondsey, and, as we have seen, had been a good deal with
Kingsley during his Torquay period.   Not only had he investigated Aeronautics and written *Aerial Navigation*, but he
had travelled in Paraguay, studied the bird life there and ex-
plored the possibilities of colonisation in the Grand Chaco.
In 1855 he had produced his *Theory of Salts* and had been
asked to send specimens of benzol to the Paris Exhibition.
While preparing these in a room hired for the purpose in St.
John's Wood, a naphtha-still overflowed and Mansfield, in an
attempt to save the premises carried the blazing still into the
street and was so badly burned that he died in Middlesex
Hospital nine days later at the age of thirty-five.   He had stayed
at Farley Court shortly before his death and was one of the
few Christian Socialist friends of whom Fanny Kingsley really
approved, but then everyone who came in contact with him had
to submit themselves to his charm.

Beside Mansfield, there passed through Farley Court Maurice,
Ludlow, Tennyson, Browning, Grant Duff, and an American
called Hurlbert who arrived in the nick of time to be put into
Two Years Ago as Stangrave.   He was a journalist who had
come to present the Abolitionist case in England and in the
novel is a denouncer of slavery.

Kingsley, who still occasionally reviewed books for *Fraser's
Magazine*, at this time wrote a homily on *Maud and other
Poems* as well as an article on Sydney Smith, stressing the
poverty of his early clerical life in Yorkshire.   Feeling very
well and belligerent we find him delivering judgement on Robert
Browning, who, he judged, could never be a poet.

> The iron has entered into his soul, he was born and bred a
> Dissenter of the *trois* [!] *état* and though he is a good fellow nothing
> will take the smell of tallow and brown sugar out of him.   He
> cannot help being coarse and vulgar and is naïvely unaware of the
> fact.   However, if he had been either a gentleman (of course I
> mean a churchman, for all gentlemen owe that name to church
> influence over themselves or their parents) or a hard handed work-
> ing man in contact with iron fact he might have been a fine poet.[1]

[1] To A. W. Gurney, October 3, 1855.

At this time Charles Kingsley paid frequent visits to London staying at Chelsea rectory and seeing a number of people.   His admiration for Carlyle had waned with his interest in Chartism and Working-men's Associations.   After an evening spent with the sage in Cheyne Row, where John Parker and Anthony Froude were also present, he came away thinking he had never heard such 'a foolish outpouring of Devil's doctrines and raving cynicism'.   It had made him quite sick, but as he confided to Maurice he had managed to keep his temper while Carlyle was denouncing sympathy with sinners as a sign of 'innate scoundrelism'.   'When I got out, I am afraid I swore with wrath and disgust—there was the ferocity of the old Pharisee without Isaiah's prophecy of mercy.   Meanwhile his wife, poor creature, is pining for want of sympathy and attention from him and is very ill.   Whatever her faults may be, he has no right to neglect her.'

Fame, and with it assurance, had come to Charles Kingsley very slowly, but very surely, in so far as he at this time became an object of pilgrimage to Americans.   When Mrs. Beecher Stowe, accompanied by her friend Mrs. Perkins, paid her second visit to England (1856) she made a bee-line for the Kingsleys' home.   'How we did talk and go on for three days', she reported to her husband, 'I guess he [Kingsley] is tired, I'm sure we were.' [1]

As descriptions of the rector are rare, it is interesting to learn that another woman, the novelist L. B. Walford, watching him in her father's house, 'was full of curiosity to see whether the author of *Westward Ho!* was like his photograph, and there could be no doubt that the camera had flattered him, for he looked weather-beaten and very red in the face.   And then his stammer was rather dreadful though it was obvious from his way of speaking that he was conscious of it, and had taken pains to overcome it by speaking very slowly—almost too slowly . . . we felt inclined to goad him on, it became so tiresome.' [2]

What between the success of *Westward Ho!* and the near certainty of preferment, Kingsley showed more buoyancy at this

---

[1] Annie Fields, *Life and Letters of H. B. Stowe,* 1897.
[2] L. B. Walford, *Memories of Victorian London.*

period than ever before. Nearly everything he thought or felt was still being poured into the ears of the long-suffering Maurice, whom he would cheer up for bad reviews and un-favourable newspaper comment in words as comforting as these:

I hope you will not bother your soul with what the *Westminster* says. The woman who used to insult you there—and I suppose does so now is none other than Miss Evans, the infidel *esprit fort* (who is now G. H. Lewes's concubine) I met him yesterday and lucky for me that I had not your letter when I did so or I should certainly have given him a queer piece of my mind to carry home to his lady.

During the Kingsleys' long absence from home a military camp had been established at Aldershot wherein to train men for the Crimea. Officers wearing swords and spurs would clank up the Eversley aisle on Sundays to hear the rector preach, and would wait about after the service to tell him how much they had enjoyed *Westward Ho!* or the hunting scenes in *Yeast*. This pleased Kingsley enormously for his heart always went out to soldiers; it was not for nothing that his direct ancestor had fought in the rose gardens of Minden! When the Queen reviewed the remnants of the army that had endured the Russian campaign, he rode over to Laffan's Plain to watch the parade. Though hardly to be compared with Gloriana at Tilbury, his sovereign lady sat her horse well and made an impression of dignity.

This was a comparatively happy summer for Kingsley, who for once in his life was care-free and not yet weighed down in spirit by 'the incubus' of imperial affairs. He played with his children, told them stories, took them out botanising, and plotted for himself wonderful fishing excursions. On the eve of one of these outings he paced his new-mown lawn gleefully snuffing the acrid smell of the grass, listening to the woodpecker's shrill cackle, to the whistling of railway engines, to drums beating in camp, and to the chiming of the Heckfield clock. As always when very happy he began to versify.

Oh blessed drums of Aldershot!
Oh blessed south west train!
Oh blessed, blessed Speaker's clock,
All prophesying rain!

Oh blessed yaffil laughing loud!
Oh blessed falling glass!
Oh blessed fan of cold gray cloud
Oh blessed smelling grass.

Oh bless'd south wind that toots his horn
Through every hole and crack!
I'm off at eight tomorrow morn
To bring such fishes back!

Discoursing to a friend in the same rumbustious mood, he said, 'What an ass Shelley was to be sure to write an ode to the south-west wind when he didn't know in the least what it was for!' He then went on to say how lucky he was to be surrounded by ponds and to have for his sole amusement fly-fishing. If he could not fish, he could always rearrange his fly-book and study the make-up of its contents—palmer, governor, stone-fly, March brown, yellow sally, black alder, and after he had gone over them one by one, he could bury himself in a book on fly-tying or on flying insects and their behaviour in the water. Anything to do with fishing always put him in good heart and sometimes between visits to a dying parishioner, he would run down to the boundary stream, flog the water hard for half an hour and then rush back to the death-bed. It was indeed a blessed faculty to be able to hurl onself into whatever one was doing just as if there were no other job on earth!

Here is a characteristic note to Tom Hughes asking him to order brass minnows and flies on his behalf and telling him:

I have at last solved the problem of my life—how to tie a cow-dung fly. . . . After haunting tackle-shops and after twenty failures extending over ten years, it is done, a fait accompli in history. But you must dye yr hackle—*how* is telling. But I'll tell *you*.

Am very hard worked, two services a day and communion (private) beside cottage visiting and a sermon every evening. Pity such good weather in Passion week.

For the summer of 1856 Kingsley had promised himself a treat in what he called Snowdonia. Tom Hughes and Tom Taylor were to go too, for not only did they like fishing but they were good companions, ready at all times to listen to his rambling discourses. What he much enjoyed and was very free with was discussion of the Bible. One day in talking over the early chapters of Genesis with two clerical friends, he threw back his head with a gasp and exclaimed, 'I've always thought that the serpent was a serpent-worshipping black tribe.' When he said, 'I've always thought', it meant that the notion had just flashed into his head for the first time. Percy Smith objected, 'Oh, but Rector—you know negroes do not go on their bellies.' 'No,' replied Kingsley, 'they don't, but then snakes don't eat dirt and niggers do!' There is no doubt that Charles dearly loved an audience of this kind; in mixed company he was always a little apprehensive of boring people with his stutter. He once said to Hughes, 'You know I should be as great a talker as anyone in England but for the stammer.' Sometimes he regarded this disability as his special thorn in the flesh, and at other times figured it as a disagreeable fault to be cured at any price. 'A man', he used to say, 'has no right to be a nuisance if he can help it and no more go among his fellows stammering than he does stinking.'

As the time drew near for his holiday, Charles was provoked by sheer excitement to write a hundred lines and more of doggerel to Tom Hughes. They show him bubbling over with restored youth.

Come away with me, Tom,
Term and talk is done;
My poor lads are reaping,
Busy every one.
Curates mind the parish,
Sweepers mind the court;
We'll away to Snowdon
For our ten days' sport;
Fish the August evening
Till the eve is past,
Whoop, like boys, at pounders
Fairly played and grassed.

When they cease to dimple
Lunge and swerve and leap,
Then up over Siabod
Choose our nest and sleep.

.   .   .   .

What are sheets and servants?
Superfluity!
Pray for wives and children
Safe in slumber curled,
Then to chat till midnight
O'er this babbling world—
Of the workmen's college,
Of the price of grain,
Of the tree of knowledge,
Of the chance of rain;
If Sir A. goes Romeward,
If Miss B. sings true,
If the fleet comes homeward,
If the mare will do—
Anything and everything
Up there in the sky
Angels understand us
And no 'saints' are by.
Down, and bathe at day dawn,
Tramp from lake to lake,
Washing brain and heart clean
Every step we take.
Leave to Robert Browning
Beggars, fleas, and vines
Leave to mournful Ruskin
Popish Appenines,
Dirty Stones of Venice
And his Gas-lamps seven—
We've the stones of Snowdon
And the lamps of heaven.
Where's the mighty credit
In admiring Alps?
Any goose sees 'glory'
In their 'snowy scalps'.
Leave such signs and wonders

For the dullard brain,
As aesthetic brandy,
Opium and cayenne.
Give me Bramshill common
(Sir John's harriers by)
Or the vale of Windsor
England's golden eye.

.   .   .   .

Tho' we earn our bread, Tom,
By the dirty pen,
What we can we will be,
Honest Englishmen.
Do the work that's nearest,
Though it's dull at whiles,
Helping, when we meet them,
Lame dogs over stiles;
See in every hedgerow
Marks of angel's feet,
Epics in each pebble
Underneath our feet;
Once a year like schoolboys
Robin-Hooding go,
Leaving fops and fogies
A thousand feet below.

The anglers were not lucky in their weather, and when a continuous downpour stopped fishing they took to writing verses in the visitors' book at the inn. One of Kingsley's quatrains ran like this:

I came to Pen-y-gwryd in frantic hope of slaying
Grilse, Salmon, three-pound red-fleshed trout
And what else there's no saying.
But bitter cold and lashing rain, and black nor-eastern skies, Sir,
Drove me from fish to botany, a sadder man and wiser.

As far as the mere killing of fish was concerned the rector told his friends that he could do better at home, for one evening on Lady Mildmay's Wansborough water, after a broiling day, he had 'grassed twenty fish weighing twenty-two pounds,' besides

losing a 'brace more whoppers'.   And all on a fly he called a
caperer, 'a fat fly with a tiny hook'!

When *Tom Brown's Schooldays* came out Kingsley did his
best to boost it, partly because he liked the book immensely
himself and partly because of his affection for the author.   After
praising it in the *Saturday Review*, he wrote to John Martineau,
'Buy, oh Buy and Puff, oh Puff Tom Brown's School Life, the
wholesomest book I've read for many a day'.   Tom Hughes,
after being warmly congratulated on his literary success, was
urged to 'buy a Farlow spoon immediately' and come and fish
with him near Eversley.   The rector boasted of having killed
'40 pounds weight of pike' on the Duke of Wellington's water
at Strathfieldsaye, and of an almost equally good catch on Lord
Eversley's lakes.   And now the Speaker has begged him to get
rid of more pike for him and this is where Tom Hughes might
make himself useful.

When reading of the extreme interest and enjoyment Kingsley
derived from sport of this kind we wonder how he had time or
inclination to bend his mind to solving the riddles of his many
correspondents or reply to the questions put to him in his
capacity of clergyman.   When he let it be known that he did
not believe in Hell people wrote to enquire how they must
interpret the biblical allusions to 'everlasting fire and the worm
that never dies.'   Kingsley took conundrums of this sort in his
stride; to his thinking, worms and fire might be entirely bene-
ficent in operation and the seeker after true doctrine would
be told:

> A fire which cannot be quenched; a worm which cannot die—I
> see existing, whether they be those or not of which our Lord spoke.
> I consider them among the most blessed revelation of the Gospel.
> . . . But in the comfort that the worm cannot die and the fire be
> quenched, I look calmly forward through endless ages, to my own
> future and the future of that world whereof it is written, 'He shall
> reign till He has put all enemies under His feet'.

Again, over the discrimination between sheep and goats in
the parable, an enquiry reaches him as to how it should be
interpreted?   And Kingsley replies with utmost sang-froid that
the words signified nations not individuals and should 'set us

THE HAPPY FISHERMAN

thinking what nations mean and how we can help to save England'.

To a clergyman's question as to whether he thought the Creator had a sense of humour he wrote solemnly:

> The matter presents itself to me thus, I see humour in animals e.g. a crab and a monkey, a parrot, a crow. I don't find this the result of a low organisation. In each of these four cases the animal is of the highest belonging to his class. Well, there the fact is; if I see it God must see it also or I must have more insight than God with God's own works.

On another occasion Kingsley was discussing the question of laughter in the divine nature and flashed out, 'What! God not laugh! What did he make a crab for then?'

Fanny Kingsley, who had no sense of values, prints much of this kind of thing, and is evidently under the impression that it shows her Charles up in a favourable light as the guide and counsellor of puzzled Christians. It would be unfair to go on quoting excerpts of the sort, for they were obviously intended to meet the difficulties of private persons and were not designed for publication.

M

Chapter 12

IMPERIALISM AND HEXAMETERS

Opinion is ultimately determined by the feelings, and not by the intellect.

HERBERT SPENCER

THE year 1857 opened quietly and happily for Charles Kingsley who, having managed to complete his new novel, *Two Years Ago*, was looking forward to receiving the thousand pounds promised him by Macmillan for the first edition. Made what is now called imperially minded by the Rajah Brooke controversy, he learned in reading the speech from the Throne of February 3 that the British flag had been insulted at Canton and that owing to the infraction of treaty rights by the Chinese authorities, British officers had been obliged to resort to force to obtain satisfaction.

Neither Kingsley nor any other private person in England being cognisant of the real facts of the case, it became possible for politicians to flog up what at best was a misunderstanding, at worst a trivial infringement of a treaty, into a first-class act of defiance. The alleged offence consisted in the fact that a party of Chinese in charge of an officer boarded a small boat built on the European pattern known as 'the lorcha Arrow', and removed therefrom on a charge of piracy the crew of twelve. The 'Arrow' was flying the British flag and was declared by its owners to be a British vessel. The Chinese governor of Canton contended that as a Chinese pirate boat it had no right whatever to hoist the flag of England, and that it was most certainly owned by Chinese who had in some surreptitious way obtained possession of the flag. This happened to be strictly true, but the British consul stood on his dignity, not only requiring the immediate return of the men deported, but sending for Sir John Bowring, our plenipotentiary at Hong Kong. On arrival at Canton, Sir John took a high-handed line demanding the surrender of the prisoners, an apology for their arrest, and an undertaking that nothing of the sort should ever occur again. If these conditions were not complied with within forty-eight

hours, naval operations would be begun. The governor sent
back the men, promised that the offence should not be repeated,
but refused to apologise as he still maintained (what was a fact)
that the vessel was a Chinese one flying the Union Jack under
false pretences. Canton was therefore subjected to six weeks'
bombardment by the British Fleet under Sir Michael Culme-
Seymour, and Governor Yeh, who was without defence, foolishly
retaliated by offering a reward for the head of every Englishman.

Lord Derby in the House of Lords on February 24 brought
forward a motion comprehensively condemning the proceedings
of the British authorities in China. Lord Lyndhurst supported
him and exposed the utter illegality of the course pursued by
Sir John Bowring. The motion was rejected. Two days
later Cobden, an old friend of Sir John Bowring, brought
forward a similar motion in the House of Commons and found
himself supported by both Gladstone and Disraeli, as well as
Lytton, Roebuck, Sydney Herbert, and Roundell Palmer.
His vote of censure was carried by a majority of sixteen. Lord
Palmerston a day or two later announced a dissolution and
appealed to the country. In his election address Yeh figured
as an insolent barbarian wielding authority in Canton who had
violated the British flag and offered rewards for the heads of
Englishmen. Yeh could hardly have been a barbarian since his
argument on the subject of International Law was endorsed by
Lord Lyndhurst and his way of arguing the political and com-
mercial case compelled the admiration of Lord Derby. Lord
Palmerston, however, romped back to power with enhanced
strength, while Cobden, Fox, John Bright, and many other
good men were left seatless.

The whole case excited Kingsley beyond measure. Sud-
denly he felt tired of the helplessness of *laissez-faire* and declared
'I am like other educated men revolting towards Imperialism.
Who knows but that I may not yet become as thorough a
despotist and imperialist as Strafford himself?' It was in a
mood like this that he wrote his *Ode to the North-east Wind*:

> What's the soft South-wester?
> 'Tis the ladies' breeze
> Bringing home their turtle-doves
> Out of all the seas:

> But the black North-easter,
>   Through the snowstorm hurled,
> Drives our English hearts of oak
>   Seaward round the world.
> Come as came your fathers,
>   Heralded by thee,
> Conquering from the eastward,
>   Lords by land and sea.
> Come, and strong within us
>   Stir the Vikings' blood:
> Bracing bone and sinew;
>   Blow, thou wind of God.

As Kingsley's Elizabethanism flared up within his heart, it made him ready to quarrel with anyone, even with his peaceable friend Mr. Augustus Stapleton.   Writing to him after a heated discussion on the Canton situation he said:[1]

> As to the boarding of the Lorcha being one of a series of acts in direct defiance of the Treaty, Lonee's speech alone shows that it was done as a deliberate insult to the British I cannot doubt.   As to the temper and intention of the Chinese the proclamation (quoted by Sir J. Ramsden) is quite sufficient.   The Treaty has been systematically and insolently violated for years.   Our people in China and at home (Palmerston especially) have had the good sense not to insist on its fulfilment so long as there was a reasonable security in Chinese ports.   The insecurity became too extreme and the Treaty was enforced (Bulwer Lytton has said that the Emperor is powerless to enforce the Treaty).   If *he* can't enforce it at Canton, then Canton is not subject to him and we must make our private terms with Canton.   As for Canton having been bombarded, it has not been so.   Certainly had I been in Seymour's place I should have done as they did (he and Bowring) relying on the common sense of the Home Government to back them in the preservation of British lives along the whole China coast.

To which diatribe Mr. Stapleton sadly replied:

> It is utterly incomprehensible to my mind how it can be that actions which appear to me the plainest and grossest violations of every principle of honour, of every rule of justice, and of every

[1] March 3, 1857.

precept of the Gospel, should appear to you right and justifiable, but so it is, and doubtless it will remain an enigma to me to the end of my life.[1]

The next excitement for Kingsley was the news from India, which was still under the nominal control of the East India Company. In March 1857 it became known that several native regiments had had to be disbanded for displaying insubordination; in April that certain Sepoys had been executed for open mutiny; in May that the native troops in Meerut had fired on their officers, released their comrades from gaol, and killed some Europeans. Meerut lay thirty-eight miles north of Delhi where lived the King of Delhi, the feeble descendant of the great Timour. The mutineers fled along the Delhi road unchecked, for the officer commanding in Meerut made no effort to stop them—a fatal error as it turned out. Throwing themselves upon the protection of the King, the mutineers proclaimed him Emperor of India and planted the standard of independence on the ramparts of his palace. From being a pensioner of John Company he was transformed into the living incarnation of the Great Mogul, and a military mutiny was converted into a national and religious war.

Amid acute panic and wild rumours Lord Canning remained clear-minded, resolute, and calm. He prudently caused the King of Oudh to be removed from the outskirts of Calcutta to his own residence within the precincts of Fort William, and realising at once that the chief objective to be struck at must be Delhi he managed to intercept English troops on their way to Canton by appealing to the British envoy in charge of the Canton expedition, an appeal to which Lord Elgin immediately assented. Lord Canning then ensured the safety of the Punjab by arranging for the disarming of the four thousand Sepoys at Meean Meer, near Lahore, and for the immediate investment of Delhi, but before this could be carried out mutinies had broken out both at Lucknow and Cawnpore.

The aged commander at Cawnpore called in his neighbour the Nana Sahib to protect him, but this potentate when he arrived made common cause with the mutineers and helped to assault

[1] Stapleton MSS.

the crumbling, rude entrenchments behind which cowered English women and children while English soldiers warded off with superhuman courage the frequent attacks of the enemy. They fought so well and killed so many of their assailants that the Nana Sahib offered the garrison a safe conduct to Allahabad. The English then made their slow way to boats on the Ganges. When the straw-thatched vessels were loaded a trumpet sounded, the thatch was fired, and the banks of the river sputtered with grape-shot and bullets. The few women and children who survived this onslaught, some hundred and twenty-five, were cooped up in a prison and made to grind corn for their captors. When the Nana learnt that Havelock was moving on Cawnpore he ordered that his captives be killed like beasts in a shambles, and their stripped bodies were thrown down a dry well. After making one stand against the victorious English before Cawnpore the Nana Sahib disappeared.

When Delhi was captured the King was sentenced to transportation for life. It was not till March 1858 a year after the beginning of the mutiny that Lucknow was completely under British control. The rebellion had been the death-knell of the government of India by John Company. A bill transferring the authority vested in the East India Company finally and absolutely to the Crown was introduced by Lord Palmerston early in 1858.

Every station in the passion of the Indian mutiny was followed by Kingsley 'in agony of mind'. Writing to Maurice he said:

> I can think of nothing but these Indian massacres. The moral problems they involve make me half mad. . . . Night and day the heaven seems black to me, though I was never so prosperous and blest in my life as now. I can hardly bear to look at a woman or a child—even at my own beloved ones sometimes. It raises such horrible images from which I can't escape. What does it all mean? Christ is King nevertheless. I tell my people so.

and again:

> Only by going into hell can one rise again the third day. I have been in hell many times in my life, therefore perhaps have I had some small share of influencing human hearts, but I have never looked hell so close in the face as I have been doing of late.

In the summer of 1857 Kingsley, in order to distract his mind from oversea preoccupations, began to arrange a volume of verse for publication with John Parker. Among the longer poems were *Santa Maura* and *Andromeda*, both dealing with a favourite theme, the martyrdom of a woman. He had no misgivings about either of these poems, for as he wrote exultingly to Ludlow, 'I can write poetry . . . there's no denying it'. Of *Andromeda* in particular he said:

> My dear man, the beauty of that whole myth; I love it and revel in it more and more the longer I look at it. If I have made one drawing of Perseus and Andromeda I have made fifty and burnt them all in disgust . . . the incompleteness of the pencil drives me to words to give it colour and chiaroscuro.

He tells of the way he rattles off hexameters while dressing and breakfasting. They run so easily from his mind.

> Onward they came in their joy, and around them the lamps of
>   the sea-nymphs
> Myriad fiery globes, swam panting and heaving, and rainbows
> Crimson and azure and emerald, were broken in starshowers
>   lighting.

Resolving to polish the poem into permanent literature, he compares this process with that of darning or cleaning wearing apparel.

> There is no more reason for not polishing than there is for walking about with a hole or a spot on your trousers, a thing which drives me mad. If I have a spot on my clothes, I am conscious of nothing else the whole day long and just as conscious of it in the heart of Bramshill Common, as if I were going down Piccadilly.[1]

Andromeda was to some degree inspired by Tennyson's *Oenone* which he read, re-read, and found 'more glorious than ever'. We cannot truthfully use these words about Kingsley's own lines in spite of the extreme facility with which he confessed to writing them.

Cassiopeia, ill-starred mother of the victim, is ordered to chain Andromeda aloft on a sea-girt rock washed by the surges,

[1] *Charles Kingsley*, vol. I. p. 341.

and begs her daughter not to curse her for consenting to her
death.   To this the tortured girl replies:

> 'Curse thee! not in the death-pang.'   The heart of the lady
>   was lightened
> Slowly she went by the ledge and the maid was alone in the
>   darkness.

Andromeda watches the sea and the sunrise, and reflects upon
life and death:

> Sudden she ceased with a shriek: in the spray like a hovering
>   foam-bow
> Hung more fair than the foam-bow, a boy in the bloom of his
>   manhood
> Golden-haired, ivory-limbed, ambrosial.

Perseus woos her and then flies upward to await the coming
of the sea-beast which he is to slay.

Kingsley was even more pleased with *Santa Maura* than with
Andromeda.   He told Ludlow that he was longing to show it
him, 'I can hardly bear to read it myself; but it is the deepest and
clearest thing I have yet done'.   To Maurice he wrote that it
came so out of the depths of his heart and induced a poetic
fervour such as he had never felt before or since.   It was the
culmination of all his reading on martyr-saints.   'I felt always
I should have a thing to say about them, though I read them
simply for pleasure.   It grew of itself as an organic whole and
I daren't cut and hack at it.'   Maurice replied that St. Maura's
story as told in the *Acta Sanctorum* 'has always been my *experimentum
crucis* of the false connection between martyrdom and
celibacy'.

The action of the poem takes place with St. Maura and her
deacon husband, both hanging on crosses and slowly expiring.
She tells her story.   Three months married and expecting a
baby, she has refused to burn incense to false gods and after
being tried, stripped and whipped, has been sent to join him.
He, with eyes gouged out, welcomes her with the words:

> Come, come to thy bride-bed, martyr-wife once more!

And she responds:

I crawled to you, I kissed your bleeding feet and called aloud
You heard me! You know all! I am at peace.
Peace, peace, as still and bright as is the moon
Upon your limbs, came on me at your smile,
And kept me happy when they dragged me back
From that last kiss and spread me on the cross, . . .

.   .   .   .   .

I cannot stir. Ah God! these shoots of fire
Through all my limbs! Hush selfish girl! He hears you!
Whoever found the cross a pleasant bed?

It is a morbid, terrible effusion, and if it really only took Kingsley, as he tells us, a day and a night to write, he must have been in a strange, excited state. In *Andromeda* and *Santa Maura* though the one martyr is pagan and the other Christian the sentiment is identical, for in both cases *Oenone* was the prototype he had in mind.

Fraser's Magazine found *Santa Maura* the only unhealthy poem in the book of 'a good man and a good sportsman'. The *Saturday Review* declared it 'too horrible, though powerful' and preferred *Andromeda*, which it likened to 'a glorious Etty picture of the best kind, but with a romance which Etty wants'. *Chambers's Journal* advised the poet not to write any more novels but to concentrate on lyrics. Chevalier de Bunsen urged him to become 'the Poet of the People'.

Chapter 13

THE RETURN OF THE GOLD-DIGGER

Against the superiority of another there is no remedy but love.

GOETHE

IN the spring of 1858 was born the Kingsleys' fourth and last child, Grenville, for whom *The Water-Babies* was to be written five years later. Though money shortage no longer worried them expenses mounted, for they had Maurice at school, Rose and Mary being educated by a governess at home, and a nurse for the new baby to budget for. The result was that Charles Kingsley had to make do without a curate. This anchored him to Eversley and obliged him to preach many sermons and to lecture on literary, historical, and geological subjects in its neighbourhood. People sometimes asked him whether he did not find country life very dull, but he always replied that he loved monotony and parochial interests.

The long winter had had its moments of anxiety, for a new disease made its appearance in the neighbourhood of Eversley. It was called diphtheria by the doctors and seemed to be scaring his parishioners almost as much as the cholera had done. Before the first case appeared in his parish Kingsley went to London to see a doctor and find out from him the best preventatives to use. He was advised to make everyone, young and old, use an antiseptic gargle and this he undertook to do. Some of his parishioners were inclined to laugh when they saw their lanky rector striding along the village roads with a huge bottle under his arm. Like his predilection for wielding the auger in sick rooms, it gave them a sense of his eccentricity. Kingsley, however, went on acting on Carlyle's principle: 'Wheresoever thou findest disorder, there is thy eternal enemy; attack him swiftly, subdue him, make order of him.'

The year 1858, as it turned out, was one of great surprises and aggravating readjustments of family relations, but there was no sign of these things when Grenville was born, and his father felt justified in planning for himself a holiday in York-

shire.   After reading in *Percy's 'Reliques'* the story of the Pilgrimage of Grace (which not so many years back had inspired
Wordsworth to write *The White Doe of Rylstone*), he had the
impulse to construct a novel on the same theme.   Froude
thought it an excellent idea, but a Catholic lady, on hearing what
Mr. Kingsley's intention was, wrote and told him he was far too
Protestant-minded to deal fairly with her ancestors who had
taken part in the Rising.   Kingsley sent her a message through
Kegan Paul to say he meant to do the Catholics of the North
'ample justice'.   He could not, of course, withdraw what he
had said in *Westward Ho!*, and he would like her to understand
that 'Romanism under the Jesuits had become a different thing
from what it had been in earlier times'.   Readers of *Hereward
the Wake* will, however, recollect that his treatment of an
earlier phase of 'Romanism' is not distinguished by overmuch
sympathy.

As W. E. Forster, the Bradford Quaker, not yet a member
of Parliament, had offered to show Kingsley the localities connected with the Rising, he went off in great spirits to Burley in
Wharfdale to scramble about the ruins of abbeys and castles.
Forster, who had a good library, proved to be an ardent genea-
logist and could enlighten his guest on the pedigrees and relation-
ships of the Pilgrims of Grace.   From Burley Kingsley was
taken to near-by Denton where he was shown round the pictures
by 'an old angel of a housekeeper who regarded the absent
owner, Mr. Ibbetson, as her child'.   He saw 'fine Dutch land-
scapes, a blue Breughel and such a delicious naked Andromeda'.
Denton was a noble place in a situation as fine as Bramshill and
the house just like Lord Portman's Bryanston, a perfect Paradise!

Kingsley was lent a gig to drive himself up the Skipton valley
while Forster was attending to business in Bradford.   Jervaulx,
Bolton Abbey, Middleham, Fountains, Norton's Tower were all
inspected and a Sunday put in at the Deanery, Ripon.   From
Ripon he went to Malham to stay with 'young Morrison, son
of the millionaire of Basildon'.   It was a charming house built
by the old Lord Ribblesdale and 'looking over a lake a mile
square with the best fishing imaginable', but unfortunately he
had brought no lake flies with him as he had not expected the
chance of such a treat when he left home.   He tells Fanny that

he is seeing far more in a short time than he has ever done in his life before and entreats her to find a stop-gap parson for a third Sunday as it would be utter folly to go back without the materials for which he came north. He had visited Hull but it seemed to him a mere labyrinth of streets and docks among which no trace of Tudor remains were to be found. All the same the Norton epic had become extremely real to him. 'I have *done* my work well, the book grows on me. I see my way as clear as day. How I will write when I get home!' But though he returned to Eversley in tearing spirits, with bulging note-books and 'never felt better in life', the book that was going to be so easy to write was never written, never even begun.

Knowing Kingsley's character, we begin to suspect that some powerful new impact had killed the impulse that animated him. Mrs. Kingsley, always secretive, states that the high spirits in which he had come home were suddenly succeeded by a period of discouragement and a tendency to depreciate his own work. He no longer found any pleasure in it and nothing she or anyone else could say put him in conceit with it again. He just moped and said it was no good.

We know that he had not only collected material for an historical novel but in odd moments had begun to write a contemporary story of which, while away, he completed some one hundred and fifty pages of foolscap. These pages of manuscript were found by his daughter, Mary, after his death and completed by her as *The Tutor's Story*. We may take it for granted that while in Yorkshire his imagination was working easily and fruitfully and that he certainly had the plans for two novels in his head. What then was it that destroyed in him the strong desire to write?

The change in Kingsley's attitude towards his own work may very possibly, almost certainly, be explained by an event that took place a week or two after his return from the north. On a day in early September a stocky, undistinguished little man of twenty-eight stepped ashore in England after an absence from his native country of five years. He had a mouth like a trap, a brown face, a fringe of hair round the chin, and his clothes were shabby and almost threadbare. Making his way from the

Port of London to Chelsea the stranger walked up and down the pavement of Church Street not daring to pull the bell of the rectory.   He was Henry Kingsley who had not written home for five years, and whom his father and mother had believed dead.   When he had screwed himself up to enter the drive and pull the front-door bell he was received by a curate who told him that he was for the time being in charge of the parish as Mr. and Mrs. Kingsley were staying at their cottage in Eversley.   The stranger had a bad manner, a colonial accent, a rather aggressive way of talking and in no way reminded the curate of Charles Kingsley.   He told him that Mr. and Mrs. Kingsley were in fair health, but ageing fast.   Henry left forthwith for Eversley.

Fanny Kingsley does not chronicle his arrival nor does she once mention his name in her two-volume biography of her husband.   This is all the odder as Henry was to live at Eversley Cross for the next six years of his life.   However pleased Charles and his father and mother were to welcome the exile home, to Fanny his appearance was totally and terribly inopportune.   Charles was just entering on a successful phase of life, he was an established author, a renowned preacher, a candidate for a canonry, and it could do him nothing but harm to have this boorish brother with a common accent picked up in Australia hanging on to him.   Moreover, he might prove a heavy financial drag upon them, for he had come back as poor as he had started.   On this score her mind was set at rest, when it turned out that though Henry had no money he had, to everyone's surprise, produced a manuscript, a very thick manuscript, which he told them was a novel.   He believed it to be a good book, it had taken years to write and if it were published it would, he was sure, keep him while he wrote another.   Charles hastened to read it and told Fanny that it put all his own work into the shade.   This was news that Fanny did not at all care to hear, in fact she was not sure that she would not have preferred to think of Henry as a penniless wastrel than as a rival to her Charles whose wretched humility would be the undoing of him.   How could anyone think that this upstart in the literary world could write a good book, a book better than *Westward Ho!*?   It was very hard on her that just as Charles had become respectable, had emancipated himself from Chartism, Socialism and the like, just when a scheme she had set going for getting him to preach before a very exalted personage was about to mature, that a creature like Henry should turn up and spoil everything. Life suddenly became discouragingly complicated, for instead of one Kingsley there would now be two competing for public approval and all her careful building up of Charles as a personality to be reckoned with and an author unique in his own line, was threatened with collapse.

After his first hasty look at his brother's book, Charles sat down to read the manuscript placed in his hands with close attention and was carried away by the power, interest and originality of the story. Fortunately for him, Henry had a neat clear handwriting very unlike his own scrawly script and he could read the sheets quickly. What a lot of life Henry had seen to be sure! How wonderful were the descriptions of scenery and atmosphere and how intimate the knowledge of crime and criminals! What an unusual opening was that of *The Recollections of Geoffrey Hamlyn*! Three men are sitting talking on a verandah in Australia, one of them is Hamlyn. In the paddock below grazes an old horse, Widderin. The men reminisce about his fine quality and staying powers and remind each other of his exploits. One of the three observes that the story of the old horse would be worth telling and so for the matter of that would be the story of the human beings concerned in his most famous ride. 'But that would take years and years!' exclaims one of the trio. Hamlyn on hearing this slips off and, returning with a great bundle of manuscript, throws it at their feet saying, 'There it is!' *Geoffrey Hamlyn* is the original of all bush-ranging tales of adventure and for sheer sustained interest and excitement eclipses most of its successors. Rolf Boldrewood, Henry Kingsley's literary descendant, as a very young man had many talks with him at his cottage, Langa-Willi, while 'that immortal work, the best Australian novel and for long the only one, was being written'. The descriptions of scenery in *Geoffrey Hamlyn* Charles thought magnificent. There could be no doubt that Henry had struck out an entirely new line in novels and was certain of many readers. His brother assured him of that and forthwith recommended the work warmly to Alexander Macmillan.   Macmillan accepted it straight away and promised publication in the spring.

When it finally appeared Henry's mother began to take great pride in her newly discovered genius.   Miss Thackeray, calling with her father at Chelsea rectory just after publication, heard Mrs. Kingsley say to him, 'You know my son Charles, I should like you to know my son Henry too'.   Taking up a new book from the table beside her, she put it into Thackeray's hands saying, 'He also writes books'.

By Christmas 1858 Eversley had become almost a Kingsley enclave.   There were Charles and his wife and four children, there were Mr. and Mrs. Kingsley, senior, there was George the doctor coming and going, his sister, Charlotte Canter (also a writer of novels), paying her parents visits from Ilfracombe, where her husband was vicar, and lastly there was Henry ensconced in a cottage attached to his parents' house.

It is a cold, queer fact that none of these relations plays any part in Fanny Kingsley's biography of Charles; indeed with the exception of old Mr. and Mrs. Kingsley who are alluded to shortly at the time of their respective deaths, no mention is made of their names.   Whether it is a proof of enormous dislike on Fanny's part or merely of a ruthless determination to blot them out of mind for posterity so that a greater radiance might emanate from Charles as the one and only Kingsley I do not know, but I do know that whatever the motive that lay behind her exclusiveness it achieved a result, for in a bookseller's catalogue to-day, as in general conversation, the name Kingsley connotes Charles Kingsley and no one else.   What an opportunity of describing a family circle of individualists unique of its kind was missed by this devoted woman as she laboriously compiled her biography.   Fortunately we are not wholly dependent on Fanny Kingsley for information.   Her mania for annihilating evidential documents was to a large degree foiled by the hoarding habit of Maurice and the preservation of letters by other friends and relations.   The figure manipulated by her had all the earthy humour and the quirky fun wrung out of it, and became a mere dummy to be draped with homilies and adulatory quotations.   In editing letters she sometimes deleted every clue to the person about whom they were written.   In the following instance the name of Ruskin is concealed by her favourite asterisks.   Mrs. Kingsley quotes:

> Physiognomy, which has been a study of mine for years gave me certain opinions of *** the first day I ever saw him, which said, 'That man and I, unless utterly changed—more changed perhaps than he ever will be in this mortal body—never can be friends. God forgive me if I be wrong. . . . But let him pass.'

And the letter as written ran:

> Ruskin, I dare say, I refused to know; though I have been introduced to him since and letters have passed between us. But physiognomy which has been a study of mine for years gave me certain opinions of the man the first day I saw him which said 'that man and I unless utterly changed—more changed than perhaps he ever will be in this mortal body—never can be friends.   God forgive me if I be wrong, but all I have seen of his writings (which then I delighted in) since that day and above all the miserable esclandre with his wife (curiously corroborating my first impression of his physique) have widened the gulf so far as I am concerned'.

Though he had been very glad to help launch Henry in the publishing world, Charles remained in a state of deep despondency for many months after his brother's return. He often asked himself whether his state of mind was not a judgement on him for the vain pleasure he had taken in the success of *Westward Ho!* and *Two Years Ago*. He had been tempted by it to think that he might become a real artist in words, one of England's great prose-writers, and now God was telling him he must let go of ideas of the kind and never aspire to the excitement of literary glory and the pleasant company that fame brought in its train.   Obviously he was intended for a country parson, and a country parson he must settle down to be.   Whatever personal set-backs and depressions he was experiencing he must go on saying to his flock what he had said so many times before, 'Don't fret, God cares for you, Christ understands you!'   In these moods he would pull his clay-pipe out of its rack, take up a rod and stump off to the one place that put all melancholy out of his mind—the banks of a stream.

There can be no doubt that the constant companionship of an

MRS. CHARLES KINGSLEY   CHARLES KINGSLEY

extremely industrious, vigorous brother of twenty-eight contributed to Charles's fatigue. It made him feel that he simply could not compete. Henry was free to spend the whole day writing, reading, or talking if he wished to. He had no parish duties, no public interests, no time-table engagements, and did not have to compose weekly sermons which though always begun on a Tuesday were never finished till the Friday following, nor did he have a host of correspondents seeking his advice on questions of doctrine. It still comforted Charles to unburden himself to Maurice, with whom he at this time discussed his own shortcomings as a writer. He knew himself to be deficient in discursive fancy and weak in the faculty which Shakespeare more than any other man possessed, the power of metaphor and analogy. Moreover he was not equipped with that most precious endowment of the poet, the instinctive vision of connections between things in heaven and earth. He was but a dull dog after all, and yet verse to him was a more congenial medium than prose. As a rhymer he felt like an otter in the water, as a prose-writer like an otter scrambling about ashore. Fanny was treated to many of these self-depreciatory reflections and they steeled her resolve to bring about a new situation. The canonry at Westminster for which she had angled had been filled up, but there were other cathedral posts. Unlike most parsons' wives she had rich and influential relations and connections in the Government. Charles must somehow be delivered from the dead-weight of his own humble-mindedness, and incidentally from victimisation by the family. By the time spring came round some of her wire-pulling might have achieved results. Meanwhile she could do nothing but acquiesce in her rector's decision 'to remain a pig in his parish where there was nothing to rouse him from pigdom save three services on a Sunday'.

Charles at this time really felt as if he had come to a full stop, and though he was only forty was ever more frequently beset by an unnatural longing for rest. Often and often he said to Fanny, 'I feel very old. How blessed it will be when it is all over! What a long life I have lived!' The constant presence of his ever-active brother was fraying him subconsciously though he would never have admitted it. He did own up,

N

however, to being deficient in vitality, 'can't ride, can't think, can't write, just like ten years ago'.

Even parish business had lost its tranquillising quality, for a new problem, that of archidiaconal jurisdiction had suddenly reared its menacing head in his preserves. Hitherto no one had gainsaid him or enquired into the way he administered his cure, but now to his intense annoyance he learnt that a quasi-official investigation into his activities was to be undertaken. Not only was the fabric of church and school to be surveyed, but an enquiry was to be made as to the way pastoral duties were carried out. He was to be asked, for example, whether he made a point of only employing district visitors who were communicants and if he made mission meetings a feature of his work. This enquiry irritated Kingsley intensely, for he regarded it as an encroachment on his freedom and discretionary power. If the independence of a rector, which he held to be 'one of the most blessed safeguards of the Church of England', should be impinged on it would really strike at the singular not to say unique character of the National Church. Regimentation of the kind foreshadowed was extremely distasteful to the rector of Eversley, who at first replied to four only of the twenty-five questions submitted, but on second thoughts answered them all. Forwarding a copy of the document he had received to the Bishop of Winchester he said that he did not recognise the *ex-officio* rights of the Archdeacon to conduct an investigation of the kind. After enjoying seventeen years of liberty under his lordship he must now ascertain his views and ask his advice as to future policy.

To Fanny's delight the storm of irritation caused by the questionnaire was swiftly and happily dispersed when out of the blue came a command from the Queen to preach in the Chapel of Buckingham Palace on Palm Sunday. At last she could feel that the situation she had schemed to bring about was materialising. It was important now the chance had come of winning royal approval to preach the right kind of sermon. Fanny had been told by a lady-in-waiting that the Queen liked the addresses she listened to to be simple and short. Choosing as his text, 'Let this mind be in you which also was in Christ Jesus. . . . Who being found in fashion as a man, humbled Himself and became obedient unto death, even the death on the cross,' Kingsley preached a short sermon, of but a thousand words. It was just like all the other sermons that he had preached Sunday after Sunday at Eversley, colloquial, simple, and stressing the importance of making one's own the thoughts in the mind of Christ. The Queen liked its directness so much and the deep feeling with which Kingsley spoke that she decided then and there to give him a Court preachership.

Consequently a letter written from Cleveland Square with a now undecipherable signature reached Kingsley early one July morning, a letter that gave both husband and wife unadulterated pleasure.

SIR,

 I have the honour to inform you that I have received the Queen's Commands to offer you the appointment of Chaplain in Ordinary to Her Majesty and I have much pleasure in being the organ [?] of the Queen's wishes to you. I shall be obliged if you will inform me whether it will be agreeable to you to accept this mark of distinction on the part of Her Majesty—at your earliest convenience. I will add that the duties are confined to the Preaching of one Sermon at the Chapel Royal, St. James' in the course of the New Year, for which there is a salary of £30 p.a.

In the press the appointment was favourably commented on, and Kingsley began to expand in the sunshine of approbation.

Soon after Easter Kingsley preached again before the Queen, this time at Windsor. Writing from the Deanery the preacher seemed pleased with the effect he had produced.

 Wellesley said afterwards that it was the most eloquent sermon he ever heard—and the most touching—odd enough. But it seems your instinct was right. Lord John Russell told Lady Sydney that it was most excellent both in matter and delivery— I have been at St. George's this afternoon with beautiful Mrs. W. [Wellesley?]. She isn't half as handsome as your Mary Bulteel with whom I have made much acquaintance and the Gladstones. There we met Sir George Grey and the Sydneys who were all very civil, my dear Sir George is always genial. And now I have to dine with her glory great Queen Victory in a pair of tights wh. Wellesley has lent me and wh. I *hope* won't pop in the middle

stop in the Middle of the
Ceremony; or get covered with
hot soup, for they are very thin.

Oh dear to think that I shd
come to this!

of the Ceremony, or get covered with hot soup, for they are very thin.

Oh dear to think that I shd. come to this!

I have had full advice what to do; but feel in horrible fear. I wish I were at home.

Fanny Kingsley, as we know, had long been trying to give her husband's career an upward twist. He had in her opinion acquainted himself quite well enough with what she termed the 'depths of society' and it was high time he should, if ever he was to be considered for a bishopric, complete his experience of life by associating, if only for a while, 'with men and women of the highest rank'. It delighted her that through the Court he would now be brought in contact with a member of the Government like Lord Carnarvon, a great lawyer like Lord Cranworth, and a rising cleric like Arthur Stanley. She had to own to herself that she had never felt much sympathy with the social reformers, nor had she found it easy to adapt herself to the conversation of John Ludlow or even listen with becoming patience to the word-spinning of Frederick Maurice which she only partially made sense of. With Charles Mansfield it had been rather different, since for him social reform had been a side-line. Hitherto she had led an extremely dull and secluded life with husband and children and except for occasional visits to her many relations had been little away from home. Now, she felt, was the moment to break away and take Charles about, to stay in country houses and mix with the great world. To begin with they went to stay with the Poet Laureate at Farringford in the Isle of Wight. Later we shall find them at Bryanston, Broadlands, High Clere, Wimpole, The Grange, Bearwood, and other houses in which they had the chance of meeting influential people. Fanny even took Charles to parties in London for we hear of him both at the Ellesmeres and the Northamptons. Mrs. Kingsley rarely let herself go, but in a letter to a woman friend, she alludes to something of what she has suffered at the hands 'of religious people and their hideous satisfaction in the saving of their own miserable souls'. She goes on to tell how her husband 'saw GOD and Christ when he was twenty-three', and of the many things he has strived against, preached against, agonised about, from the time he first saw the truth of things. For all of which he was suspected and avoided by Clergy and laity, and abused by the press till—he preached before the Queen and became acquainted with the Prince Consort! Then the tide turned! Such things do not raise one's respect for poor human beings—who nevertheless were made in the image of GOD.[1]

Here we have the real Fanny speaking the real truth. Who can fail to admire her courage and determination, and her unwavering loyalty to a man who over and over again upset her well-laid plans?

When Georgina Grenfell, his wife's niece, became engaged to the Taylorian Professor of Modern European Languages at Oxford, a pleasant new element was introduced into Charles Kingsley's life. Not only did he take enthusiastically to Max Müller as a friend, but the connection opened doors into the historian's world, and it was through his new nephew-in-law that Kingsley later made acquaintance with Ranke and other distinguished Germans. Max Müller was a great admirer of Kingsley's drama and of his historical novels, so much so that he told him quite seriously that he was the only man in England who could carry on Shakespeare's work. The Kingsleys lent the rectory to their niece for her honeymoon and on the Sunday after the wedding Kingsley administered Communion to the newly married pair and lunched with them afterwards 'in his own dining-room'.

Now that Kingsley was a royal chaplain the congregations at Eversley church were swollen by strangers, for since his Court appointment his sermons had suddenly won universal approval. What a comfort it was to Fanny to know that Charles now abhorred politics and never alluded to anything that even savoured of political interest. His new frame of mind led him to make some rather strange statements. We find him for instance telling listeners from the pulpit:

The only politician now living is the Lord of all and He has principle and principles; whoever has not. It is a fearful look out when God has to govern a nation because it cannot govern itself.

[1] Mrs. Henry Cust, *Echoes of a Larger Life*, p. 68.

What precisely these enigmatic words were intended to mean cannot now be explained, but like other peculiar phrases in his sermons they went down very well. A sermon on 'National Privileges' may have proved more intelligible to those who heard it preached than to us who read it to-day. In it Kingsley said:

> We in England live in the garden of the Lord and have but to stretch out our hand to the tree of life, and eat and live for ever. But hands are not stretched out and sacraments are neglected. If you despise Christ, Christ will despise you—it is no use saying, 'we are church-goers—we are safe'—I say to you, 'God is able, from the Negro and the wild Irishman—nay God is able of these stones to raise up children to the Church of England'.

No comment would serve to elucidate the moral here. One can only marvel that edition after edition of the Rector of Eversley's sermons were printed and absorbed by the reading public.

In addition to writing sermons, Kingsley was intently studying a new book in which Charles Darwin had set forth his conclusions as to the existence and cause of evolution. The title of this book was *On the Origin of Species by Means of Natural Selection of the Preservation of Favoured Races in the Struggle for Life*.

For a long while Kingsley had assiduously kept himself posted in the investigations of Hooker in botany, Lyell in geology, and Wallace in the principle of natural selection. All were working closer and closer to a perception of the secret that first revealed itself to the humble, patient genius of Darwin. In 1856 under pressure from Lyell, Darwin had begun the abstract of an essay which was to develop into the book that now electrified the world.

Not every clergyman had trained himself as Kingsley had done to accept scientific discovery as the very voice of God. In many orthodox minds the publication of *The Origin of Species* produced a spiritual cataclysm. Let us glance for a moment at its effect on the mind of Philip Gosse. Deeply perturbed to realise that two incompatible theories of the origin of human life should exist, he tortured himself by endeavouring to uphold the truth of the account of creation to be found in Genesis against the doctrine that splintered it. Gosse maintained that the theory of evolution was untrue and sought support for his contention by asserting that there had been no gradual modification of the surface of the globe nor any slow development of organic forms. The act of creation was sudden and by its means the earth presented itself as if life had long existed on the planet. In the same way Adam had appeared complete and full-grown. When it was pointed out to Gosse that Adam displayed a navel (though no umbilical cord had ever attached him to his mother) it did not seem to him to refute the tenets he held or to imply that the first man bore false witness as to his origin. Living creatures apart, Gosse was then asked how, if God created the world in a week out of chaos, he could account for the fossils embedded in the rocks? Had they, as suggested by flippant pressmen, been hidden there by God to tempt man to infidelity?

In a strange, fanatical book, *Omphalos*, Gosse earnestly set out to justify geology in the eyes of godly readers of the Bible and to reconcile scientific discovery with the statements of Holy Writ. The book reads to-day almost like the work of a lunatic or, at any rate, of a man with an *idée fixe*. Kingsley, whom Gosse hoped might help him and must surely sympathise with his state of spiritual turmoil, wrote:

> If we accept the fact of absolute creation, God becomes a *Deus quidam deceptor*. I do not mean merely in the case of fossils which *pretend* to be the bones of dead animals, but in the one single case of your newly created scars on the paudanus trunk, and your newly created Adam's navel, you make God tell a lie. It is not my reason but my conscience which revolts here.

Kingsley added that he found himself unable to 'give up the painful and slow conclusion arrived at over twenty-five years study of geology and believe that God has written in the rocks an enormous and superfluous lie'.

He did more than this for in a footnote to a new edition of *Glaucus* he wrote:

> It is with real pain that I have seen my friend Mr Gosse, make a step in the direction of obscurantism, which I can only call desper-

ate, by publishing a book called *Omphalos*. In it he tries to vindicate what he thinks (though very few good Christians do so now) to be the teaching of Scripture about Creation by the supposition that fossils are not the remains of plants and animals which have actually existed, but may have been created as they are, for the satisfaction of the Divine mind; and that therefore the whole science, not only of palaeontology, but (as he seems to forget) of geognosy also is based on a mistake, and cannot truly exist, save as a play of the fancy. It seems to me that such a notion is more likely to make infidels than to cure them. For what rational man, who knows even a little of geology, will not be tempted to say—If Scripture can only be vindicated by such an outrage to common sense and fact, then I will give up Scripture, and stand by common sense.

To Gosse's immense chagrin *Omphalos* was laughed at by Christians and atheists alike, and its author, fearfully cast down by failure, devoted himself more closely than ever to the study of corals and sea-anemones and two years later produced his best book on marine biology.

To Kingsley, however, every great scientific discovery was a message from God, and worship became for him what Carlyle said it ought to be for everyone—'limitless wonder'.

Chapter 14

SANITATION AND *ESSAYS AND REVIEWS*

The candid incline to surmise of late
That the Christian faith proves false, I mind,
For our Essays and Reviews debate
Begins to tell on the public mind.

ROBERT BROWNING, *Gold Hair*

IT is in reading Fanny Kingsley's narrative that we see how from the time Henry settled at Eversley, Charles devoted more time and thought than ever to public health. In addition to lecturing on the subject in the neighbourhood of his parish we find him going to London to sit on the platform at the first meeting of 'The Ladies Sanitary Association' at Willis's Rooms presided over by Lord Shaftesbury. Dr. Southwood Smith and Dr. Lankester, pioneers in reform, both addressed the audience and Charles Kingsley made a speech which was printed later as *The Massacre of the Innocents*.

In the course of this speech he entreated the ladies present to weigh well the effect of the work they proposed to undertake. If successful it will produce 'a serious if not dangerous change in the state of the nation', for it will mean saving the lives of some 30 to 40 per cent of the babies born in England. He has heard it said that the country is already over-populated and that if 'kind Nature' is prevented from carrying off surplus infants the problem of finding enough food for the masses will become difficult of solution. He values human life himself, he values it in fact above that of all dumb animals, and he believes the English race to be the finest in the world and as capable as the Roman of adapting itself to all climates; he also reminds himself and his hearers that four-fifths of the world is still uninhabited. It is to his thinking the noblest of duties to help increase the English race as rapidly as possible and to see that every child born into 'this great nation of England' be developed in physical strength, beauty, intellect, and virtue. Lord Shaftesbury has told them that at least 100,000 preventable deaths take place in England every year. Though it is a fact, we do not make a fuss about these as we do about deaths in war, war the clumsiest and most expensive of all games, because Nature working silently, insidiously, sends no roar of cannon, no glitter of arms to warn us that she is out to kill and will go on killing till men have learnt her laws and act on them. Every woman in the room will certainly have the chance of saving three or four human lives during the next six months. Let her do it, for 'it is not the will of your Father in Heaven that one little one that plays in the kennel outside should perish, either in body or soul'.

The speech exhausted him, and he returned to Eversley completely de-magnetised, and declaring to Fanny, 'I am tired of most things in the world but of sanitary reform I shall never grow tired!'

There was nothing very cheering about daily life in the parish. Much of it is recorded in private letters, sometimes querulous, sometimes tart in tone. There are references to rebuilt pews, to preferential seats for the households of the gentry, to enclosures of common land, to enlarging the churchyard and so on. No one seemed to be anxious to oblige the rector or to consider his interest. When, for example, the question arose of finding extra land for graves everyone seemed to take it for granted that the rector should surrender part of his glebe. It was even broken to him that the parish had set its mind on his rick-yard. From time to time Kingsley's relations with his flock tended to irritate him, and had it not been for his innate unselfishness and amiability, open quarrelling might have ensued.

The rectory lawn was six feet lower than the churchyard and Fanny Kingsley would greatly have preferred to have the new graves as far as possible from the house, but she was aware that whatever she did or said Charles would be imposed on and that in his tiresome spirit of humility and appeasement, he would yield to the demands of farmers and parishioners without putting up a fight. And she was of course right, for as he told her, 'I fell in with the golden rule—if you can't help doing a thing do it willingly and gracefully—which is the secret of all good government'. Fanny just hated hearing that 'a parish is a corporation of free men, who have by law a right to their own opinion, and it is a most blessed thing that it is so, for it is the root of English strength'. The expression of sentiments so correct and platitudinous can hardly have consoled her for the substitution of corpses for ricks.

Life fortunately was too full of distractions ever to become really unbearable to Charles, whose mind was soon diverted from parochial squabbles to a squabble of far greater dimensions, stirred up by the publication of a podgy little volume entitled *Essays and Reviews*. The preface stated that it was the work of seven authors all writing 'in entire independence of each other' and 'without concert or comparison'. The editor was a clergyman, Henry Wilson, and the contributors were Frederick Temple, Mark Pattison, Benjamin Jowett, Baden Powell, C. W. Goodwin, and Rowland Williams. Though the essays with which the volume opened and closed were as different as they could be in earnestness and ability from those between, none of them strengthened the doctrinal position of the Church of England. Williams was flippant about the divine claims of the Old Testament; Baden-Powell contemptuous about miracles; Wilson perhaps gave more pain to the devout than the other authors, for having twenty years earlier denounced Tract XC, he now argued in favour of the mode of interpretation he had once condemned. Temple, a future Archbishop, was responsible for *Tendencies of Religious Thought in England, 1688–1750*, and Benjamin Jowett, future Master of Balliol, for *On the Interpretation of Scripture*. These two essays had originated as sermons, in which form they had had no publicity, but rewritten and printed they attracted great attention as in them Anglican divines admitted that the Bible might be criticised like any other book. The disapproving murmur of Rural Deans throughout the country swelled into clamour for proceedings to be taken against the authors. As the agitation grew Dr. Temple and Mr. Jowett in quick succession were interviewed by Bishop Tait at Fulham, who appears not to have made any definite pronouncement on their essays nor, so far as his visitors could make out, to disapprove of them. He merely urged the two clergymen to take a more positive attitude towards the central figure of Christianity.

The agitation did not die down as Tait had hoped it might, and presently Archbishop Sumner summoned twenty-five bishops to Lambeth to discuss the book and the situation it had created. A letter was drafted by the Archbishop of which they approved and to which they appended their signatures. One of its clauses ran as follows:

> We cannot understand how these opinions can be held consistently with an honest subscription to the formularies of our Church, with many of the fundamental doctrines of which they appear to be essentially at variance.

Having made up their minds on this point the gathering of bishops had to determine whether the publication should be judged in the ecclesiastical courts or whether it should be synodically condemned. Action of some kind was necessary if only because the newspapers had taken the question up, and a curious public was demanding new editions of the book. Far from being the storm in a clerical tea-cup that Bishop Tait hoped it might prove, the controversy bade fair to blow up into a hurricane which would shake the English Church to its foundations.

Dr. Temple felt the cold draught of disapproval at Rugby School, of which he had recently become Headmaster. Parents manifested uneasiness in entrusting boys to his care and it became necessary for him to disassociate himself with some of the views expressed in the *Essays*. This upset him, for he felt that he had been badly let down by his old friend, Tait, who should have warned him when he visited Fulham of the attitude the hierarchy was likely to adopt.

Presently the *Essays* were debated in Convocation and intemperate things were said in the Lower House. The book was alleged to contain all the poison to be found in Tom Paine's *Age of Reason*, and one clergyman spoke of the young as 'corrupted and thrust to hell by the action of the book'. The Bishop of London expressed himself as pained and ashamed to learn that it was a clergyman who had characterised the writers as *Septem Contra Christum*. After due consideration Convocation synodically condemned the work.

Lord Houghton, in the House of Lords, asked the Lord Chancellor whether Convocation had not exceeded its rights and exposed itself to penalties by this Act of Condemnation. Lord Westbury in reply contemptuously referred to the condemnation as illegal but unworthy of notice. He did not spare the clergy and said their judgement was couched 'in terms so well-lubricated, so oily, so saponaceous, that no one could grasp it; it simply meant nothing at all'.

As soon as it was known that *Essays and Reviews* were disapproved of in high places the Archdeacons of England received instructions to find out how their clergy were reacting to the book. Kingsley received another enquiry, 'Did he or did he not agree with the views expressed?' Instead of answering the question direct, he wrote:

Dear Mr. Rural Dean,

The circular you have sent me puts me in a disagreeable position.

I should have been most happy to express to you or to the Archdeacon my opinion of the *Essays and Reviews* as one private gentleman to another.

But this address sent by the Archdeacon and with his sanction, implies a power on the Archdeacon's part officially to ascertain my sentiments on that work.

That power I deny—I know what by law the functions of an Archdeacon are. It was with much pain that I saw them gradually and at last grossly surpassed by the late Archdeacon, the Bishop of Rochester. He sent to me the last time a set of questions simply inquisitorial, as to the condition and working of my parish. Only four out of some twenty-five was I bound by law to answer. I had my doubts as to whether I ought not to answer those four simply and return the rest blank; but having reason to know that he would soon be translated and being a man of peace, with a parish (thank God!) whose interior organisation is not of the worst in the diocese I filled them all up, I fear foolishly.

It seems to me that the independent and quasi-episcopal position of the Rector is one of the most blessed safeguards to the Church of England; that it saves the priesthood from slavery to popular fanaticism, slavery to many in high places, slavery of every kind; that the man who for fear or favour allows any higher functionary to encroach on his parochial independence betrays his order and his Church.

I have marked with deep concern a growing desire under Lord

Palmerston's government to throw more power into the hands of the Bishops and their representatives. If that scheme has a chance of taking effect then I at least will meet it with whatsoever powers God has given me whether of logic or oratory, ridicule or denunciation, and all the more because it proceeds from that section of the clergy who have the lowest views of a Bishop's office and who magnify that office in the hope that the existing majority of Bishops if their power be increased will enable them to establish a doctrine which is contrary to Episcopacy, to the Liturgy, and (as I believe) to the Articles viz. the modified Puritanism which is now called Popular Protestantism.

Against all encroachments of superior authority therefore, I shall protest. I am Englishman enough to revere and obey authority humbly while I yet, as a freeman governed by law, bid it remain within its own legal limits.

If it be answered to this that the Venerable the Archdeacon does not send round this circular officially as Archdeacon, but merely as a private person asking the sense of his clerical brethren, I fear I must demur even more strongly.

For the effect of this circular is inquisitorial and nothing else. It is virtually and practically asking each gentleman who happens to hold a cure in the diocese 'Do you, or do you not, agree with these "Essays and Reviews" '? There is the plain honest fact. It will be known through the Archdeacon to the Bishop and to dozens more whether or not I have signed, whether or not A, B, and C have signed and those who have not signed, as the Venerable the Archdeacon (being a man of the world) must well know, will be exposed to the obloquy of *The Record*, *The Morning Advertiser*, and any and every other periodical as well as that of their clerical brethren.

To draw inoffensive men (who have nothing meddled with E & R, *the* Bishop or anyone else) into such a storm (?) is a move which I should not have made against the Venerable the Archdeacon. I am sorry that he has thought fit to make it against gentlemen who have never injured him.

That the Bishop can wish for such an inquisition of the sentiments of his clergy I cannot believe. His rule has been 'Live and let live' and by that rule of unvarying kindness and liberality he has won the affection of me and of us all and has made his diocese the happiest, the most rapidly improving in England. God grant no storm may darken his honourable old age. You are at liberty (and

I shall thank you to do so) to show this letter to the Archdeacon and to anyone else you like.[1]

What Kingsley's views were we learn from an address made to some candidates for ordination, in which he said, 'I thrust the book away in disgust. There is nothing like the old paths and the old truths and one must learn one's divineness by sick beds and in everyday work. Don't darken your minds with intellectual puzzles which may breed disbelief, but can never breed vital religion or practical usefulness.' And writing to his 'affectionate Arthur Stanley', who had reviewed the *Essays* favourably, but anonymously, in the *Edinburgh Review*, he expressed regret that the book should be selling so well. What could one, however, expect after the advertisement it had been given by Convocation? He could not help being amused to hear that two of the essay-writers had been prosecuted in the Court of Arches and after being sentenced to a year's suspension had appealed to the Queen in Council thereby setting in motion the cumbrous machinery of a Judicial Committee under the Lord Chancellor who granted an acquittal. How badly handled the controversy had been, but what else could one look for from comfortably ensconced Erastian bishops! Carlyle thought the behaviour of Convocation lamentable and feared the hierarchy would end by destroying 'a great institution' or making it appear ridiculous.

Stranger troubles than those originating in *Essays and Reviews* were in store for the Church of England and as usual were brought about by one of her office-holders. Many clerical dovecotes were upset by the investigations of a colonial bishop into the statistics of the Bible. Bishop Colenso, whose diocese was Natal, had adopted the study of mathematics as the principal interest in his life, and he applied his knowledge to every book he read, proving for example that the authors of the 'Book of Pentateuch' were ignorant of arithmetic, otherwise they would not have made statements from which it followed that every priest had to eat over eighty-eight pigeons daily. The Bishop was fond of telling a tale about an intelligent Zulu chief who had refused to believe that Noah ever built an ark and how he

[1] From Cambridge, March 1861.

had come to agree with the Zulu. There seems to have been little or no doctrinal stability about Colenso as he went on to prove to his own satisfaction that 'Deuteronomy' was a pious fraud of Jeremiah. The spectacle of the Church of England being systematically attacked by its own personnel with apparently complete irresponsibility is as extraordinary to the present-day observer as it was to Carlyle.

To Lady Hardwicke, who had complimented him on two sermons and had asked his opinion of Colenso, Kingsley replied:

> I cannot see why people should throw away the main truths of the Bible, the very message that made it precious to all Christians just because it seems likely that a few dozen texts, or even a few whole chapters are not genuine; and because one or two books were not written by the authors whose names they bear. If all that Colenso says were proved to be true it would not take away from Scripture anything concerning God, Christ or our own souls, which is of the least importance to us.
>
> No doubt there are passages in the O.T. wh. I cannot understand: but how do I know that they are rightly translated? How do I know that they were in the original document? Why shd I torment myself with what I can never know, while there is so much invaluable truth in the Bible of wh. I can be sure?
>
> I don't know, for instance, what is meant by woman being created from a rib of man. I don't know what is meant by Adam having *every* living thing brought to him. It seems as physically impossible as that every living thing should have got into Noah's Ark. Whether these sayings are allegories or literal truths, I cannot decide. But it is enough to me to take the moral lessons. That woman is a part of and equal to man, and not his inferior, his puppet and his slave, as he in his brute force has always tried to make her. So with Adam's naming the animals. 'Every' is used in the O.T. like 'everlasting' quite loosely, to signify a great number—or all that were around—just as everlasting only signifies a long time. But what of that? *The* point is that God brought the animals to Adam to call out in him that power of descriptive *naming*, wh. logicians now tell us, and rightly, is the great function of the human reason, as distinguished from the brute. And in that sense I see the great truth wh. comes out more and more as we read on in Scripture that God wishes to teach man and actually

does teach him; and does so by throwing opportunities in his way which call out the divine gift of reason. And it sanctifies to me my own study of Natural History, telling me that when a naturalist sees a new animal or plant, God has brought it to him, that he may study it and see its place in God's system of the universe, and like Adam of old give it a name which *shall be the name thereof*, a describing and defining name of practical use and meaning. And therefore I believe that the honest and single hearted man of science is fulfilling the very vocation to which that text says God called Adam. And that is a far grander thought to me than that a miracle (of which Scripture never speaks) should have been wanted to enable Adam to see every microscopic fly or animalcule and give them names which certainly have been forgotten, for there are no such in Hebrew or in any tongue till the last fifty years.

In February 1860 Charles joined his two brothers at Chelsea rectory as his father was not expected to live more than a few days. 'Never, never pray for a long life', he wrote to Fanny after taking his turn as a watcher by the sick bed. Mr. Kingsley had 'ruled the parish of Chelsea for twenty-four years', and when death took place they buried him in Brompton Cemetery with those words inscribed on his tombstone. John Martineau went to the rectory before the funeral and talked to Mrs. Kingsley, whom he found 'a most charming old lady'. She told him that she had decided to live for the rest of her life at Eversley.

Straight from the funeral Charles went back to his parish, making it his first duty to consecrate the new part of the graveyard. Fanny was not there to welcome him, for on hearing that her sister Charlotte Froude was very ill she had rushed off to Torquay during his absence. She was not in time to see her sister alive. Charlotte seems to have died almost without warning, and her husband and Fanny decided between them that her body should be conveyed to Eversley. It was the first to be laid in the newly consecrated ground. Charlotte's death was a very sharp grief to both Fanny and Charles as well as to Anthony Froude who, in his loneliness, came to depend on them for companionship. In order to comfort the widower Charles helped to plot a fishing excursion to Ireland for the summer.

Connection with the Court had brought Charles into direct

contact with the Prince Consort, who was a man after his own heart. It rejoiced Fanny to hear him say, 'I have fallen in love with that man,' for she knew from other sources that the Prince had taken a fancy to her rector and had talked over his merits with the Queen, whose favourite preacher he was rapidly becoming. What a good manly influence Charles might exert over indolent Prince Bertie if he could be given a post that made it possible for him to exert it! Her mind strayed to Cambridge, whither the Prince was being sent after he had finished his terms at Oxford. Supposing Charles could get to Cambridge in some capacity or other all might work out for good. Presently somebody—we do not know who, but Fanny had an immense acquaintance—somebody suggested to Lord Palmerston that Kingsley should take the place of Sir James Stephen who was resigning his Chair of Modern History. In May 1860 there arrived at Eversley a letter from Lord Palmerston offering the Regius Professorship of Modern History to Charles Kingsley. Whatever negotiations had gone on were unknown to him and it came as a great surprise. His first reaction was to think himself unworthy and he accepted the appointment with the greatest diffidence. Fanny waited for this mood to pass off and then despatched him to take his degree as M.A. which hitherto he had not been able to afford. Dr. Whewell, the redoubtable Master of Trinity, received him with such welcoming kindness as to make the whole experience 'as beautiful as a dream'.

He has quite forgotten, he writes, how exquisitely clean is the atmosphere of Cambridge, how rich the stone-work of the Colleges, how peaceful the scene as he looks from his windows into Trinity Walks, 'the first green walks in England'. He feels that a new chapter in life is opening, that all the writing and struggling is over and that congenial work and a settled position now stretch in front of him. This, of course, was just the way Fanny would have had him feel, but it annoyed her to know that even in the excitement of the new work he should still sound the sickly *ritournelle*: 'Would that it were done and kindly death near to set me off again with a new start somewhere else'. Perhaps the excursion to Ireland would put fresh vigour into him.

It was a wildly exciting plan that Froude had contrived for

their holiday. Nothing less than fishing for salmon in the West of Ireland in water renowned for big catches. They went first to stay with the Coopers of Markree Castle whence Charles wrote to Fanny:

> I have done the deed at last—killed a real, actual, live salmon of 5 lbs weight. I lost a whopper from light hooking. Here they are by *hundreds* and just as easy to catch as trout. This place is full of glory, very lovely, very well kept up, altogether as well as in England; lavish healthy expenditure—and the windows of the cabinet don't open!!!! But a large foot-tub suplies the place of bath and a handsome Kidderminster that of a bath-cloth. If I don't ruin carpet and ceiling before I leave so much the better.

While at Markree he had several talks with his host on a subject he found of fascinating interest, the making of a salmon river. When Mr. Cooper had come into the property he had found himself the owner of a good stream draining Loch Arrow and emptying itself into the sea at Ballisodare. Owing to a fall of limestone a bar had formed at the mouth of the river which entirely prevented salmon from running up it. To enable them to surmount this rocky barrier Mr. Cooper had made a zigzag stairway with troughs for landings. He repeated this experiment in two other falls higher up the river and then introduced salmon by artificial spawning. The whole outlay, under £2000, was quickly recouped. These improvements had been carried out three years earlier and in consequence of them Charles had the intoxicating pleasure of 'hooking with a fly ten salmon in one morning', and this despite the fact that seine nets were being worked at the mouth of the river at every tide. Charles eagerly made notes of Mr. Cooper's story as he could think of half a dozen rivers in England that might be susceptible to similar treatment. In the end he was glad to leave Markree as 'salmon-fishing is such very severe work that one wants to sleep in the evening instead of being expected to talk'. Kingsley when invited to go yachting or sea-fishing refused with disdain saying, 'Now that I have tasted blood, I can think of nothing but salmon'. As a holiday the trip was a huge success as Fanny was quick to realise.

Kingsley must have known far more about conditions in

Ireland than Fanny's narrative suggests, for S. G. O. had investigated the administration of the 'distressed districts' for the *Times*, and had examined the system adopted to deal with the population of the country immediately after the famine. It shocked Charles very much to drive past the ruined villages in Sligo destroyed in order to stamp out the cottier system which was alleged to be responsible for the shortage of food. The cots were in process of being replaced by prosperous farms of roots and grass, and the land, but not its inhabitants, was being reclaimed from 'universal potatodom'. The appearance of the 'natives' worried him a good deal. What was it that made them look like human chimpanzees? 'To see white chimpanzees is dreadful. If they were black one would not feel it so much, but their skins are as white as ours.' And then he set his own doubts at rest by pretending that all was better than it looked by saying, 'I don't believe it is our fault. . . . I believe they are happier, better, more comfortably lodged under our rule than ever before.' There is a note in the British Museum which shows that he did not succeed in deluding himself on these points. He owns up to being 'horrified' at the condition of the people and says:

Bring love and care to bear on them, give them leases, give them votes, let them vote for Satan if they like. If this goes on the Irish landlord will have to be civilised off the face of the earth. If I were a tenant in these parts I should be a Fenian at heart.

The summer of 1860 had been a very wet one in England. Rain had fallen almost continuously for three months and farmers, nervous lest the harvest go to waste, approached the clergy to pray for fine weather. The people of Eversley asked their rector to help them in this way, but he refused, for he believed that rain, since it cleansed drains and swept away refuse, was a safeguard against the cholera. He explained his views from the pulpit in a short sermon entitled, 'Why should we pray for fine weather?' This he had printed and circulated, for he felt he must get it out of the villagers' heads that they knew better than God. He does not dare himself to set up his own wisdom or rather his own ignorance against God's wisdom. It would be the utmost presumption on his part if he were to ask

God to alter the tides of the ocean, the form of the continents, the pace at which the world spins round, the force, the light, the speed, of sun and moon. And if he really did beg God to alter the skies, even for one day, he would be doing all these things.

While Charles Kingsley was in Ireland, his brother, Henry, had stuck to his task of completing his second novel *Ravenshoe*. It is markedly different from his first, for a new influence, probably that of his sister-in-law, is discernible in the book. We become aware in reading it that it is no longer the observant, authentic Henry who speaks, but someone who is trying to adapt himself to a *milieu* with which he is unfamiliar. People of rank and fashion appear, wicked earls, changed children, and ladies so flighty as to be mere lights o' love. A sinister priest, who has the key to everyone's secrets, lurks in the background of the Ravenshoe establishment. There is a deal of gambling, and the stilted, incredible, and complicated plot is only relieved here and there with passages of obvious autobiographical interest, —the row at the University, for example, and the boat-race of 1852.

Henry, like other members of his family, was an ardent naturalist and at his best when describing the Australian bush, the pictures of which are sharply focused and new. To take but one example, a ride through the tea scrub:

> Piles of drifted sand scored over in every direction with the tracks of lizards of every sort and size: some of which slid away with a kind of muscular waddle into dark places, while others refusing to move opened their mouths at him or let down bags under their chins to frighten him.

Ravenshoe was ready for publication in the autumn of 1860 and appeared serially in *Macmillan's Magazine* from January 1861 to June 1862. For the next fourteen years Henry produced at least one novel a year to say nothing of essays and short stories. In his third novel *The Hillyars and the Burtons* he went back to the scenes he knew so well in Australia. Henry's greatest Australian friend, Henry Campbell, describes the writing habits of the novelist at Eversley. After dining and prolonged smoking, he would shut himself up at about 11 P.M. in the study at the back of his cottage, place at his elbow a jug of rum and water, and write without intermission till 6 A.M.   No one saw him till luncheon time and then he would either go out for a long walk or fish or shoot.   He would live this life without variation week after week and month after month.   It is no wonder that Charles, who worked by fits and starts, always called him 'my most industrious brother'.

Chapter 15

THE PROFESSOR AND *THE WATER-BABIES*

Froude informs the Scottish youth
That parsons do not care for truth.
The Reverend Canon Kingsley cries
History is a pack of lies.
What cause for judgements so malign?
A brief reflection solves the mystery—
Froude believes Kingsley a divine,
And Kingsley goes to Froude for history.

WILLIAM STUBBS

IN the autumn of 1860 Charles Kingsley moved with his family to St. Peter's Terrace, Cambridge, leaving his parish in the charge of young Frederick Stapleton. The change was welcomed by Fanny Kingsley, who was thankful to escape the dreaded winter at Eversley and who did not for an instant doubt that her husband would be a great success in his new sphere. As November 13 drew near Kingsley's nerves began to let him down and it was with considerable trepidation and with a strange and half-frightened look on his face that he took his place at the desk in the Senate House to the sound of the cheers of the undergraduates assembled to listen to his inaugural address, 'The Limits of Exact Science as applied to History'. He began to speak in a hesitating way, but seemed to gain confidence as he proceeded. John Martineau says, 'Buckle's book [*The History of Civilisation*] was not mentioned by name but the whole [lecture] was an answer to it'.

The lecturer began by defining his attitude to his subject in these words, 'The belief that God in History is educating man is no mere hypothesis: it results from the observation of thousands of minds throughout thousands of years'. He suggested that if this idea was firmly grasped, facts fell into perspective revealing a pattern in which the apparent horrors of war, massacre, pestilence, would declare themselves as wisely and deeply benevolent. In short, the more science and history students absorbed, the more firmly would they believe in God.

He accepted the providentialist interpretation of history 'so long as it was limited to the Chrisitan era'.

Men spoke of the laws of matter, said the lecturer, as inevitable and immutable, but what about the laws of human life which he would call the everlasting judgements of God? And could they be so sure of an inexorable law in Nature when any one of them in the simplest manner could prove for himself that the supposed law of gravitation was not by any means the rigid and universal sort of thing that Newton assumed it to be. If he chose to catch a stone he could hold it in his hands; it did not fall to the ground and would not till he let it. 'So much for the inevitable action of the laws of gravity!' When this lecture was printed, it was reviewed, not too kindly, by Justin McCarthy and many other critics.

Critics of the Freeman school had their eye on him, and though they were ready to admit that the new Regius Professor could write a spirited historical novel they soon decided that he was incompetent to deal with scientific history. On being appointed to his Chair, Kingsley had written to Dean Wellesley:

> I will do my best at Cambridge to teach young men what I hold right views of history; above all that great truth which has been my lode-star for several years past—that the cause of loyalty and the cause of progress instead of being antagonistic are identical.

This intention we find him carrying out. He told his hearers that no scientific discovery can set aside 'the great root-law of the Universe', that 'the fruit of righteousness is wealth and peace, strength and honour, the fruit of unrighteousness is poverty and anarchy, weakness and shame'. He went on almost in a tone of admonishment:

> Not upon mind, gentlemen, not upon mind, but upon morale is human welfare founded. The true subjective history of man is the history not of his thought, but of his conscience: the true objective history of man is not that of his inventions, but of his vices and his virtues.

Leslie Stephen, who heard one or two of the lectures, said that Kingsley had a good deal of charm but gave an impression of weakness. Stephen was past the undergraduate stage himself, but the very young men were fascinated and crowded in ever larger numbers to listen to a lecturer of whom no one could predict what he might or might not say. Justin McCarthy's opinion of the lectures was that though they were intended as an onslaught on the positivist view of history, on Comte, Mill, Buckle, Darwin, yet the lecturer had made it perfectly clear that he did not know what it was these authors professed to teach. This way of dealing with the question

> must seem to many readers as it did to him nothing better than downright buffoonery. But Kingsley was grave as a church and earnest as an owl. He felt quite certain that he was refuting the pedants who believe in the action of the law of gravitation when he talked of holding a stone in his hand. That an impulsive, illogical man should on the spur of the moment talk this kind of nonsense even from a professor's chair is not wonderful but it does seem a little surprising that he should see it in print, revise it, and publish it without ever becoming aware of its absurdity.[1]

Other reviewers handled the lectures quite as severely, the *Athenaeum* dubbing them *Impressions de Voyage* and the *Westminster Review* describing them as 'feeble, confused and pretentious'.

For a clergyman accustomed to the freedom of the pulpit it was second nature to sermonise, but preaching is one thing and printing is another, as McCarthy justly observed. The effect of the hostile criticism was to prevent the Professor from printing any more of his Cambridge lectures, though one or two somehow found their way into *Good Words* a few years later. *Good Words* was the magazine to which Mrs. Kingsley secretly sent sermons, and it may be that at the conclusion of Kingsley's time at Cambridge she sent lectures too without saying anything about it. It is permissible to assume this on the strength of a letter from the editor of *Good Words* gratefully accepting a sermon on 'The Self Education of Young Men'. On this is a note in Kingsley's handwriting, 'So! you have been sending my sermons to press without consulting me, you thoroughly delicious sly puss! Well! be it so.'

In his second lecture, 'The Dying Empire', the Professor

---

[1] Justin McCarthy, *Reminiscences*, vol. II, pp. 266-7.

found occasion to tilt once again at Salvian's doctrine of the dignity of celibacy and the defilement of marriage, than which 'few more practically immoral doctrines have ever been preached'.

I have little doubt that Salvian was a prudent man, when he thought fit to bring no more human beings into the world. That is an ugly thought—I trust that you feel how ugly, unnatural, desperate a thought it is. If you do not, think it over till you do, till it frightens you. You will gain a great step thereby in human sympathy and therefore in the understanding of history.

The lecture concluded by quoting Salvian's explanation as to why the Romans had been ousted from control by the barbarians, 'Do we wonder if we are surpassed in power by an enemy who surpasses us in decency? We have been conquered only by the vices of our own morals.' There, Kingsley told his auditors, was the story of the death of Rome, and he hoped that in pondering over what he had just said the young men listening to him might be given 'a calm and steady brain, and a free and loyal heart; the energy that comes from health; the self-respect that comes from self-restraint; and the spirit that shrinks from neither God nor man, and feels it light to die for wife and child, for people and for Queen'.

In the third lecture which dealt with the overrunning of Italy in the fifth century by tribes from the north, he told the undergraduates that they would find many particulars of the first sack of Rome in St. Jerome's *Letters* and in St. Augustine's *City of God*.

But if you want these dreadful times *explained* to you, I do not think you can do better than take your Bibles, and read the Revelations of St. John the Apostle. I shall quote them more than once in this lecture. I cannot help quoting them. The words come naturally to my lips, as fitter to the facts than any words of my own. . . . Its awful metaphors give me more living and accurate picture of what went on than any that Gibbon's faithful details can give.

There were twelve lectures on the Roman and the Goth, the last of which was labelled 'The Strategy of Providence'. In this he tried to show how a small and uncivilised people like the Teutons could conquer a vast and civilised people like the Romans. It had been achieved by a war lasting two hundred years, and which included not only the campaigns of Alaric but the reconquest of Africa and Italy by the Romans. The lecture ended in a paean on the Arabs who, taking the Eastern Empire in rear, saved Europe. And now for the moral. If Trafalgar could not have been won without the mind of Nelson, or Waterloo without that of Wellington, was there no single mind to lead those innumerable armies, on whose success depended the future of the whole human race? If man believe in Providence as he does, it follows that though the war had no general upon earth, it may have had a general in Heaven, and the hosts of our forefathers, in spite of all their sins, were truly the hosts of God.

In his inaugural discourse he had said that he knew that a certain prejudice existed against him in the minds of better men than himself. That prejudice he hoped his lectures would dissipate. The rambling discourses delivered during 1860–1 did not have this result, but they had another that gave more satisfaction to Fanny Kingsley than donnish approval could ever have done. Charles was appointed tutor to the Prince of Wales.

The Prince had already kept three terms at Oxford and now, according to the arrangement of the Prince Consort, was to keep an equal number of terms at Cambridge. He was to live at Madingley, ride in twice a week for a class with Professor Kingsley composed of specially chosen undergraduates, and then go through the week's work each Saturday morning at his tutor's house.

While at Eversley during the Christmas vacation 'the Professor', as Mrs. Kingsley now called her husband, suddenly received orders through Mr. Herbert Fisher, the Prince's private tutor, that his royal pupil was to be instructed in History from the reign of William III to the battle of Waterloo. This was a fearful blow to one who for months had been working on early German history and his first reaction was to think that all the work he had done for the lectures was wasted as it found him unready for the cardinal task of his life. Further correspondence showed that his prepared lectures need not be altered, and that no original reading would be needed for the instruction of the special class of ten or twelve suitable undergraduates selected by Whewell to study with the Prince. The Professor declared he knew little or nothing of eighteenth-century history but that he thought the Georges, and he had in mind Thackeray's lectures, were much maligned human beings and that he would most willingly take up their defence.

John Martineau went to see the Kingsleys at Cambridge and found the Professor busy with the Prince of Wales on his hands three times a week, and Fanny very happy. They were both reconciled to the fact that their son Maurice was no scholar and wished to leave Cambridge without taking a degree in order to work at farming or engineering. Though in May all was well, by the summer Charles had had one of his curious failures in vitality and Martineau received a note from Mrs. Kingsley saying he was very ill from overwork, and had been unable to walk even a mile, much less do any thinking since his return to Eversley.

The Prince of Wales had made a very good impression on his tutor. Writing to Mr. Augustus Stapleton, Kingsley said:

> The Prince is very interesting, putting me in mind of his mother in a nice manner, free and everything. I had him in private today and we had an interesting talk on politics, old and new, a free press and so forth. I confess I tremble at my own responsibility, but I have made up my mind to speak plain truth as far as I know it. It would be base not to do so when such confidence has been reposed in me.

This happy state of affairs was put an end to in December when the Prince Consort died of typhoid at Windsor, and his son was sent abroad after his father's funeral in the charge of Arthur Stanley. The Prince Consort's place as Chancellor of the University of Cambridge was taken by the Duke of Devonshire, for whose installation the Regius Professor of Modern History wrote an ode which was set to music by Sterndale Bennett. The sober bachelor Duke was romanticised by being linked with an Elizabethan ancestor, a great Cavendish who sailed

Round the world and over the main
Breasting the Thames with his mariners bold,
Past good Queen Bess's palace of old;
With jewel and ingot packed in his hold,
And sails of damask and cloth of gold;
While never a sailor-boy on board
But was decked as brave as a Spanish lord,
With the spoils he had won
In the Isles of the Sun,
And the shores of Fairy-land
And yet held for the crown of the goodly show,
That queenly smile from the Palace window
And that wave of a queenly hand.

Novel-writing had, as we have seen, been laid aside for some time, but in the spring of 1862 something of the old Kingsley came to life in response to a demand by five-year-old Grenville for a book by papa all for himself. Papa was pleased to oblige, and without answering the request went off to his study for half an hour. At the end of that time he emerged with the first chapter of *The Water-Babies*. The rest of the story came to him as easily. It was composed for the most part on the banks of the Itchen, but the fact that the names of people and places were the same as in *The Tutor's Story*, which had been written on holiday in Yorkshire, seems to indicate that the book had for long been hatching in his head.

When read with innocent eyes the story has bewitching fragrance and charm, for a sense of fun and love of country sights infuse the narrative, and we cannot help smiling as we read of the ancestral beetle setting out for his wedding looking 'as smart as the gardener's dog with a polyanthus in his mouth', nor enjoying the description of the limestone fountain at the foot of the limestone crag, as it rose 'quelling and bubbling and gurgling so clear that you could not tell where the water ended and the air began', and how neatly 'it ran away under the road amid blue geranium and golden globe-flower and wild raspberry and bird-cherry with its tassels of snow'. As little Tom bumps down the grass slopes and limestone ledges, we hear about the rock-roses, the saxifrages, the thyme, the basil, over which he slides in his precipitous descent. After Tom has run away 'with bells ringing in his head' from the schoolmarm's house, he stumbles to the river and sinks into its depths to become a clean little water-baby and brother to the fairies. And then begin an enchanting series of interviews with caddis, gnat, dragon-fly, and other denizens of the warm shallows, and finally meetings with trout and otter, eel and salmon, till the sea is reached. Tom catches flies for the lazy trout and feeds them with caperers and cock-tailed duns, spinners, yellow, brown, claret, and grey, and alder flies. It is all most lovingly done in the spirit in which in moments of leisure Charles turned the leaves of his own fly-book.

With the introduction of the Professor, Mrs. Bedonebyasyoudid and Mrs. Doasyouwouldbedoneby, a new sort of book begins, full of moral lessons and sound advice, and Tom, grown up, after seven years goes adventuring to the Other End of Nowhere. His visits to the Shiny Wall, the pool of the whales, the floor of the sea, the mollys, and Mother Carey remind one of the Voyage of Pantagruel to the islands.

Re-reading *The Water-Babies* after many years one finds it studded with the pricks of old controversies and the prejudices peculiar to the author. When Pandora's box is opened out of it fly things that Kingsley most disapproved of—monks, popes, measles, tight stays, and so on. The most remarkable feature about the book is that much of it is written in the idiom of Rabelais. The French author loved stringing lists of nouns, adjectives, or verbs together. Montaigne imitated him in his *Apologie de Raimond de Sébonde* where he uses 68 consecutive verbs in the first person plural of the present indicative. Corneille makes Matamore in *L'Illusion* pour out an uninterrupted stream of 41 nouns, but what is accidental and rare in these authors is the common habit and use of Rabelais. With obvious pleasure he arranged long lists of words in columns in emulation of the 240 games of Gargantua or the 208 epithets applied to the name of Triboulet. On a lesser scale, instead of saying that a countryside had been pillaged, he would say that cows, calves, sheep, goats, bulls, had all been carried away. A man does not lose his groceries, he loses wax, pepper, incense, saffron, wall-flower, spices, cassia, and rhubarb. Dickens was probably a reader of Rabelais too, for we find him rather unexpectedly making use of the same trick in *Edwin Drood*.

Kingsley read his Rabelais through every year and used to say that the right way to describe a gentleman in France was to say, 'Il sait son Rabelais', whereas in English one might say, 'He knows his Bewick!'   We find Kingsley asking, 'Are there not water rats, water flies, water crickets, water crabs, water tortoises, water scorpions, water tigers, water hogs, water cats, water dogs and if so why not water babies?'   Of the doctrine of his fairy tale he says, 'It is orthodox, rational, philosophical, inductive, seductive, deductive, logical, irrefragable, nominalistic, productive, salutary, comfortable, and on all accounts to be received'.   On other pages we find a catalogue on the key of the backstairs, lists of 'divers and sundry medicines' and of the contents of a cutler's shop.   There can be no doubt that the author enormously enjoyed composing this fantasia.   The manuscript was sent to Macmillan without any material correction and on publication had an immediate and phenomenal success.

Fanny Kingsley could now preen herself on having steered her bark into quiet water, not a backwater however, for she thought of Charles as on the broad tide-way to advancement. He had placated the prejudice that existed against him on account of certain early writings in his frank preface to his lectures: he was no longer associated with Reform or Chartism, and he was at long last associating with the right kind of people.   Visits to Lady Ashburton at The Grange had caused him to meet on equal terms men like the Duke of Argyll and the Bishop of Oxford.   He was no longer regarded as a trouble-making, unreliable clergyman, but as a pillar of the established order. Had Fanny but realised it, it really was not safe to think of him as a reformed character, for Charles had an unaccountable, irresponsible streak in him that might at any moment destroy the position she had built up.

It was extremely pleasant during the vacation to take Fanny and Maurice to stay with the Duke of Argyll at Inveraray, 'an incomparably lovely place', and it was very enjoyable to fish the Tay from Murthly, and it did not matter to Fanny that the weather was marvellously fine, so fine that anglers could only watch the fish flapping and smacking about in the shallows and swirling in the pools. Perhaps Charles kept it dark that he poached a salmon with a triangle near the tail and ran up and down the bank after it for two hours in high enjoyment.

During the course of 1862 the Prince of Wales became engaged to the lovely Princess Alexandra of Denmark and for the wedding in March Mr. and Mrs. Kingsley were invited to Windsor. For both of them it was a sublimated experience. Fanny was well placed in a box close above the Queen, in full sight of the altar, and could hear every response. Her Professor as a royal chaplain was in the Household Gallery opposite, whence he could watch every shade of expression that passed over the 'martyred face' of his Sovereign. To him it was a dream-like experience,—the dear old chapel, the knights of the Garter, the banners, the billowing bridesmaids, the serried ranks of European royalty were woven into a shimmering texture of delight. The behaviour and the reverent dignity of the 'Young Master' were perfect.

In their absence John Martineau helped to make the wedding festivities at Eversley go. A sheep was roasted whole; beer flowed; there were hurdle races, foot races, and a big bonfire. At the height of the blaze the Kingsleys got back from Windsor. They were in court dress and Charles carried a cocked-hat full of bonbons and wedding cake. They were still almost in a state of ecstasy over their day and the ceremony that had caused their hearts to brim with loyalty.

The enormous pleasure derived from witnessing the royal wedding was succeeded by a cold douche of an unusual and unexpected kind. Fanny Kingsley did her best to make light of the incident, but it caused great mortification to her husband. It originated in this way. A deputation from Oxford University, which included Max Müller, had waited on the Prince in the winter of 1862 to offer congratulations on his impending marriage. The Prince and Princess announced their desire to attend Commemoration in the May after their wedding and, as was the custom on such occasions, H.R.H. sent in a list of the names of those whom he wished to receive the honorary degree of D.C.L. Among the names was that of the royal tutor and chaplain, Charles Kingsley. Despite the occasion, despite the backing, Dr. Pusey at once opposed the granting of a degree in Council on the grounds that *Hypatia* was an immoral book and its author an unworthy recipient of the honour. Kingsley's friends, who thought it his best book, were highly indignant and tried to get Dr. Pusey to withdraw his opposition, but unsuccessfully. Arthur Stanley, at that time Professor of Ecclesiastical History and Canon of Christ Church, made use of a marked copy of *Hypatia* lent him by Max Müller when arguing with Dr. Pusey over the condemned passages. He made no headway against that formidable controversialist the Professor of Hebrew, who had no respect for regius appointees as such. It was less than a year since he had challenged brilliant Benjamin Jowett, Regius Professor of Greek, before the Vice-Chancellor's court with disseminating opinions that were not in accordance with the doctrine of the Church of England. Dr. Pusey feared no one and spared no one. Given the particular circumstances in which Kingsley's name had been put forward, it was thought it might have been carried by votes in council, but when Dr. Pusey threatened to call out *non placet* in the theatre in the very presence of the Prince and Princess, Kingsley's friends decided to withdraw his name in order to avoid so scandalous a scene. Writing to Tom Hughes about the matter Kingsley said:

> The Council and Stanley behaved excellently well and not at all cowardly. They would have fought the thing through if old P. had not declared his intention to cry *Non Placet* in the theatre and have a fracas before the Prince's face and that had to be avoided at all risks.

Kingsley put a good face on the matter, and Fanny pretended that her real reason for regret was that she would never now have the pleasure of seeing her husband in a scarlet gown. To Max Müller, whom she thanked for the great kindness and chivalry he had shown, she said that it had helped her to forget the vindictive thoughts roused in her breast by the un-Christian conduct of Dr. Pusey.

Three years later Charles Kingsley was invited to preach at St. Mary's, Oxford. In thanking Bishop Wilberforce for the invitation he said:

As a Professor at Cambridge, and still more as a Chaplain of the Queen, and allowed at times to preach in her private chapel and to approach her Royal Person, I do not think it stands with my honour to appear publicly in Oxford till some public retractation and apology has been made for that scandalous imputation which though privately made, was allowed to become notorious through the public press.

The very book on which that imputation was grounded, had been read and graciously approved by Her Majesty; therefore it is for Her sake, and for that of my University, and not from any paltry pride about myself, that I fear I must, with very great regret, decline at present the honour which you are so good as to offer me.[1]

No apology or retractation was ever made, so Kingsley never had the opportunity again of preaching at St. Mary's. *Hypatia*, so far as Oxford University was concerned, was registered as an immoral book and its author as an inaccurate historian.

[1] May 29, 1866.

Chapter 16

CROSSING SWORDS WITH
DR. NEWMAN

*Dogma has been the fundamental principle of my religion:
religion, as a mere sentiment, is to me a dream and a mockery.*

J. H. NEWMAN

NO allusion to the encounter between her husband and Dr.
Newman, says Fanny Kingsley, would have been made in
her biography but that she feared complete silence might be
misconstrued into tacit acknowledgment of defeat on the main
question. She would like, however, to mention the fact that
word had been conveyed to Mr. Kingsley that Dr. Newman was
in bad health and deprecated the idea of polemical discussion.
Out of consideration, therefore, for his delicacy, Mr. Kingsley
was 'put to a great disadvantage in the issue'.

For the right understanding of the difference between the
two clerics Fanny Kingsley feels that she cannot insist too em-
phatically that it was on behalf of truth and truth alone that
Mr. Kingsley contended. He had asked Dr. Newman a plain
question, 'Were Roman Catholic priests encouraged to pursue
truth for its own sake?' and it was a question to which he never
obtained a reply. One can only assume that this rather
distorted version of the origin of the controversy was the one
presented to her by her husband, and finally registered in his
mind as well as hers as the gist of the affair.

In order to understand the steps that led up to the quarrel we
must look over Charles Kingsley's shoulder in the first days of
December 1863 as he turned the pages of volumes seven and
eight of Froude's *History of England from the Fall of Wolsey to
the Defeat of the Spanish Armada*. He was about to review
them for *Macmillan's Magazine* and they gave him the opportunity of indulging himself in having a shot or two at his
favourite quarry the 'Romish priests'. So accustomed had he
become in *Westward Ho!* to using violent and depreciatory

language about them [1] and to coupling the profession of Catholicism with squalor of conduct and ferocious cruelty, that it must have seemed a very harmless thing to him to say in his review that Romish priests in general disregarded truth. He had no misgivings in the matter; for him it was a self-evident proposition that required no proving. Least of all did he envisage opposition. No protests had been made over *Westward Ho!*, which was treated as an imaginative work of fiction. But had he stopped to think, he would have realised that he could hardly look to receive the same indulgence for an historical review, a review, moreover, in which he had been so rash as to mention the name of the most acute controversialist of the day as his authority for stating that the 'Romish priests' had no regard for truth. The offending paragraph, containing an implicit gibe at celibacy, ran as follows:

> Truth for its own sake has never been a virtue of the Roman clergy. Father Newman informs us that it need not and on the whole ought not to be; that cunning is the weapon which Heaven has given to the saints wherewith to withstand the brute male force of the wicked world which marries and is given in marriage.

This passage in the review was offensive and odious to Newman, because it revived in an off-hand, careless sort of way as if it were indisputable, an old and familiar charge against the Church he had entered. To Kingsley, on the other hand, it was on all fours with saying, 'John Morley is a follower of Gladstone'.

A day or two after the review was printed the firm of Macmillan received a communication from Dr. Newman [2] couched in the following words:

> I should not dream of expostulating with the writer of such a passage, nor with the editor who could insert it without appending evidence in proof of its allegation. Nor do I want any reparation from either of them. I neither complain of them for their act, nor should I thank them if they reversed it. Nor do I even write to you with any desire of troubling you to send me an answer. I do but wish to draw the attention of yourselves, as gentlemen, to a

---

[1] We may remind ourselves that Amyas Leigh's cousin, Eustace, was 'sent to be made a liar of in Rheims'. Eustace, a little older, 'is a man no longer; he is become a thing, a tool, a Jesuit'.

[2] December 30, 1863.

grave and gratuitous slander with which I feel confident you will be sorry to find associated a name so eminent as yours.

The protest was passed to Kingsley to deal with, and it is evident that he was able to assure Alexander Macmillan as to his capacity to do so, for in a note written to Maurice, Macmillan says, 'Charles Kingsley is going to write to Dr. Newman as kindly as he can.   Old passages about Froude have left a bitter flavour in his thoughts and feelings about the great pervert.' [1] Kingsley's reply was ingenuous in tone.   He believed his words to be just and the document he had specifically in mind was a sermon entitled 'Wisdom and Innocence'; he is glad to learn that he has mistaken Dr. Newman's meaning, and adds, 'I shall be most happy on your showing me that I have wronged you, to retract my accusation as publicly as I have made it'.

'Wisdom and Innocence' was a sermon preached on the trouble-making text, 'Behold I send you forth as sheep in the midst of wolves; be ye therefore wise as serpents and harmless as doves'.   The preacher explained that since Christians were forbidden to defend themselves by force they had to use prudence and skill, *i.e.* be wise as serpents.   It was remarkable that Christ should have chosen the serpent as a pattern of wisdom.   Christians in the days of persecution and oppression often appeared crafty since to be frankly angry meant to invite death.   The world must always have translated their meekness and silence as craft and hypocrisy.   There again, instead of using the wisdom of the serpent, they had abused it, and were wise without being harmless.   Newman defined harmlessness as simplicity in act, purity in motive, purity in aim, and acting conscientiously without caring for the consequences.   It is obvious that Kingsley had not read the sermon for some time, but had drawn on some old impressions of its being casuistical and encouraging deceit.   His conviction was that a truth-lover could never have uttered it.

Dr. Newman expressed what seemed like disingenuous surprise at being informed that the initials at the end of the review, C. K., stood for Charles Kingsley, and immediately took his stance, not on the general question on which he had preached his sermon, but on the actual words supposed to have been ascribed to him by Kingsley, thus narrowing the controversy down to one specific point.   At the time the sermon had been preached he had been an Anglican and his discourse had no words in it expressing the opinion attributed to him by the reviewer.

Of the factual part of the disclaimer Charles Kingsley took no notice because for him it was all a matter not of actual statement but of interpretation.   He was able, therefore, to write, 'The tone of your letter makes me feel, to my very deep pleasure that my opinion of the meaning of your words was a mistaken one'.[1]

Satisfied with the magnanimity of his personal attitude he enclosed the apology he proposed inserting in *Macmillan's Magazine*.

> Dr. Newman has, by letter, expressed in the strongest terms his denial of the meaning which I have put upon his words.   No man knows the use of words better than Dr. Newman; no man therefore, has a better right to define what he does or does not mean by them. It only remains, therefore, for me to express my hearty regret at having so seriously mistaken him, and my hearty pleasure at finding him on the side of truth, in this, or in any other matter.

This missed the point as there were no words to explain away. Submitted to Newman, the draft was objected to in several particulars.[2]   Kingsley deleted much of it but refused to change his position, and the *amende*, in an abbreviated form, was printed in the February number of *Macmillan's Magazine*.   The real issue, which was that Newman had had words attributed to him that he had not used, had been evaded.   It may be that Kingsley never understood what the charge against him really was, else could he have been satisfied that he had 'done all that could be expected of him as an English gentleman' in penning the following words?

> In your last number I made certain allegations against the teaching of Dr. John Henry Newman, which I thought were justified by a Sermon of his, entitled 'Wisdom and Innocence.'   Dr. Newman has expressed in the strongest terms, his denial of the meaning I

[1] January 14, 1864.   [2] January 16, 1864.

have put upon his words.   It only remains therefore, for me to express my hearty regret at having so seriously mistaken him.

The next move was made by Dr. Newman who printed the correspondence between himself and his assailant [1] in a pamphlet analysing and summing up Kingsley's arguments in a way that was found particularly irritating by the rector of Eversley and his wife.   To have one's 'method' and 'thoughts' interpreted in a humorous way was distinctly trying.   To invent a dialogue on the basis of such correspondence was just something one did not do.   Kingsley felt that he had 'by an act of courtesy put himself into the power of an unscrupulous opponent'.

The dialogue that gave such offence took the fancy of the journalists, who gave it a good deal of publicity.   It ran like this:

'Oh, the chicanery, the wholesale fraud, the vile hypocrisy, the conscience-killing tyranny of Rome!   We have not far to seek for evidence of it!   There's Father Newman to wit;—one living specimen is worth a hundred dead ones.   He, a Priest, writing of Priests, tells me that lying is never any harm.'

I interpose: 'You are taking an extraordinary liberty with my name.   If I have said this tell me when and where.'

Mr. Kingsley replies: 'You said it, Reverend Sir, in a Sermon which you preached when a Protestant, as vicar of St. Mary's and published in 1844; and I could read you a very salutary lecture on the effects which that Sermon had at the time on my opinion of you.'

I make an answer.   'Oh *not* it seems as a Priest, speaking to Priests; but let us have the passage.'

This was tiresome enough for Kingsley, but when it came to making fun of his magnanimity it was altogether unbearable. To be depicted as relaxing and saying to Dr. Newman:

'Do you know I *like* your *tone*.   From your *tone* I rejoice, greatly rejoice—to be able to believe you did not mean what you said.'

I rejoin: '*Mean* it!   I maintain I never *said* it whether as a Protestant or as a Catholic!'

Mr. Kingsley replies: 'I waive that point.'

[1] *Mr. Kingsley and Dr. Newman: A Correspondence on the Question Whether Dr. Newman Teaches that Truth is No Virtue.*   (Price 1s.)

I object: 'Is it possible? What? Waive the main question? I either said it or I didn't. You have made a monstrous charge against me; direct, distinct, public. You are bound to prove it as directly, as distinctly, as publicly:—or to own you can't!'

'Well,' says Mr. Kingsley, 'if you are quite sure you did not say it, I'll take your word for it; I really will.'

'My *word*' I am dumb. Somehow I thought it was my *word* that happened to be on trial. The *word* of a Professor of lying that he does not lie!'

But Mr. Kingsley reassures me. 'We are both gentlemen,' he says, 'I have done as much as one gentleman can expect from another.'

I begin to see: he thought me a gentleman at the very time that he said that I taught lying on system. After all, it is not I, but Mr. Kingsley who did not mean what he said.

Though Newman's dialogue did not amuse the Kingsleys, it was thought 'famous sport' by the *Athenæum*. 'How briskly', it said, 'do we gather round a brace of reverend gentlemen when the prize for which they contend is which of the two shall be considered the father of lies.' The *Saturday Review* praised the liveliness of the humour. Most unexpected of all, the *Spectator*, edited by R. H. Hutton, a friend and admirer of both Maurice and Kingsley, printed an article on the controversy based on a psychological study of the characters of the two men. The writer, Hutton, said what pleasure literary people had derived from the drawing out of Father Newman's powers of sarcasm by the unwary Kingsley. But some people might think of Kingsley as too helpless a victim to be operated on in this way. His rough and manly intellect was only too accurately characterised in the sub-title of one of his books, *Loose Thoughts for Loose Thinkers*. Hutton continued in the same vein:

A more opportune Protestant ram for Father Newman's sacrificial knife could scarcely have been found; and the thicket in which he caught himself was, as it were, of his own choosing he having rushed headlong into it quite without malice, but also quite without proper consideration of the force and significance of his own words. . . . Mr. Kingsley made a random charge against Father Newman in *Macmillan's Magazine*. The sermon in question certainly contains no proposition of the kind to which Mr. Kingsley alludes. . . . Mr. Kingsley ought to have said, what is obviously true, that on examining the sermon no passage will bear any colourable meaning at all like that he had put upon it.[1]

The castigation was certainly severe and Kingsley's next impulse was to snatch up his pen and write the pamphlet entitled, 'What then did Dr. Newman mean?' 'I am answering Newman now, and though I give up the charge of conscious dishonesty, I trust to make him and his admirers sorry that they did not leave me alone. I have a score of more than twenty years to pay, and this is an instalment of it.' [2]

Kingsley was much pleased with a sentence from Ward's *Ideal of a Christian Church* to which a correspondent had drawn his attention. It seemed to justify everything he thought and was about to write. 'Candour is an intellectual rather than a moral virtue, and by no means either universally or distinctively characteristic of the saintly mind.' It was grand to be able to taunt the perverts with their own words! He was careful to discount in advance Newman's possible line of defence by identifying his opponent's method with that of Liguori, Scavini, and Nyeraguet in order to whirl him away into a gulf of quibblers, hypocrites, and rogues. Admitting that he went in fear of anything Dr. Newman might write, he asked what proof he had that when this priest says "*mean* it! I never *said* it!" he does not mean, "I did not *say* it, but I *did* mean it"?'

The pamphlet was a source of some satisfaction to Kingsley, who really seems to have thought he was giving Newman his quietus. Its impact on Newman produced a totally unexpected result—that of goading him into the composition of the *Apologia pro Vita sua*. The new attack involved not one preacher only, but Catholic teaching generally and the sincerity or otherwise of all priests. The duty of vindication and explanation had quite definitely, he felt, been laid upon his shoulders. He must do his best to carry the responsibility of championing the Church.

Rumour of Dr. Newman's intention may or may not have reached Kingsley before he had one of his nervous breakdowns. By great good luck he was able to make an immediate get-away, for Froude, who was obliged to go to Madrid to consult docu-

[1] *Spectator*, February 20, 1869.
[2] Father Dudley Ryder, *Recollections*, p. 351.

ments, offered to take him abroad. Fanny Kingsley felt the situation saved when she saw him off to Paris in March. Soon after he had left, the *Apologia* began making its appearance in weekly parts. Charles was not told anything about it by Fanny till his return in May.

Carefree as a boy (he had never been to Paris before) Kingsley rushed round the principal Catholic churches on Good Friday and assisted at ceremonies of which he could make neither head nor tail. At the Madeleine he watched a grand ceremony 'consisting of a high priest brushing people with a handkerchief'. At Notre Dame 'old women were adoring the Sacrament in a Tombeau dressed up with cloth and darkness and two argand burners throwing light on it from above. Over all "a fold of white drapery exactly in the form of the sacrificial *vitta* on the Greek vases from which it is probably unconsciously derived".' He found it a relief to get away to the open spaces of the Landes where he could forget all about papists and their tortuous ways. The Landes were not unlike Hartford Bridge Flat, but far more attractive owing to the presence of *pinus maritima* and Mediterranean heath, to say nothing of 'the little long-woolled sheep', 'the cows you could put under your arm', and the boys on stilts tending them, who wore sheepskin coats and sheepskin pads on their feet. The travellers went to Bordeaux, Bayonne, and Biarritz, where Froude said good-bye and slipped into Spain.

'The air is like champagne and the cliffs are covered with red and white stocks just as fine as garden ones. It is all more exciting than words can say', wrote Charles to Fanny. He has found a sea-urchin that bores into limestone, and pools filled with beds of cluniasters of loveliest colours, primrose, sea-green, dove, purple, crimson, pink. One letter is illustrated with sketches of a vulture. He has discovered it chained in a tree dripping and sulking after a shower of rain, and trying to dry itself by expanding great concave wings as big as windmills. The attractive, happy side of Kingsley was once again to the fore.

'Oh, the blessed, blessed feeling of having nothing to do!' he exclaimed after a morning spent lounging on the rocks smoking penny cigars, picking up skate purses, and watching grey lizards dart in and out of the crevices. Tearing himself away from the shore he made for Pau, that 'beats all cities seen for beauty', then Toulouse, Marseilles, Narbonne, Carcassonne, and Nîmes—'a delightful place where people do nothing but *live*.' The most remarkable things in the city were 'the Roman ladies' baths in a fountain bursting up out of the rock where under colonnades they walked about in or out of the water as they chose. All is standing and could be used to-morrow, if the prudery of the priests allowed it.' At Avignon as at Nîmes he found Viollet-le-Duc restoration in full swing. At every stopping-place he wandered off into the country and marvelled at the flowers he found. Bee-orchids, lithospermum, blue lily, broom, asters, such days of wonder as never were! All this he described to Fanny, and then, almost as if conscience-stricken at his own intense enjoyment and uplifting excitements, he would add in conclusion, 'yet there is one thing more glorious and precious than the whole universe—and that is a woman's love'. As he turned homewards he began to wonder 'if Newman is answering again' and if *he* was returning 'to fresh trouble and battle'.

After nights at Orange and Lyons he went to Fontainebleau where he found 'the cool greenness' very restful and the whole place reminiscent of fairyland. 'Acres of palace built by Francis I, Henry II, and Charles IX,—wasteful scoundrels, while the people were starving. . . . Forest such as I never saw before with huge rocks of sandstone rising among great trees.' Hitherto he had done no thinking and had slept like a child, but at Fontainebleau his mind clouded over with the shadow of old controversy and he wrote to his young curate, Frederick Stapleton:

> I will tell you volumes of what I have seen of the Mari-idolatry of France. I could not have conceived such things possible in the nineteenth century. But I have seen enough to give Newman such a revanche as will make him wince, if any English common-sense is left in him which I doubt.

He got home towards the end of May, and the last section of the *Apologia* came out during the week of his return. It was entitled 'General Answer to Mr. Kingsley'. What could be more de-magnetising than to find oneself once again up to the

neck in controversy? Everyone seemed to be reading and
discussing Newman's story, which as a specimen of polemical
method was said to be masterly.

There can be no doubt that Dr. Newman had set himself a
very hard task when he determined to disarm the British public
of their strong prejudice against priests; he did not underrate
the difficulties which in a way acted as spur to his mind and
courage. In addressing his fellow countrymen, he describes
them as

> the most suspicious and touchy of mankind; unreasonable and
> unjust in their seasons of excitement, but I had rather be an English-
> man (as in fact I am) than belong to any other race under Heaven.
> They are as generous as they are hasty and burly, and their repent-
> ance for their injustice is greater than their sin.

Newman presented himself in the *Apologia* as gratuitously
slandered and showed how 'blundering, impulsive, and prejudiced was the mind of the man' who had failed to understand
him, even 'as children do not apprehend the thoughts of grown-
up people, nor savages the instincts of civilisation'. Kingsley
had thought of himself as the manly Englishman showing up
the shifty papist, but there was little left of manliness when the
shifty papist had done with him.

The *Apologia*, in the serial edition, appeared as Part I, 'Mr.
Kingsley's Method of Disputation', Part II, 'True Mode of
meeting Mr. Kingsley'. Both were bantering in tone. With
Part III began the autobiography proper. The whole book
was published in seven weekly instalments by Longmans.[1]

Alexander Macmillan wrote to Kingsley on his return from
abroad advising him to read every word of the *Apologia*.

[1] *Apologia pro Vita sua*

A Reply to a Pamphlet entitled 'What
then does Dr. Newman mean?' Issued
by Longman in buff paper-bound parts.

Part I. 1/–   Mr. Kingsley's Method of Disputation.
„ II. 1/–   True Mode of meeting Mr. Kingsley.
„ III. 1/– ⎫
„ IV. 2/– ⎪
„ V. 2/–   ⎬ History of my Religious Opinions.
„ VI. 2/6 ⎭
„ VII. 2/–   General Answer to Mr. Kingsley.

'Nothing could possibly be more soothing I should think.   But Mrs. Kingsley should judge.   As I understand the matter the second number put the battle substantially into your hands.' [1]

Kingsley at once sat down to read Newman's book.   He then wrote to Alexander Macmillan: [2]

> Here is my ultimatum on the Newman question which please shew privately to anyone and everyone you like, including Mr. Hutton.
>
> I have determined to take no notice whatever of Dr. Newman's apology.
>
> (1) I have nothing to retract, apologise for, explain.   Deliberately, after twenty years of thought I struck as hard as I could. Deliberately I shall strike again, if it so pleases me, though not one literary man in England approved.   I know too well of what I am talking.
>
> (2) I cannot trust, I can only smile at the autobiography of a man who (beginning with Newman's light, learning and genius) ends in believing that he believes in the Infallibility of one Church, and in the Immaculate Conception.   If I am to bandy words it must be with sane persons.
>
> (3) I cannot be weak enough to put myself a second time by any fresh act of courtesy, into the power of one who like a treacherous ape, lifts to you meek and suppliant eyes, till he thinks he has you within his reach, and then springs gibbering and biting at your face.   Newman's conduct in this line has so much disgusted Catholics themselves that I have no wish to remove their just condemnation of his doings.
>
> The world seems inclined to patronize Dr. Newman and the Cafard [3] just now, because having no faith of its own, it is awed by the seeming strength of fanaticism.   I know them too well either to patronise or to fear them.   I wish poor dear Thackeray had been alive.   He knew what I know and would have taken a tone about this matter which would have astonished too many literary men.   He was too true a liberal to pat lies and bigotry on the back.

The 'ultimatum' shows, if nothing else does, that Mr. Kingsley had learnt nothing from crossing swords with Dr. Newman. It is open to question whether he ever understood what the fight

---

[1] May 19, 1864.   [2] June 8, 1864.   [3] Cafard = hypocrite.

was about.   In a famous epigram by a *Quarterly* reviewer the matter was summed up, 'Charles Kingsley goes down to history as the embedded fly in the clear amber of his antagonist's apology'.

Having made his case, received the congratulations of bishops and priests, and been publicly thanked at the Provincial Synod of the Birmingham clergy at Oscott,[1] Newman, who found it difficult to be angry with a man he had never seen, deleted Parts I and II from all subsequent editions of the *Apologia*.

Though Kingsley had no wish whatever to make acquaintance with Dr. Newman, Newman used to say that he hoped the chance might come his way of having a talk with his opponent. They never met face to face, but when he heard of his death,[2] Newman said a Mass for Charles Kingsley's soul.

[1] June 1864.   [2] Ward II. 45.

Chapter 17

WINDSOR CASTLE, AND JAMAICAN RIOTS

Life is an art in which we are too often mere dabblers. We must take our degree in our heart's blood.

CARMEN SYLVA

ENGAGEMENTS to preach and the preparation of lectures kept Kingsley from fretting about the *Apologia*, and his wife says that his chief interest for the moment was the threat to enclose common lands in the parish. She represents him as 'really distressed' over the matter 'from the aesthetic point of view', since he felt 'that the characteristic beauty of the parish he loved so well would be destroyed and that old associations and old cricket grounds might be broken up which nothing new could replace'. She even reported him as saying, 'Eversley will never be the same Eversley to me,' and added, 'it was a wound to his heart and to his poet's fancy, and it never healed'. After reading her book, Sir William Cope protested to Cowley Powles that he could show him letters and a memorandum by Charles Kingsley recommending, for a variety of practical reasons, the enclosure of the Eversley Commons, which were mainly moor. The reasons adduced by Kingsley were that

Common lands encourage bad farming. Freeholders depend on these lands for spring feed for their sheep. Kingsley has himself seen sheep staggering about the commons in April in a state of starvation, just because the users have failed to sow rye grass to come on when the turnips are finished.

Common lands encourage dishonesty. Men of small means keep more cattle than they have land for on the chance of their living on the commons.

Common lands encourage poaching, wood-stealing and other wild habits. Game, straying on to common land, is regarded as common property.

Common lands never get drained as repeated and hap-hazard turf-cutting reduce the acreage to bog. Common land should be enclosed, cultivated, and turned into a *parish* enclosure.

THE RECTORY AT EVERSLEY

The cricket ground lamented over by Fanny Kingsley was never threatened, for Sir William Cope and Mr. Powles contributed five pounds each towards remaking the pitch.

In the spring of 1864 Henry Kingsley announced that he intended to get married and to live in the cottage at Eversley, which worried Charles and Fanny a good deal as it meant finding other accommodation for old Mrs. Kingsley. Campbell, the friend on whom Henry relied for companionship and for copying his manuscripts, had returned to Australia early in the year. The bereft author missed him dreadfully and consoled himself by constantly visiting Mr. and Mrs. Blunt, the successors to his father and mother at Chelsea rectory, with the result that he fell in love with the children's governess, Sarah Kingsley Hazelwood, a second cousin of his own. Their marriage took place at St. Mary's, Brompton, in July 1864, the Charles Kingsleys, George Kingsley, and about thirty others being present. Mrs. Blunt records that they amused themselves after the wedding by playing croquet on the rectory lawn.

From Charles Kingsley's letters we learn that he liked neither the bride nor her mother, in fact that both he and Fanny deplored the connection. Henry's life from now on became a kind of treadmill for he had to support not only a penniless wife but a penniless mother-in-law. He had never been good at managing money and during his six years at Eversley had been free of domestic worries as his mother looked after him. Henceforth he involved himself in borrowings and debts innumerable. His letters to Macmillan from the time of his marriage are full of requests for advances on royalties to meet bills already incurred. In 1864 he writes, 'May I draw on Child's for my salary?' In 1865 he asks help in 'an alarming financial crisis'. In 1866 he *must* have money to pay his Christmas bills for he is 'terribly pinched'. 'Please make it safe for me to present a cheque at Child's.' In 1867 he says, 'I am without the ready. Can you pay me for *Silcotes* as we go along?' and in the same year, 'Could you pay £12 : 10 : 0 to my wife's solicitors?' In 1868 it is, 'Can you lend me £35 out of your private pocket?' In 1869 he begs for a further £22 for his wife's solicitors. One pathetic appeal must close the list. 'I am as poor as ever. Buy me body and bones.'

Q

When in the long run even kind Alexander Macmillan did not see his way to continue helping him with money advances, Henry appealed to outsiders, sometimes to friends of his brother, Charles. It would seem from letters written by Charles that both Sarah and her mother also wrote begging letters on their own account. It is little wonder that the marriage was looked upon as a disaster by the rector of Eversley and his wife.

While at Wargrave Henry Kingsley took to writing literary essays on Ben Johnson, Kit Marlowe, Andrew Marvell, Old Sussex Worthies, and the Fathers of the *Spectator*. They are very well written and the better written they are the more we note a decline in the quality of his novels. The essays are interesting in so far as Henry makes his taste known to all readers. He shows great familiarity with and appreciation of Dickens, hatred of Swift and all his works, intense dislike for 'that splendid little viper Pope', and warmest admiration for Addison. He feels about these men just as if they were alive and gives the impression not only of having read their works but everything available about them. He is far more sharp-edged than his brother Charles, whose essay-writing is often flaccid and styleless.

Henry's departure from Eversley had the effect of making Charles feel he wanted to write novels again, and he began to put together a story based on the exploits of Hereward the Wake who, outlawed for robbing a monastery, headed a rising of the English against William the Conqueror at Ely in 1070. That he merely revised and strung together notes made as an undergraduate is suggested by the fact that the sentences are short and the book more shapeless than *Westward Ho!* and more overcrowded with characters and incidents than *Hypatia*. Descriptions of fenlands and of birds living in sedge-fringed lagoons are less skilful than in *Prose Idylls*, written later and published earlier. *Hereward the Wake* gave Kingsley the opportunity of descanting on campaigns, clothes, customs and life in Ireland, Flanders, France, and all the other scenes of the outlaw's adventurings. The author probably did not think very highly of the production himself, as he allowed Fanny to arrange that it should appear serially in *Good Words*. Thomas Wright, the antiquary, whom he consulted during its composition wrote to him at some length objecting to the use of 'handkerchiefs' and 'fabliaux', told him that Windsor Castle was not built in Hereward's day and corrected him on certain anachronistic statements connected with the Confessor. According to Kingsley, Hereward's favourite mount was a mare called Swallow. Wright told him that no knight would choose a mare as a mount, but Kingsley stuck to Swallow, as he had read in some chronicle that she was the ugliest and fastest mare of all time.

Invited in January 1865 to be one of the University preachers at Cambridge, Charles Kingsley chose 'David' as the theme of his four discourses. In the first sermon on David's weakness, he interpreted true Christianity as 'a healthful, manful' religion, a religion that 'does not exalt the feminine virtues to the exclusion of the masculine'. He recognised a close resemblance between Hereward the Wake and David; both were mighty fighters, both sweet singers to the harp, and both sinned with a woman. In the sermons, as in the lectures, Kingsley managed to get in a thrust or two at monasticism and developed a theory, new to his audience, that the monks of the Middle Ages, in aiming exclusively at the *virtues of women*, copied little but their vices. According to Kingsley their strenuous efforts to unsex themselves diseased their mind and heart. They became personally cowardly, as their own chroniclers declare; querulous, passionate, prone to unmanly tears; at times cruel—cruel with that worst cruelty that comes from cowardice. He reminded his hearers that it was chivalry that saved the world from the pernicious results of monastic influence.

In May Mrs. Kingsley told John Martineau that her husband had had a delightful visit to Windsor and 'a long private interview with the dear Queen, who is certainly a most remarkable woman with priceless qualities of heart and mind that are little known'. He had preached to her on 'Ezekiel's Vision' and had also dined with her in private. It pleased her too to learn that at the Chapel Royal, St. James's, a select congregation had been 'electrified' by his sermon on 'The Wages of Sin is Death'. As his reputation in royal circles was augmenting so rapidly, surely some tangible recognition would soon be forthcoming!

Lady Knightley tells us that she was present at a service taken by Mr. Kingsley in the Queen's dining-room. It consisted of Litany, Communion, and a short sermon. The text of the sermon was, 'Say not thou, what is the cause that the former days were better than these? for thou dost not enquire wisely concerning this'. 'The burden of the song', says Lady Knightley, 'was that the nineteenth century with all its imperfections, is better than all that ever went before it and that we should make a great mistake if we tried to exchange. The language was good and the sermon very different from those one generally hears, but I don't think it was heart-searching or likely to do one much practical good.' [1]

During one of his sermons at Windsor a telegram was handed to the Queen. It announced the death of her much loved uncle, Leopold, King of the Belgians. The Crown Princess of Prussia, who was staying with her mother at the time, at once asked the preacher-poet to commemorate the sad event by writing some lines in her album. Very willingly did Mr. Kingsley inscribe the following impromptu in the book:

> A king is dead! Another master mind
> Is summoned from the world-wide council-hall,
> Ah for some seer, to say what lurks behind—
> To read the mystic writing on the wall!
> Be still, fond man: nor ask thy fate to know.
> Face bravely what each God-sent moment brings.
> Above thee rules in love, through weal and woe,
> Guiding thy kings and thee, the King of kings.

In June 1865 Mrs. Kingsley noticed signs of a coming nervous breakdown in her husband and somehow arranged that the family should transfer itself from Cambridge to the Norfolk coast where Charles could indulge himself in sea-shore studies and have a three months' rest from the pulpit. After this holiday he might be able to face the Eversley winter, a winter which, unexpectedly enough, was to bring an interest into his life that for the time being banished personal worries.

His brother Henry had spent part of the year in 're-narrating' tales of old travel for *Macmillan's Magazine*. Among them was

[1] Lady Knightley's *Journal* (1915).

one entitled *Eyre's March*, an account of a trek round the great Australian Bight undertaken by John Edward Eyre in 1840–1. Eyre was a man of enterprise and courage who had started life as a sheep farmer and was supposed to know more than any other white man about the aborigines of Australia. In consequence of his interest in their welfare he had been made official protector of natives for the Lower Murray. He did his work well, sparing no pains to save his charges from the squatters who formed a powerful pastoral aristocracy. So highly was he reported on from Australia that in 1846 the Secretary of State for the Colonies commended him to the Queen as Lieutenant-Governor of New Zealand, a post he filled satisfactorily for seven years. From New Zealand, Eyre was transferred to St. Vincent in the West Indies where he spent four years, leaving in 1861 to become Acting-Governor of Jamaica of which island he was appointed Governor in 1864.

Early in 1865 Mr. Eyre wrote to inform Mr. Secretary Cardwell in London that there was considerable unrest among the coloured people and that rebellion might be brewing. He did not, however, represent the situation as urgent or even of great seriousness. One has to remember in judging subsequent action on the Governor's part that the Indian Mutiny had only been suppressed after serious campaigning and that the memory of the Cawnpore massacre, like a black spectre, haunted the minds of English administrators the world over. The Mutiny had made civil and military authorities perpetually conscious of the fearful responsibilities attaching to the offices they held. There was also the memory in the West Indies of the wiping out of the white population by negroes in Hayti. The white inhabitants of Jamaica could hardly be expected to take an Exeter Hall view of such situations.

Towards Christmas 1865 reports began to circulate in England that there had been a mutiny in Jamaica. Letters from English officers, who had helped to quell it, contained the first news that reached the public. Henry Kingsley, who was living at Wargrave on the Thames, felt his creole blood rising within him when he heard a rumour that an insurrection had taken place necessitating the proclamation of martial law followed by a round-up of negroes. Some said that the ring-

leader had been hung, others that several hundred coloured
men had been put to death.

Mr. Eyre, the Governor, though he had warned the Secretary of
State for the Colonies of symptoms of unrest in the island, appears
to have been taken by surprise at the suddenness with which a
menacing state of affairs developed. It is not easy to put the
story together fairly, but such material as is available in reports
and official enquiries seems to indicate that the events which took
place in Jamaica in October 1865 originated as follows.

Jamaica at the time was divided into three counties, Surrey,
Middlesex, and Cornwall. The seat of government was at
Spanish Town in Middlesex, and the Colony was administered
by the Governor, his Council, and the House of Assembly.
One of the members of the House, George William Gordon, a
coloured man and a Baptist, had for some time regarded himself, and had been regarded, as the advocate of the rights of
negroes in the matter of land-ownership, taxation, and other
questions affecting their welfare. Though an avowed consti-
tutionalist, he was supposed to favour the elimination of white
rule and to wish to turn Jamaica into another Hayti. When
posters appeared in the county of Surrey urging negroes 'to
shake off their sloth, rise, and free themselves', it was presumed
that Gordon must be the author of them, just as it was presumed
that he must be the instigator of certain acts of violence against
the property of planters in the neighbourhood of Morant Bay
and Port Antonio in the county of Surrey. Gordon lived close
to Kingston and had an office in the town. On hearing that
the Governor in Council had decided to issue a warrant for his
arrest, he went to the general in command at Kingston and
explained that he had been working in his office during the
disturbances and was completely innocent of the offences of
which the warrant accused him. He placed himself unreservedly at the disposal of the authorities.

On October 7 a meeting of magistrates took place in the
Court House at Morant Bay, a small town to the south-east of
the Island. As a consequence of this meeting the chief magis-
trate, or Custos, issued warrants for the arrest of various persons
who had taken part in disturbances prior to that date. When
the warrants were about to be put into execution, resistance was

offered and the police were overpowered. The Governor, on learning of this, summoned his Council, but they were not quick enough in decision or action to prevent the very unpleasant occurrences of October 11 when negroes, armed with the cutlasses used for reaping sugar-cane, gathered in the square of the Morant Bay Court House while the magistrates were in session. On seeing them pressing forward in a threatening manner the local volunteers came up to protect the building. The Riot Act was read, the mob threw stones and the volunteers retaliated with a volley which brought some negroes to the ground. This enraged the rioters who attacked the handful of volunteers and overpowered them. The Court House was then set on fire and eighteen persons were killed, including the Custos. Over thirty persons were wounded. For those who had to maintain law and order it was altogether a very alarming business.

Governor Eyre, having learnt from Baron Ketelholt, a Dutchman living in Spanish Town, that he feared a situation might arise in which white men would be done to death, took prompt measures to anticipate such a contingency, and by advice of his Council proclaimed martial law at Morant Bay and despatched a hundred men of a West Indian Regiment to the scene of the rising. It appalled him to learn that his friend Baron Ketelholt had been beaten to death soon after giving him warning of impending trouble, that a white clergyman had had his tongue torn out before being killed, and that twenty-two volunteers had lost their lives. Great capital was afterwards made by the Jamaica Committee in London of the fact that no organised resistance was offered to the soldiers on landing at Morant Bay. By the time they got there, however, the worst was over, and the negroes, drunk with blood and wearing charms of white men's fingers, had dispersed, some said to burn the sugar crops.

I have before me the unpublished diary of a man on the spot. In his opinion the Governor was wrong in assuming that Gordon was responsible for the Morant Bay mutiny. Gordon had taken no ostensible part in inciting the negroes; indeed, on hearing that a warrant was out for his arrest he had, as we have seen, given himself up at Kingston. Notwithstanding this fact the Governor at once ordered his removal from

Kingston, where civil law still ran, to Morant Bay, where martial law had been proclaimed.

The court martial set up at Morant Bay was composed of two young naval lieutenants and an ensign in the West Indian Regiment. By this inexperienced and unsuitable tribunal Gordon was tried and sentenced to death. The sentence was approved by the Governor on October 21 and on October 23 Gordon was hanged, protesting to the end that he was innocent of disloyal conspiracy. On the day of his execution a general amnesty was proclaimed, though martial law remained operative till November 12.

No attempt was made by the rioters at Morant Bay to oppose the landing of the West Indian troops, but this parish was not the sole cause for the Governor's anxiety. It had been reported to him that negroes were out of hand in several plantations and that men and women in outlying districts had been murdered —a gentleman and his friends at Amity Hall, and a book-keeper at Blue Mountain. Petitions for protection from people scared by the irresponsible attitude of their employees were reaching him from all over the island. White families were said to be flying to the cane brakes or putting out to sea in boats. Some were being rescued by H.M.S. 'Wolverine', others by an American ship, 'Reunion'.

Eyre, who had never in all his career had to deal with a real crisis, now had to take decisions of enormous gravity. He knew himself responsible for protecting the whites from the annihilation they feared. There was no time to hesitate, so supported by his Council he decided for severity, the continuance of courts martial, and the rounding-up of negroes suspected of having taken part in the rioting or known to be disaffected. The net result was that four hundred and thirty-nine persons were put to death and over six hundred flogged, some of them women.

As soon as detailed accounts of what had happened reached England, Mr. Cardwell was besieged at the Colonial Office by deputations from the Aborigines Protection Society, the Anti-Slavery League, and certain Nonconformist bodies all urging that an immediate enquiry be held on the conduct of Governor Eyre in suppressing what some people called the mutiny and others the rioting in Jamaica. Mr. Eyre was temporarily suspended from office, and a commission of enquiry was sent to the Island to investigate and take evidence on the spot.

This Royal Commission, which held sittings from January to March at Kingston, after careful sifting of evidence and equally careful deliberative discussion drew up a report which commended the Governor for promptitude in action but blamed him for unnecessary rigour. When recalled to London by the home Government he found an unofficial Jamaica Committee ready to indict him for murder and cruelty. The Committee was composed of intensely respectable people. Its chairman was John Stuart Mill, who was supported by Professor Huxley, Herbert Spencer, Goldwin Smith, and Thomas Hughes, by this time Liberal member for Lambeth. Eyre, who had already lost his livelihood and had a wife and children to support, was stunned by the threat to his freedom involved in making him defendant in legal proceedings which aimed at bringing him to trial for murder.

To Henry Kingsley it was a matter of grave concern that the ex-Governor should be attacked in this way. After discussing with his brother and the Macmillans the possibilities of coming to his assistance they agreed to try and form an Eyre defence association. A fund for this purpose was started by Sir Roderick Murchison and supported by Alfred Tennyson, John Ruskin, Thomas Carlyle, and Charles Dickens. These men (with the exception of the last named) formed themselves into a committee. Carlyle had a talk with Eyre in London and found him 'visibly a brave, gentle, chivalrous and clean man whom I would make dictator of Jamaica for the next twenty-five years—something of the Grandison in him mildly susceptible'.[1]

To Froude, Carlyle said that the situation in Jamaica was that of a ship on fire which the captain by immediate and bold exertion had put out. He had then been called to account for having flung a bucket or two of water into the hold beyond what was necessary. He might have damaged some of the cargo, but he had saved the ship. The action of the Government seemed to Carlyle base and ungenerous, and as if unemployment

[1] *Carlyle's Life in London*, vol. II, pp. 328-9.

and disgrace were not sufficient punishment, Eyre was now threatened with persecution. He would help if he could, and beaten though he felt to the ground, would 'take weapon in hand again and stand forward with such feeble support as he could find for an unpopular cause, in defence of a grossly injured man'.

Froude says of himself that he was one of the cowards holding back, but that Ruskin was brave and spoke out like a man. Writing to Miss Bromley Davenport [1] Carlyle reported:

> Yesterday in spite of the rain I got up to the Eyre committee and even let myself be voted into the chair, such being the post of danger on the occasion, and truly something of a forlorn hope. . . . We seem so far as I can measure, to be a most feeble committee; a military captain, a naval ditto, a young city merchant, Henry Kingsley, Charles still laying back afraid, old S. C. Hall of the Art Union . . . a secretary who had bright swift eyes, but showed little knowledge of his element . . . I had to set my own shoulders to the wheel. . . . Poor Eyre! I am heartily sorry for him and for the English nation that makes so dismal a fool of itself.

The whole affair stirred Henry Kingsley's hereditary instincts and he did all that it was possible for a poor man to do. Charles was with him in spirit, though less anxious for obvious reasons to fight or get into the limelight. He believed Eyre to be a much calumniated man who had done his best in a terrible emergency, but he was constrained to inactivity from fear of attracting the notice of the press.

The proceedings instituted by the Jamaica Committee dragged on and on, for the bills of indictment they sponsored were always thrown out by the grand jury. Meanwhile Mr. Eyre was reduced to poverty. In 1872 the Liberal Government in office decided to pay the unfortunate ex-Governor the expenses he had been put to in defending himself against the various prosecutions to which he had been subjected. A resolution to this effect when put to the House of Commons was endorsed by a large majority. There seems little doubt that whatever mistakes he may have made, John Edward Eyre by acting as he did saved the British Government an infinity of expense and trouble,

[1] August 30, 1866.

and preserved Jamaica from the anarchical terrorism that had overtaken Hayti not so many years earlier.

All unpleasant thoughts about negroes were dissipated by a visit to the rectory during the autumn of 1865 of the Queen of the Sandwich Islands. In describing the novel experience of entertaining black royalty, Fanny Kingsley wrote to her sisters:

Eversley Rectory

Dear Queen Emma's visit has been one of the most interesting passages of one's life, & will ever remain in our memories as a very perfect & most strangely interesting event.—perfect because everything went well & smoothly, & she & *we*, & the Wellington College boys & Authorities were *perfectly satisfied*—strange—because the feeling of having a Queen, civilized & yet of savage even cannibal ancestry sleeping under one's roof, in Charlie's & my room—eating at one's table—talking of Tennyson & Tom Brown's School Days (!) of the delight with which she & the late King 'her dear Husband' had read 'the Waterbabies' to 'their little Prince'; strange—it was passing strange, & made me feel when she took my hand in the carriage as we stopped at the Railway Station going away, & with tears in her sad bright eyes said 'It has been such a real *privelege* to me being in Mr. *Kingsley's house & with you all*,' that we had been living for 28 hours in a dream! It was only on Friday that we knew she was coming—so we busied ourselves all Saturday in preparing for her that we might not have anything to disturb our minds on Sunday. I dashed over to the Wellington College Hotel to order a carriage & Posters for Monday & Tuesday & to the Head Master to make out our Programme; who in his turn announced it to the 6th Form (in which is my beloved Maurice now!) upon which Ponsonby the head of the school agreed to get up a Cricket Match for her Majesty, & the Choir proposed to get up a special Choral Service for the Chapel on Monday Night—this done I secured my waiter for the dinner, who was first to figure at the Luncheon at the Wellington & then to return in the Carriage to Eversley to look like a footman. This done, I returned, Susan being already plunged into the Plate Chest, out of which all the old Kingsley silver-handled knives & forks & dishes & cream jugs & candlesticks were rapidly exhumed. Rose & I plunged into the China Cupboard. Mrs. Hedges the old fat cook, assumed a royal air, & stepped into a small pony cart at the risk of her neck, to have a private interview with the Butcher & sit with him upon saddles of Mutton & joints of Beef (which I vainly endeavoured to persuade her wd. not appear as it was to be strictly a Russian Dinner). the Fishmonger was ordered to procure a Turbot or a whale if he cd. get one; Lord Eversley was written to for Fruit. Every body who came into the Kitchen received a hint, that Game wd. be acceptable & each of us assuming an air & step of Majesty, endeavoured calmly to suppress our strong emotion; & not be upset even by a Queen in this well regulated Parsonage—old furniture was humped into cupboards; windows cleaned, pink calico & white muslin were cut up regardless of Expense—& the Queen's Room (Charlie's & mine) soon looked very pretty—the Nursery sitting room was turned into a Bedroom for the Black Chaplain & Lady in Waiting who happily being man & wife can occupy one room. The suite usually consists of this Dark Chaplain (a delightful man) & the Lady in Waiting, an Aide de Camp (Brother of the Consul General at Hawaii) Major Hopkins by name, who acts as Secretary—a Footman (English) who has lived with the Queen 9 years, & a French Lady's Maid—& possibly dear Lady Franklin & her niece Miss Cracroft & Lady's Maid. I just arranged to hold them all by sending the Children Nurse & Disie to the Cottage. Well on Saturday Night, all was in progress—& we were calm on Sunday—but still Royal in our manners—Rose said the Cook's dignity was so great that she did not dare go into the Kitchen, & Susan was so grand—I was afraid of speaking to her—the children were all in Extacy.

I asked nobody to dinner but the Headmaster of the Wellington College Mr. Benson & his wife—& *Maurice*. No one to breakfast but the Under Secretary of State Mr. Murray (who lives in our Parish & who had been employed by our Queen to engage Emma's apartments in London & see to her comfort—) & Mrs. Murray—for I felt the dear Queen wanted quiet & comfort, & not crowds of people & hot rooms—for if I had asked *one* I must have asked all.

On Sunday morning we heard that Lady Franklin & her niece wd. not sleep which enabled our children to stay at home. On Monday morning, all the flowers were arranged—the house was *full* of flowers—and at 11 o'clock the sun shone out & we started Charles Rose & I dressed in our Sunday's best in a Basket-carriage to Wokingham—where the Queen's carriage with Grey Posters

& a very choice postillion were in readiness—also a cart for the
Luggage—& we crossed the line to await the Train—feeling not
a bit flurried but deeply curious & interested—at 12.27 the Train
came in—& Charles & the Station Master with heads uncovered
handed out Queen Emma & the most enormous dark (not to say
Black) Lady in Waiting 6 foot high.   Lady Franklin Miss Cracroft
& the Aide de Camp following—the Chaplain Mr. Hoapili cd. not
come.   I was presented & we all went to the carriages; into the
first stepped Queen Emma, Mrs. Hoapili & I—the Aide de Camp
& Charles on the box—Rose in our carriage with Lady Franklin
& her niece—the servants going straight to Eversley to strike
terror into the hearts of our maids who did not expect them till
4 hours later.   As we got into the carriages the rain began to
pour down & continued in such a deluge that no one cd. see an
inch of Country from the Windows.   It was despair! but Queen
Emma cd. just see enough of the Fern & Heather & Fir Trees
by the road side to interest her—and we talked of Mr. Walter &
the Times (going thro' his land) & of schools & Education &
Churches—& I said how kind it was of her to come to us, & she
said how kind it was of us to ask her—& in $\frac{1}{2}$ an hour we arrived
at the Great Gates of the Wellington, where the Head Master in
his gown, Mrs. Benson, (Sir Heron & Lady Maxwell who happened
to be there to see their boys) & the servants all in the old Duke's
liveries were ready to receive us.   The Great Gates were thrown
open Mr. Benson walked with the Queen, & I with matchless
presence of mind marshalled the procession sending Charles with
the Lady in Waiting, such a huge gentle savage, the Aide de Camp
with Mrs. Benson, &c &c   The rain poured in torrents, the
boys swarmed after us—but we were happily under the corridor.
first the Great School was visited—then a Dormitory—then the
Kitchens, the Library which is so full of the Queen's Gifts—the
Museum with many contributions from Lady Franklin—things
belonging to Sir John! the Cloak the old Duke wore at Waterloo
was looked at with deep interest—then the Exquisite Chapel—
Queen Emma asking the most intelligent questions about every
thing—then the Boys were to be seen in Hall at dinner.   This
was most interesting.   Queen Emma stood at the high Table &
asked in a low voice for a half holiday—upon which Ponsonby
(head of the School) said in a loud voice 'Three Cheers for Queen
Emma'.   It was the first time she ever heard English boys cheer—
& you may imagine her amazement.   It was a sound she said she

shd. never forget all her life.   She then tasted their pudding which enchanted them & after staying a few minutes we all went to the Head Master's house to Luncheon the little children meeting her with bouquets—from the windows of which we saw the first Eleven (my Maurice among them) preparing for the Cricket Match in pouring rain.   Oh! it was grievous—but after Luncheon Queen Emma put on a waterproof borrowed a pair of clogs & though she had a bad cough insisted on going down to the Boy's Pavillion & sitting to see the Match which interested her intensely. She had all the cricketing apparatus, pads & gloves &c brought to her & felt them & asked the boys questions about them which delighted them—& at 3.30 the carriages came to the Pavillion & we drove home, with the addition of the above mentioned waiter personating a footman.   The rain poured on—& all our poor people standing at their cottage doors cd. hardly get a glympse of the Queen's face—but when I told her how they wished to see her, she leant forward, & waved her nosegay to them.   When we got home I begged her to come up straight to her own room to rest for an hour & half before dinner which she gratefully did. We had to dine at 6 because of the Chapel Service—& in that hour & half I did all the dessert.   The table was very pretty—I used all my drawing room china for the Fruit & flowers—Lord Eversley's grapes & Melon were magnificent.   We were 12 at dinner—Queen Emma sat at the side in the middle between Charles & Mr. Benson & I opposite with the other people.   Rose & Maurice top & bottom.

I forgot to say when she arrived Mary & Granville met her at the door with a beautiful bouquet.   I had to do all the introductions & felt quite the High Chamberlain.   At 7.30 we all got into our carriages again & went to the Service which was beautiful. The reverent manner of the boys delighted Queen Emma who said they looked as if they never forgot they were in the House of God.   & after the Choral Service all the School went out except the Choir who sang the Queen a beautiful Anthem in Isaiah.   & then we came home—a pretty supper & tea was laid out.   & then I took Queen Emma to her room.   I was up at 6 putting in order & putting back my china into its place in the drawing room—so that the little dessert fraud shd. not be perceived.   at 9.45 Mr. & Mrs. Murray arrived—& at 10 Queen Emma came down with that look of sad dignity & yet perfect simplicity which so distinguishes her—& all the servants & children & Queen Emma's

servants & our School Masters assembled for Prayers in the
Drawing room.   We had the Psalm for the Day—reading verse
by verse—& a beautiful selection of Collects.   & when Charles
prayed for Jews Turks infidels & *Heathen* it gave one a most
peculiar feeling.   Then Breakfast, after which I went all thro' my
Autograph & Photograph Book with Queen Emma—she *knew
about every body* in such a curious way.   Then as she wanted to
write Letters & humbly asked if she might go with her Secretary
into the Dining room, we all retired giving her up the Drawing
room till Luncheon & having great fun ourselves with Mrs.
Hoapili who wrote in Rose's Book of Favorite things.   At 1
Luncheon & then to Wokingham—Charles & I with dear Queen
Emma & the others in our carriage.   *Most* interesting was our
conversation.   I wish I cd. tell you all instead of having lingered
over all these silly details—I hav'nt told you half or a quarter—
but must now stop.   All our servants & children were assembled
in the Hall as she went away—& a good many people on the Lawn
to see her get into the carriage.   And our people with hats off
at their cottage doors.   Oh! it was such pleasure except for the
thought of her *deep sorrows*.   She is a dear creature—we all quite
love her.   & her gentleness & dignity, & humility combined with
her cultivated mind & great powers of observation make a remarkable character.   I quite long to see her again . . . she was getting so
happy with us when she went that I cd. have cried to lose sight
of her.   I hope we shall have her dark Chaplain to preach here.
He preached admirably at Lord Charles Hervey's.

The enjoyment derived from the Royal Visit was great, but
the collapse, as far as Charles was concerned, was also great.
He had found it a strain to entertain Queen Emma.

In January 1866 a proposal to endow a Chair of American History was put forward at Cambridge.   Interest in the
United States had been stimulated in the University both by
Kingsley's lectures on the subject and by the Civil War.   Mr.
Yates Thompson of Liverpool had offered to endow the lectureship and Kingsley took up the idea enthusiastically and circu-
larised the M.A.s.   He was painfully aware how little was known
about the subject in England.   The University Library had
since his lecture course been supplied with American books,

and it seemed only natural that the books should be followed up by an American professor. The 'proposal', he assured his correspondents, had come from representatives of that class in America which regards England with most love and respect. Such men would not become propagandists of revolutionary principles. It seemed to him of the highest importance that English undergraduates should get 'to know as much as possible about a country destined to become the greatest in the world'.

In February 1866 he drafted what he called 'my Harvard address, a broadsheet':

> I trust that it will not be considered impertinent, if I, as Professor of Modern History, address a few words on this matter to the Masters of Art in this University.

He goes on to explain that the proposal comes from Harvard and should be looked on as a very graceful compliment.

> The gentlemen of Harvard are painfully aware of our ignorance about them.
>
> We need not fear americanisation or democratisation and we should not judge America by the Ku Klux Klan any more than we should be judged by the Newgate Calendar.
>
> Suppose that in the second century before the Christian era the Romans had offered to send a lecturer to Athens that he might tell what the new Italian State was like and what their intentions, laws, and customs were would Athens have been wise or foolish to reject it?
>
> A sensitive people like the Americans will be but too likely to take up our refusal as a national insult . . . we should be doing all in our power to promote mutual good will and understanding.

The proposal was rejected by the Senate of the University to the regret of many dons.

From Mrs. Kingsley's point of view the year 1866 was an agreeable one, though at one time she had been apprehensive lest Charles get himself into fresh trouble by backing so unpopular a cause as the defence of Governor Eyre. The fact that he did not take a very active part and that Carlyle and Tennyson, the laureate, were on the same side to some extent allayed her anxiety, but time was passing and there was still no bishopric or even canonry in sight. Visits to Wimpole, Ampt-

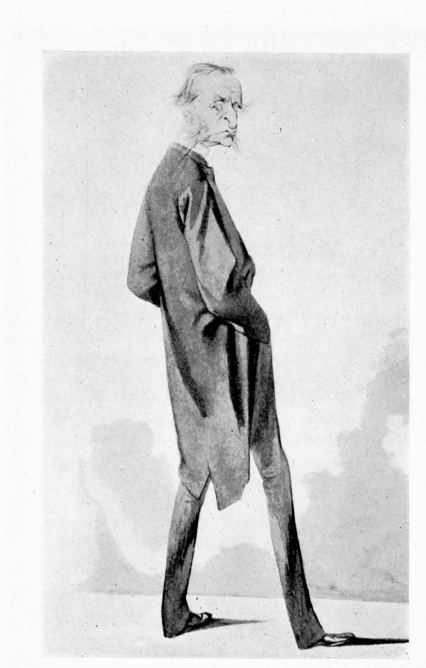

THE CANON OF CHESTER.

hill, and Woburn not only brought about important and agreeable social contacts but introduced Charles to the picture
galleries for which two of these houses were renowned. George
Howard (the future Lord Carlisle) who took him round the
Woburn pictures never forgot a remark made by Kingsley about
historical portraits: 'It was formerly the habit of portrait painters
to flatter their sitters by making them as like the reigning king or
queen as they could '. And it was the Professor, says George
Howard, who first initiated him into an appreciation of Greek
Art by showing him at Eversley a book containing repro-
ductions of the figures on Sir William Hamilton's vases.

Towards the close of the year Kingsley delivered two
lectures at the Royal Institution, published as *Health and
Education*, but at the time labelled *Science and Superstition*.
He also was given by Arthur Stanley his first opportunity of
preaching a sermon in the nave of Westminster Abbey. It
was entitled 'The Water of Life' and delivered in aid of the
Bishop of London's Fund.

The Austro-Prussian War of 1866 claimed Kingsley's interested admiration. Few Englishmen had believed Germany to
be justified in her invasion of Schleswig-Holstein in 1864 and
the fact that a Princess of Denmark had so recently come to
this country as its future queen had made everyone tend to
sympathise with the small country being bullied by the large.
Even Kingsley had been 'wroth' with the Prussians over it, but
in the new war with Austria he saw

> a great and necessary move for the physical safety of every North
> German household and the honour of every North German woman.
> To allow the possibility of a second 1807–12 to remain when it
> could be averted by any amount of fighting, were sin and shame,
> and had I been a Prussian I would have gone down to Sadowa as a
> sacred duty to wife and child and fatherland.

So he wrote to his dear Max Müller, who was a passionate
German patriot.

R

Chapter 18

METEORS AND HERMITS

Earth's crammed with heaven,
And every common bush afire with God;
But only he who sees, takes off his shoes,
The rest sit round it and pluck blackberries.

ELIZABETH BARRETT BROWNING

THE great meteor shower of November 1866 affected
Charles Kingsley deeply. In a state of high tension,
manifested by pacing the Eversley churchyard in 'trembling
excitement', he spent the night watching the display of 'red
meteors with bluish-green tails' as they sped through inter-
stellar space. To him the most striking, awful phenomenon
was their point of departure in Leo, where, again and again,
meteors appeared and hung for a moment, their tails so much
foreshortened as to be wholly or almost unseen. Thrilled to
the marrow by this display of heavenly fireworks, he decided to
preach his next Chapel Royal sermon on 'the pitiless laws of
Nature'.

Horrible, I say, and increasingly horrible, not merely to the
sentimentalist, but to the man of sound reason and sound conscience, must the scientific aspect of Nature become, if a mere
abstraction called law is to be the sole ruler of the universe; if, to
quote the famous words of the German sage,—If, instead of the
Divine Eye, there must glare on us an empty, black, bottomless
eye-socket; and the stars and galaxies of heaven, in spite of all their
seeming regularity, are but 'an everlasting storm which no one
guides'. It was but a few days ago that we caught a strange and
startling glimpse of that everlasting storm. . . . We were swept
helpless, astronomers tell us, through a cloud of fiery stones. . . .
Did the thought occur to none of us, how morally ghastly, in spite
of all its physical beauty, was that grand sight, unless we were sure
that behind it all there was a Living God . . . and the question is not
whether there be a God, but whether there be a Living God . . . a
King who is actually ruling His kingdom, or an epicurean deity who
lets his kingdom rule itself. Is there a Living God in the universe

or is there none? That is the greatest of all questions. Has our
Lord Jesus Christ answered it or has He not?'

The facts revealed by science 'or what the world calls Dar-
winism' fascinated him more and more. Writing from Cambridge to his 'dear and honoured master', Darwin, he said that
the younger dons were standing up to the new theories, and that
even the older ones were facing the whole question 'in a different
tone' from what they had done some time back. 'I trust you
will find the old University to be your firmest standing-ground
in these isles.'

Since Froude had to go to Spain to study archives, Kingsley
took over the editorship of *Fraser's Magazine* during his
absence.[1] This brought him into contact with new correspondents about articles submitted, rejected, and accepted and
gave him a good deal to do. By the summer he was ready for
a holiday and took it in Scotland ostensibly to attend the meeting
of the British Association at Dundee. He then spent over a
month paying visits to Mr. van de Weyer at Abergeldie Castle,
and to Mountstuart Grant Duff at Eden.

The meetings of the British Association took place at Dundee,
and its members were the guests of the University of St.
Andrews. At a banquet of welcome Professor Campbell of
St. Andrews proposed 'The Literature of Science', coupling
with it the name of Professor Kingsley. In responding the
Professor could only speak for 'the camp-followers of science'.
There was great applause when he said that he thought children
should be trained in what he called the scientific habit, that they
should be made to understand that in Nature the great Maker of
the universe was speaking even to quite little children face to
face; if the camp-followers of science could get a few little
children to understand that, they would save the British Association in the future a great deal of trouble. He was not very well
and found the racket of the Conference terrible; the continual
talking and the catching of the train into Dundee and back with the
steamer at Broughty Ferry thrown in, were altogether too much
and he was thankful to escape from the meetings and go fishing.
Though he wanted to catch salmon the weather was so dry

[1] March–April 1867.

that he began to listen to the gillie's stories of the Celtic hermits who had once lived in that part of Scotland. This localised interest led him on to study the subject of hermits in general and finally to publish a book about them.

While working on *Hypatia*, he had read the life of St. Anthony by St. Athanasius, that of St. Paul by St. Jerome, and those of many other solitaries of the desert. In epitomising the Athanasian biography, which is alleged to have converted St. Augustine, Charles inserted a spirited account of the history of Treves, a memory of his visit there with Henry fifteen years earlier. The essays on St. Anthony the Abbot and on St. Paul the Hermit were followed by short notices of St. Basil, St. Simeon Stylites, the European hermits, the Celtic hermits, and finally the English hermits, winding up in the fens with St. Guthlac who had been tormented by 'develen and gostes', and over whose dead body rose the mighty Abbey of Crowland.

Having recounted a great many of the legends connected with his subject the author, after 195 pages, feels bound to give us his own views. He has refrained from doing this earlier as he wanted to begin by saying, 'everything on behalf of those old hermits which could honestly be said to prejudice readers in their favour'. He does not himself believe in their wonder-working powers, and though one side of him no doubt would have liked to believe in the grave-digging lions which came to help St. Paul, aged 87, bury St. Anthony, aged 113, he concludes, 'The hermits worked no real miracles and saw no real visions. They had merely managed by continual fasts and vigils to work themselves up into a state of mental disease, a state in which the mind cannot distinguish between facts and dreams', and adds that 'the more pious and the more ascetic the man, the more utterly would their brains be in a state of chronic excitement'. And yet he has to admit that by giving up all that makes life worth living for the sake of becoming good and making others good, they must have accomplished something for their fellow men, and should not be accounted altogether negligible in the history of civilisation.

A far more congenial subject was dealt with in *Madam How and Lady Why*, a series of papers on geological matters, covering volcanoes, earthquakes, the ice-age, the testimony of the rocks and geological problems generally. These papers were written for Grenville and his schoolmates. They had been instigated by Fanny Kingsley, who was quick to realise that there was money in children's books. She had already sounded her friend the editor of *Good Words* on the subject, but like a sensible woman had kept quiet about this until Charles had occasion to go and see Strachan on other business. When offered £1000 for all rights in *Madam How and Lady Why*, he was tremendously surprised and wrote that evening to his Fanny, '*What* a wise woman you seem to have set me writing about physical science!!!'

One of Kingsley's favourite books was Lyly's *Euphues*, but when asked to provide a preface to a new edition he declined to do so saying he thought Sir Walter Scott had quite ruined it for the public by the travesty of Euphuism presented in Sir Piercie Shafton in *The Monastery*.

It was with disapproval [1] that Kingsley at this time read John Stuart Mill's denunciation of the doctrine of discrimination and superiority in race that we now call racialism. 'Men are not', he wrote to Professor Lorimer, 'congenitally equal.' A quarter of a century spent in educating parishioners, his own children and other people's children, had taught him that congenital differences and hereditary tendencies really existed. With characteristic impetuosity he went further and, taking the Irish Celts as an illustration, said that they seem to him entirely unfit for self-government and almost for the self-administration of justice involved in trial by jury. He was sure that no Roman Catholic country would ever be fit for constitutional government. 'Anyone who knows the difference between a French lycée and an English public school ought to know what I mean.'

Alluding to the House of Lords 'as representing every silver fork in Great Britain', *i.e.* all hereditable property as well as hereditable products of moral civilisation, such as hereditary independence, chivalry, and honour, he stated:

No elective body can represent the hereditary principle. The House of Lords are the true representatives of everyone who has

[1] December 17, 1866.

anything—a picture, a fork—a Yankee clock to hand to his children. Even Mr. Bright's house-plate and linen is represented by them. If the House of Lords were abolished Mr. Bright's children would discover the fact by the introduction of laws which would injure the value of all hereditable property, would tax (under the name of luxuries) the products of art and civilisation, would try to drive capital into those trades that supplied most necessities for back and belly, would tax the rich for the sake of the poor with very ugly results to civilisation.

At Cambridge he lectured in January on the Congress of Vienna, and then opened his course on the sixteenth century. These lectures were attended by about one hundred undergraduates who seemed to enjoy listening. Academic authorities, however, were not so easily pleased and criticised the lectures severely, as did two leading London newspapers. This discouraged Kingsley so much that he thought it would be best for him to give up his Chair. Fanny was very much puzzled by the persistence of the attacks made on him and worried at their stringency. 'One day', she says, 'when the secrets of all hearts shall be revealed will it be known how many young men owe the first dawn of a manly spiritual life to the very lectures on which severe strictures have been passed.' Charles tried to comfort her by saying that such attacks were a perfectly normal feature of university life and that any man who had attained any mark must expect to become a cockshy. This explanation only partly satisfied her, and she went on hoping that a way out of Cambridge might be provided by patronage of the highest kind.

It was known to her that the Queen would have desired long before this to see her well-liked chaplain translated to some sphere more suited to his preaching talent than a country parish. In private, Fanny's fancy strayed to a deanery or even a bishopric, but for the moment she had to exercise patience. When the Queen suggested in 1868 that Mr. Kingsley should be appointed to a vacant canonry at Worcester, she was informed by her advisers that 'the preferment of Mr. Kingsley just now, would be seriously prejudicial to Mr. Disraeli'.[1]

---

[1] *Letters of Queen Victoria*, 2nd series, 1926, vol. I, p. 519.

Disraeli had but recently become Prime Minister in succession to Lord Derby, and his tenure of office was threatened by Gladstone who soon afterwards carried a resolution against the Government by a majority of 65. Disraeli then tendered his resignation, but was persuaded to postpone a General Election until the autumn. At the General Election Gladstone and 393 supporters were returned as Liberal members, while Disraeli found himself at the head of 265 Conservatives. Fanny, though no Liberal at heart, was delighted with the result for it might mean that Charles would at last come into his kingdom.

For several months, seven or more, Kingsley worked on Comte, and the thesis he had evolved that through study of the phenomena of society we should be able to deduce sociological laws and construct a system of human conduct with almost the same degree of precision as Newton deduced his physical laws. What Comte set out to teach was no novelty to him and he was 'not dazzled', though he found it 'difficult at times not to be cowed by his self-sufficient glibness and cheerfully naïve sophistry'. His aim for his Lent term lectures was to take the work of three living teachers as revealed in their books, Maurice in *The Kingdom of Christ*, Carlyle in *The French Revolution*, and Bunsen in *God in History*, and to demonstrate that all three held one view while Comte held an entirely different one. Kingsley saturated himself in Comtism, and could not make up his mind as to its value. Was it definable as a Catholic framework devoid of Christian content?

After meeting Arthur Gordon again at the Shaw-Lefevre's house, Heckfield, Kingsley made up his mind to accept an invitation to go and stay with him at Government House, Trinidad. It might be possible for him to leave England in April and journey with him to Caracas. But for reasons that will presently transpire the trip had to be postponed till Christmas.

Though Kingsley's head may have been fully occupied with Comtism, he found time to try and brighten the life of his parishioners by providing a room for a club, where they could drink light beer and read the newspapers. For this club he collected books, organised readings, and set up a bagatelle board. All went well at first, but in the end the counter-attraction of 'the seven pubs of the parish' proved too strong and the club was deserted by those it was designed to please. A helpful curate of the name of Harrison (later to become his son-in-law) supported him at this time. Both he and the rector were great walkers and on one of their long tramps they came one day on a newly felled and very large tree. Kingsley stopped, looked at it, and to the curate's surprise burst into tears. 'I have known that tree ever since I came to the parish', he said.

Conducting the services of the church with the most reverent attention, he nevertheless noticed everything that happened during service. One Sunday morning on his way from altar to pulpit he disappeared from view and was found searching for something on the ground which when found he carried to the vestry—it was a battered butterfly. 'He prayeth best who loveth best' was a quotation often on his lips, and it was usually followed by, 'It is God's world not the Devil's'.

Harrison has left it on record that he never had to do with a more uncompromising opponent of Rome than Charles Kingsley. He seemed to draw his spiritual sustenance from everywhere and anywhere and had little sympathy with consistency in religious belief. The volumes on his study shelves were of all kinds from theological treatises to books on fly-fishing and voyages of adventure. One of his most prized folios was the works of St. Augustine given him by Carlyle, which had once been used by Sterling. Kingsley's favourite position for reading was lying in the hammock slung from beams in his study.

It was a very great pleasure to him and Fanny when Cowley Powles, after spending a few days with him at the rectory, decided to lease a house in the neighbourhood. He was shortly followed by John Martineau, who settled at Park Corner four miles away. This meant that congenial company was always available for both Fanny and Charles.

In April Kingsley wrote to the Master of Trinity (Dr. Thompson) to inform him that he had obtained leave from the Queen to resign his professorship and that he had already informed Mr. Gladstone of his decision and had received a very kind note in reply. An unpublished letter from Mrs. Kingsley to a friend indicates quite plainly that the Prime Minister had promised her husband preferment when a vacancy made it possible. She expresses the greatest relief at his retirement from the Chair at Cambridge and her joy that he should be back in 'his own dear little study freed from the necessity of *drudging* at lectures', and she was right, for it had been sheer drudgery for him to prepare them. In his letter of resignation Kingsley explained that he had had to work for eight or nine months to produce the twelve lectures he had delivered in the Lent term 'and was half-witted by the time they were delivered'. He had children to provide for and could not afford to waste time in this way. Time for him meant money and almost anyone else could do the work far better.

The great experience of his last term at Cambridge was attending the F. D. Maurice lectures on 'Conscience'. A clergyman, who sat next him while the lecturer was discussing the inadequacy of Bain's theory of conscience, says 'Professor Kingsley's fighting blood was evidently roused when Nelson's famous signal was referred to. I had to shrink into very small compass, for a strong right hand shot out straight from his shoulder, passed quite as near as was pleasant to my face. I looked and saw that Professor Kingsley could not see for tears.' The lecturer proceeded to quote Sir Hastings Doyle's lines on the sinking of the 'Birkenhead' and, the clergyman continues, 'at the end we all rose, as near to tears as anything else, and cheered'.

Visits were paid to Sandringham by both Fanny and Charles. On one of his preaching visits he took a sentence from *Euphues* as his text. 'The virtue, gentlemen, that maketh the poor rich, the base-born noble, the deformed beautiful, the subject a sovereign.' On another occasion he was taken out hunting and watched 'the Princess more beautiful than ever' jumping ditches. After dinner they played General Post and Kingsley was so scared when he found himself clutching a lady's wrist that fearing it might be the Princess he had caught, he staged a stumble and let go, but when the kerchief was pulled off his eyes he found it was 'only Lady Spencer'. That evening he had just undressed when the Prince of Wales came in to his room to ask him to witness his will, and they had 'an earnest touching talk together'.

On his next visit to London he met Mr. Longfellow at dinner.

Writing from the Crystal Palace, whither he had repaired for a day's rest, he says:

> I have seen Mr. Longfellow. The dinner last night went well. Tennyson was not there: but instead what was better Maurice and the Orator (W. G. Clark of Trinity) who had come all the way from Cambridge. Longfellow is far handsomer and nobler than his portraits make him. I do not think I ever saw a finer human face. I had an opportunity of telling him something of what we all felt for him, and of the good work he had done in England—and to get a promise out of him that he would come to see *us* when he comes back in May.

Kingsley at this time joined the National Education League and preached a sermon in London reminding his congregation that it is the disputes, not of unbelievers, but of Christians, which have made it impossible for governments to fulfil one of their first duties, namely to command and to compel every child in the realm to receive a proper education. He is quite alive to the work hitherto done by religious and voluntary bodies, but the voluntary system must be superseded because it is a failure. Thousands of children go to no school. In Birmingham alone 21,000 out of 45,000 youngsters grow up unlettered. Our social system must be condemned as nothing less than barbaric.

A visit to Dr. Perceval, head of the new public school, Clifton College, to attend a Social Science Congress, gave Kingsley a further opportunity of speaking his mind on this important subject. Henry de Bunsen, who was one of the speakers, said that in spite of his embarrassing stammer Kingsley managed to give a stirring address on compulsory education for both sexes and all classes. He doubted whether the education of the young should be entrusted to clergy at all, even to an ideal and perfect clergy. Their function should rather be to educate children in divine things, in their spiritual relations to God and to their fellow men. More than that he did not think it should be their duty to teach. He went so far as to confess himself the enemy of the denominational school as he believed it fostered internecine quarrelling among Christians and had hampered and must hamper successive governments in legislating for efficiency in education. He has but to state that 1,250,000 children are at that very moment growing up in illiteracy for his auditors to grasp how immediate and serious the problem is. After supporting the National Education League for compulsory education for a while, he later gave his warm approval to Mr. Forster's Elementary Education Bill of 1871 as an instalment of the reforms he longed to promote.

Chapter 19

HYMNOLOGY AND PROMOTION

It has been said that the true test of a hymn is that it would make a love poem, and the test of a love poem that it would make a hymn.   NOVALIS

BEFORE the humane atmosphere generated by the Tractarians had percolated into country churches, singing at morning and evening services, as we know from Charles Kingsley and many other incumbents of rural parishes, had been limited to the droning of the metrical versions of the Psalms printed at the end of the Book of Common Prayer. By degrees these chants were superseded by hymns with sentimental, gay, or even militant tunes. This change was not to Charles Kingsley's taste, for on the subject of hymnology he held definite if old-fashioned views. As a matter of fact he deplored the introduction of any hymns into the stereotyped service and would have gone back to the metrical psalms of his boyhood had public opinion not been against him. It was not with him a matter of prejudice so much as a firm belief that praise was best expressed in psalms, and that praise, not petition, should be set to music. He thought *Benedic anima mea* (Psalm civ) with its allusions to forests, beasts, and waters, *Laudate Dominum* (Psalm cxlvii) with its cosmic inclusiveness, *Laudate Dominum* (Psalm cxlviii) with its sweeping in of the elements, dragons, mountains, worms and feathered fowl, and best of all *Benedicite omnia opera* examples of songs of praise that could not possibly be improved on. The inclusion of hymns from various sources seemed to the austere rector to break up the unity of morning and evening services and introduce a personal note of prayer, often of suffering, into what should in essence be a pure and communal effort to praise God in His works.

Among the volumes of hymns in use at this date were Bishop Heber's *Hymns*, Keble's *Christian Year*, and the *Lyra Apostolica*, written by Newman, Keble, R. H. Froude and other authors of *Tracts for the Times*. These writers had made available to

English congregations many beautiful verses, notably the Greek hymn, *Hail, gladdening Light*, which was sung in the early Church at the lighting of the lamps, *Come, Holy Ghost, our souls inspire* (attributed to Charles the Great), *The Royal Banners forward go* (by Venantius Fortunatus, Bishop of Poitiers), and *All glory, laud and honour* (by Theodolphus), a hymn that ran only second in popularity to the *Te Deum*. Even Charles Kingsley came somewhat reluctantly to admit that these particular hymns did not infuse the service with the personal note he so much disliked.

By looking at the marginal comments made by him on Faber's hymns we may glean something of his fastidiousness. On one of the most romantic of them—

> Hark! hark, my soul, angelic songs are swelling
> O'er earth's green fields and ocean's wave-beat shore
>
> .   .   .   .   .   .
>
> Angels sing on! your faithful watches keeping,
> Sing us sweet fragments of the songs above,

he wrote, 'I have always objected to this hymn as a direct invocation of angels, and also as "unreal". People do not hear angels singing over fields and sea.' Of another Faber hymn—

> For thee, O dear, dear country,
> Our eyes their vigils keep;
> For very love beholding
> Thy happy name they weep.

he said, 'I have always objected to the first four lines of this hymn. Congregations do not lie awake or weep thinking of heaven. I dread all exaggerated language. It should be left for non-conformists.' But then nothing written by Faber really pleased him.

> O Paradise, O Paradise!
> The world is growing old
>
> .   .   .
>
> O Paradise, O Paradise!
> I want to sin no more
> I want to be as pure on earth
> As on thy spotless shore.

was condemned on its phraseology. 'I want to' was used
instead of 'I long', or 'I desire', and in a pernickety mood he
enquired where had the author learnt that the world was growing old?   Another hymn beginning,

> Sacred heart of Jesus
> Heart of God in man

provoked the comment, 'Surely the second line should run,
"Heart of man in God?" ' adding, 'Not by the conversion of the
Godhead into flesh, but by the taking of the manhood into
God—beautiful, but not for congregational singing.

All hymns tinctured with mysticism, puritanism, and romanism were according to Kingsley's standards inadmissible.   He
deprecated the adaptation of verses from the Canticles and
disliked the mention of vine, olive, or fig in the songs of a
country in which they did not grow.   Most of Kingsley's
objections were swamped when the great collection known as
Hymns Ancient and Modern made its appearance in 1861, for it
was soon adopted as the hymnary of the State Church.   But
although it might be declared the official hymnal Charles Kingsley still recoiled from such a hymn as that then attributed to
St. Bernard of Clairvaux, *Jesus, the very thought of Thee*, and
Jesus Thou joy of loving hearts, and he did not like Wesley's
Jesus, Lover of my soul any better.   Such verses were, he felt,
too personal and too warm.

Some of Kingsley's observations on the Canticles and the
Psalms give an impression of eccentricity.   He had always pronounced the 'Song of Songs' to be the highest tribute ever paid
to monogamy and *Domine, probasti* (Psalm cxxxix) was esteemed
by him as a marvellous essay on natural theology foreshadowing
and stressing the importance of the study of embryology, a
subject that at the moment he wrote was filling the minds of
Owen, Darwin, and Huxley.   When composing *Hypatia*,
Kingsley had made great use of the *Letters of Synesius*, but it
is doubtful whether the hymn written by this author, *Lord
Jesus think on me!*, so lovely in its simplicity and feeling, would
have found favour in his eyes.

There is no way now of ascertaining what hymns were usually
sung in Eversley church, but there is no doubt that Kingsley

was careful to supervise the choice. The sort of hymns that one imagines would have appealed to him strongly were *Onward Christian soldiers* and *Through the night of doubt and sorrow*, but we have not got his comments on them as they were only published in 1870 and only attained parochial circulation in the last years of his life.

Sir William Cope who was musical wrote an air, to match which Kingsley provided the hymn entitled *Easter Week*. 'I believe,' he told his patron, 'that Tom Moore's plan was the right one, that the air should inspire the poet and not the poet the air.' In a tiny note he once insisted that his whole name— The Revd. Charles Kingsley should be printed on the cover of the hymn as he did not approve of the 'modern custom of alluding to poets and writers simply by their Christian and sir-names.' At the London Library Mr. Charles Kingsley corrected an assistant who addressed him thus, with 'the Revd. Canon Kingsley by your leave'.

Another Church question that engaged Kingsley's attention at this time was the proposal to delete the Athanasian Creed from the Articles and Prayer-Book. When invited to join a committee for the defence of the Creed he consented, despite the fact that he had in the past signed addresses to Archbishops recommending modification of its damnatory clauses. The idea of jettisoning the Creed was more than he could bear; he would far sooner have no alterations than deprive public worship of 'that precious noble creed'.

In a very English, and it would seem unpractical, way the committee called meetings in defence of the Creed. At a gathering of citizens in St. James's Hall this doctrinal, philosophical matter was discussed as if it were a question of practical politics, and part of a letter written by Charles Kingsley to the committee was read aloud to a rather surprised audience. He advised that a fresh weapon should be used in defence of the Creed 'by bringing forward a somewhat neglected Catholic doctrine, that of the intermediate state'. He went on to explain that he had always held this doctrine, though it had been put out of most people's minds by the Romish variation known as Purgatory. There was no doubt that the Creed had been drafted by one who believed in an intermediate state. 'I have reason to believe,' he added, 'that the English mind is specially ripe just now for receiving once more this great Catholic doctrine.   Unless this course is taken, we shall lose to our extreme injury not only the so-called "damnatory clauses", but for all practical purposes the Creed itself.'   This communication caused a sensation; no one quite knew how to take it or how to reply.

To follow Kingsley closely along the theological byways he traversed would be neither an easy nor a profitable task, though it is clear, in this particular instance, that his old desire to weaken or eliminate the damnatory clauses was at the back of his intervention.   He was always double-crossing himself intellectually and losing his way in a maze of inconsistencies.   The American writer who said that Charles Kingsley's strong influence was due to the fact that he never did any thinking, but always spoke from the heart at the inspiration of the moment, explains these vagaries in so far as they are susceptible of explanation.

In writing to John Stuart Mill to acknowledge the receipt of *The Subjection of Women* Kingsley tells him what a deep pleasure it is to him to find 'many passages in which you treat of what marriage ought to be, and what marriage is, corroborating opinions which have for more than twenty-five years been the guides and safeguards of my own best life'.   A fortnight later he accepted an invitation to attend the first Women's Rights meeting called for the following month.   He is extremely anxious to discuss with Mill the whole question of 'woman' as his own ruling idea has always been that which his friend Huxley had lately set forth as common to himself and Comte— that the reconstruction of society on a scientific basis is not only possible but the only political object much worth striving for.

I beg you to do me the honour of looking on me, though (I trust) a Christian and a clergyman, as completely emancipated from those prejudices which have been engrained in the public mind by the traditions of the monastic or canon law about women and open to any teaching which has for its purpose the doing woman justice in every respect. . . . Mrs. Kingsley begs me to add the expression of her respect for you.   Her opinion has long been that this movement must be furthered rather by men than by the women themselves.

HENRY KINGSLEY

Gladly did Kingsley accept an offer of hospitality from Mill for the night of the Women's Rights meeting.   On his return from London he told Fanny that he was as much struck with his host's courtesy as with his vast learning.   'When I look at his cold, clear-cut face, I think there is a whole hell beneath him, of which he knows nothing, and so there may be a whole heaven above him.'

Mill's book made many converts, among them Lord Houghton, who signified his conversion by promising to sit on the platform at the meeting.   Kingsley wrote to him before-hand telling him of the satisfaction he derived from thinking that so influential a man should become a platform supporter of Women's Rights.

A few weeks after this meeting the Kingsleys' private horizon was irradiated by the promise of promotion.   At long last Fanny's efforts on Charles's behalf were to come, at any rate, to partial fruition.   In a letter to her 'dearest Miss Bulteel' Mrs. Kingsley says:

> The Queen has most kindly given him [Charles] the vacant canonry at Chester which lapsed to the Crown on the elevation of Dr. Moberley to the see of Salisbury.   It is not a rich canonry, being £500 a year, but it enables us to remain at Eversley and to have a nice change once a year for three months . . . a good furnished house which the four canons inhabit by turns.   It will be a rest from the heavy work of the professorship.

The canonry was a by-product of Mr. Gladstone's electoral victory and it was Mr. Gladstone who wrote on August 13, 1869:

> I have much pleasure in proposing to you that you should accept the Canonry of Chester, vacated by the appointment of Dr. Moberley to the see of Salisbury, and if you agree, I need not impose on you any obligation of even temporary secrecy, as I know that the act will be very agreeable to her Majesty.   The cathedral of Chester is under an energetic Dean, and nave services are now carried on in it with excellent effect.

There can be no doubt that it was a great support to the self-respect of both Mr. and Mrs. Kingsley when the stall at Chester was offered to them.   It was not a first-class appointment nor

S

one that would give a preacher the chance of influencing the great world; but it was better than nothing, for Charles was just fifty and, except for the honour of having been appointed Chaplain in ordinary to the Queen ten years earlier, had received no preferment of any kind, though, as he often reflected, other parsons, less literary than he, slipped into deaneries and canonries without having to wait.

Alexander Macmillan, in writing to Henry Kingsley in August 1869, said in a postscript, 'Delighted to learn Charles has a Canonry. It should have been something better.' And that was Fanny's private opinion too.

At Chester there was a slight trepidation over the appointment, for Dean Howson, having read *Yeast*, was aware that Kingsley held strange views as to the use a cathedral might be put. To the Dean the new Canon, being also responsible for *Alton Locke*, loomed up as something of a subversionist. Would he upset the Chapter, and how would he manage to fit himself in with the staid round of duties entailed by his new post? In November his curious fears were allayed. The new Canon came among them, and seemed most orthodox and fair spoken, docile and perfectly amenable to the atmosphere of the precincts. After the formalities of installation had been gone through Kingsley took his leave, assuring the Dean and Chapter that he would return in plenty of time from his trip to the West Indies to take up his duty in May, June, and July of the following year.

Preparations for the voyage to the Caribbean occupied him during December and he arranged in advance to contribute 'Letters from the Tropics' to *Good Words*. The Reverend William Harrison would take care of the parish in his absence. The attraction of the West Indian islands had always been dormant in Kingsley's mind. His mother's stories of her girlhood there, her cabinet of coloured shells, vegetable coral and scarlet seeds, shown to good children on Sundays, had set the islands apart in his mind as a kind of secret garden. When the chance had come to him unexpectedly at Heckfield of going to stay with Mr. Arthur Gordon, the Governor, he accepted it with glee. Mr. Gordon was married to Miss Shaw-Lefevre, daughter of his neighbour, the Speaker, and had just been warned of his coming appointment as Governor of Mauritius, so it was Kingsley's last chance of being with him in Trinidad. The prospect of spending two months in the tropics was like the realisation of a dream.

The rector first set foot on land at St. Thomas where, hurling himself into a bum-boat, he made feverishly for the shore to be overpowered by the luxuriance of nature—'the first tropic shells, the first orchids, the huge green calabashes—playthings of childhood [he was writing to his mother] the flocks of pelicans, the flying fish!' It was a land of enchantment.

Again on Christmas Eve he wrote to his mother:

> Here am I writing with a fan-palm looking in at the window 6 ft. off and an orange and flower fence next to pines at the bottom of the dell and over the house an enormous tree: above that hills dotted with grey palms.
>
> Hindoo prisoners, some with felon marked on their backs make excellent outdoor servants, a wilderness of tame monkeys, a young jaguar, ditto puma, a toucan all the colours of the earth, a spider monkey hanging on by its tail among creepers a Duke would give any money for, warm water pouring out of the cloud in pailsful, a ruffling breeze which makes the fan-palm rattle like a lot of loose boards and at night frogs and fire-flies by the thousand with a spice of mole-crickets and mantises, oh, it is the queerest paradise. But a paradise it is and a most healthy one so make yourself easy about us and send this on to Fanny. I delight in the coolies who are graceful and well-mannered and will be the saving of the West Indies I verily believe.

The 'Letters' contributed to *Good Words* (eventually to appear as the book, *At Last*) were edited by Fanny who had remained at home to look after the children. Charles made his letters as realistic as possible, since he had to explain much to Fanny and even more to the readers of *Good Words* who knew even less than she did. He loaded the first part of his narrative with history and when he reached port invited readers to consider the July day of 1498 on which Columbus caught his first glimpse of the three hills to the south-west of the island. Reminded of the Trinity, he forthwith named the island Trinidad. The next picture is of Sir Robert Dudley in ruff and trunk-hose going about among 'gentle people all naked and painted red'. Sir Robert soon tired of idly waiting for the arrival of Sir Walter Raleigh, and sailed away to plunder Spanish ships and hunt for El Dorado. Before leaving Trinidad, however, he put the Spanish 'Corps de Garde' to the sword. Kingsley ploughed through the rest of the island's story till he had shepherded it into British hands. He then felt free to give his own impression of the place.

Port of Spain was a place of 'multitudinous stinks' and he was furious that no one had told the denizens of the port that cholera and even yellow fever derived from odours less appalling than those that assailed his nostrils. The coarseness of the young negresses nauseated him. How immodest and 'incondite' was their behaviour! 'I'm afraid I don't like negroes,' he wrote home, 'specially the women', but it was too painful a subject for him to enlarge upon. Presently he stifled his moralisings and allowed himself to revel in the treasures of the Botanic Gardens, to listen to singing fish, to gaze at the flaming draperies of bignonia and the curtains of scarlet morantia.

The communion service at which he officiated on Christmas Day seemed to him inspired with the true spirit of equality, and it was with a full heart that he watched persons of all ages and shades of colour kneeling side by side in great humility. When asked to preach a Sunday sermon he found himself addressing a very smart congregation of Chinese ladies and brown ladies all arrayed in Paris bonnets and voluminous skirts of satin and brocade.

Kingsley got home in March and felt the rigour of the Eversley climate 'almost as cruelly' as did his son Maurice back from South America. At once the Canon began to prepare his May sermons for Chester, sermons that were so great a success that 'whole cathedral congregations went wild about them'. Fanny records that Charles found the 8 A.M. and 5 P.M. daily services a great help as 'they seemed to anchor his soul'. In order to avoid interruption from oversea visitors he had taken to reading in the Chapter House, but Americans would catch a glimpse of him sometimes owing to the verger's habit of pointing him out as one of the sights. They led a quiet life and they did not dine out as Charles liked going to bed very early and anyway had to lecture on two evenings of the week. Not long after his arrival a bishopric fell vacant and tongues began to wag. It was certain that their renowned and eloquent Canon would be promoted, said the people of Chester, but nothing happened and Kingsley jogged on very contentedly with his new duties.

Less than a week after the Canon had completed his first term of residence at Chester the Franco-Prussian War broke out in Europe. It was an exciting moment for Charles when he learnt that his brother, Henry, was to go abroad as correspondent for the *Daily Review*, an Edinburgh paper of which he had been for some months editor. This gave the Canon an even more personal interest in the conflict than he had had in the Crimean War to which his brother-in-law, Sydney, had made two visits.

At once he wrote to Sir Charles Bunbury, 'Were I a German I should feel it my duty to my country to send my last son, my last shilling, and, after all, my own self to the war, to get that done which must be done, done so that it will never need doing again'. To Max Müller he wrote more emotionally, 'Accept my loving congratulations to you and to your people. The day for which dear Bunsen used to pray, with tears in his eyes, might not come till the German people were ready, has come, and the German people are ready.' Many people of his acquaintance turned out to be unqualified admirers of Germany. To Professor Freeman, who had attacked Kingsley over his Roman and Teuton lectures, the war seemed the most important historical event since the French Revolution and, on the strength of it, the two men became warm friends.

Feeling as he did about the glory and exaltation of battle, it required some self-control on Charles's part to reconcile himself to remaining quietly at Eversley while Henry was preparing to go to France. The monotonies of parish life became unattractive in the extreme as his bellicosity welled up within him.

Henry, who seems to have had no official pass of any kind, left Rotterdam for Luxembourg on August 7. There he learnt that the French had suffered one set-back after another. No one in England had told him that Douay's division had been crushed at Wissembourg, and Macmahon defeated at Froeschwiller, both by the armies of the Crown Prince. As details and accurate bulletins were not available, Henry made up his mind to try and get to Metz where it was reported that Napoleon III was forming the Army of the Rhine. From high ground to the north of the city he viewed 'the splendid cathedral riding like a ship in full sail above the sea of forest'.   He knew nothing at all about the situation and so lay down ear to earth and eyes on Metz waiting for something to happen.   Stray Englishmen turned up along the front on the same errand as himself, Sir Henry Havelock, for instance, at one moment and Auberon Herbert at another.   They enquired of Henry Kingsley what he had seen, what he knew, and then trudged on to try and find out more for themselves.

Like many English people Henry Kingsley was a firm believer in the capability of the French Army to win battles and he was puzzled at first to realise that it was not doing too well. He could not have known, for probably the German High Command alone was in possession of the information, that the French Command was nerveless and incompetent, still less could he have known that when Napoleon III handed over control of the Army of the Rhine to the incapable Bazaine, that Marshal had, after some hesitation, decided to retreat towards Verdun and ordered the whole French Army to march on Gravelotte without taking the trouble to find out whether the road was still open or not.   As Henry Kingsley says, 'I was on one side of the hill north of Metz and poor Bazaine the other. He believed the country to the north was open when it concealed 120,000 Germans!'   Henry had discovered for himself that communications between Metz and France had been completely severed and was not surprised when the unfortunate French troops having just got clear of the fortifications were given the counter-order to retreat into Metz.   By the action at Gravelotte and the engagements that led up to it the fate of the French Army was sealed.   The equanimity with which Marshal Bazaine accepted defeat combined with the misleading reports he was transmitting to his government caused those in charge of National Defence to order their last bodies of organised troops to move to Malmédy, a decision which resulted in the disaster of Sedan.   In his novel, *The Harveys*, published in 1872, Henry gives an account of the glacis and fortifications of what he calls the 'land Gibraltar of Luxemburg', and tells of the commandant sitting in the Café de l'Europe while 500,000 Germans hunt 300,000 Frenchmen past his frontier at Esne.

With glengarry on back of head, hands in Norfolk jacket pockets, and knapsack on back, Henry strolled about the countryside sometimes meeting Prussian Hussars feeling their way from one patch of forest to another, sometimes watching Brandenburg Cuirassiers in their scarlet tunics, sealskin busbies with scarlet cap, lunching on the grass beside their tethered horses. Long before he had finished admiring their gay appearance they would be up-saddled and cantering away. By dint of cadging lifts off anyone who was heading in the right direction Henry Kingsley actually managed to watch Macmahon fighting on September 1 and 2 with his back to the Belgian frontier. Wave after wave of Germans swamped the French under his very eyes. 'It must be the greatest battle in the world,' he remarked to the casually encountered *Times* correspondent, Captain Maclaine. Ziethen Hussars and Saxon infantry he recognises as he began to follow the track of the by now fugitive Emperor. On the fields around Sedan he seems to have derived a melancholy kind of satisfaction from gazing on 'hecatombs of rotting dead' as well as 'thousands and tens of thousands of prisoners'. How he wished the Emperor could be at his side to see what he is responsible for. He really ought to come and have a look at his work, 'for', as he continued ironically, 'the sight of it is immensely beautiful: the dead men look so pretty from a little distance they group themselves as they fall, and even when they crawl away to die, they look well, for death is generally beautiful'.

The French had certainly been outnumbered and outgeneralled but they had not been outfought, Henry Kingsley was sure of that. The trouble was that the Germans had prepared their campaign too thoroughly, they knew the ground too well and the French scouting had certainly been appallingly inefficient. The way the German artillery fired over the heads of their infantry was altogether too accurate, too deadly. The barrage struck him as horrific. With strange ghoulish satisfaction did Henry congratulate himself at being on the scene 'of the grandest slaughter which the world has ever seen'. At Ulm 40,000 had capitulated; at the passage of the Beresina 30,000 had been killed, but at Sedan '80,000 have capitulated and it is said there are 40,000 dead'. But what chance had men armed with the *chassepôt* that fired but a little bullet against the *Zundnadel-gewehr* that fired a bigger bullet of higher velocity? We may see in Daumier's grim caricatures that Frenchmen of the day were under no illusion as to the chief technical cause of their defeat.

The approach and the boulevard of trees that led to the gates of Sedan are journalistically described. On either side of the road horses were picketed and eating hay, while 'a blonde Ritt-meister inspected their condition'. Doffing his glengarry, Henry enquired whether it was permitted to enter Sedan. 'By all means!' was the reply, and as he advanced he took note of the unaccountable numbers of muzzle-loading French cannon. As the gates of Sedan were closed he made his way into the town through an open sewer to find as many disarmed French as armed Prussians crowding the streets. In trying to make his way to an hotel he had to wait till a column of 12,000 prisoners had passed. They looked tired and dejected as they shambled along, but every now and again one of them managed to swagger by in a devil-may-care sort of way. By this time Henry was half mad with thirst. The sweltering heat and an empty stomach made him very anxious to obtain food, but when he entered the hotel he found nothing could be ordered by a vagrant like himself; though he was allowed to drink wine. With two French officers as 'beaten as the men who fought at Thermopylae', he had some conversation. 'Vae victis! Glorious old France is not dead yet!'

Unlike the military doctor with whom he spent some time examining corpses, Henry found himself always on the verge of arrest, since he had no credentials of any kind to show. The only wonder is that he was not clapped into prison as a spy. With horrid gusto he described the sun-blackened faces of the dead, and the red cloth of trousers blended with bleeding entrails. 'Forty thousand men of the pretty French army lie out on the hill-side a mere heap of rags, bones, entrails, and brains.' What an overrated business was *la gloire*!

Henry, with his inherited love of flowers, was interested to find that the desolate, trampled countryside was remarkable for two herbs, clover and autumn crocus. The crocus grew on the very bosoms of the dead, on the earth of their graves, just as the dwarf iris had done in the wild Crimean spring of 1854. With the exception of 'these two brave plants' the land was utterly brown for miles and miles, its only garniture here and there a helmet, a shako, a leather strap, or the *petits-livres* of the dead Frenchmen. Fresh battlefields are everywhere of an identical monotony and no one who stumbled through Nonne-boschen Wood a few weeks after the conclusion of the first world war or saw the rags and bones being dug up at Hill 60 and on Vimy Ridge can feel anything but horror for the criminality and folly that can organise such deliberate waste of young lives. In the 1914–18 war visitors to the battlefields spoke much of the beauty of the flaming Flanders poppy. In the last world war no one seems to have noticed whether the ground was putting forth flowers or not.

Coming home, Henry found himself discharged by his paper and penniless. Till he could get something ready for the press he must have money, and at this point we become aware through correspondence of his machinations to this end. First he borrowed money from his near relations and then when their lending capacity gave out began to write appeals to persons he knew but slightly, if at all. Finally he approached the Royal Literary Fund. Of these activities and the embarrassment caused to Charles by his brother's methods of raising money we have ample evidence. A letter written to Lord Houghton in 1871 professes to give the reason for his insolvency. It begins 'My Lord' and the second paragraph runs like this:

In 1865 I had lost everything, since then I have been making a severe and terrible struggle to put matters right. I have nearly succeeded, and should in fact be comfortable with £200. But I have been writing against time in the newspapers for an income and have been republishing things out of my portfolio which in better times would never have seen the light at all. *This will not do*. People naturally suppose that I have written myself out, whereas the simple fact of the matter is that these later things were all written before my hand was as good as it is now. The only new novel in four years is *Oakshott Castle*, which Macmillan and Bentley competed for without looking at it, (Macmillan saw the first chapter) Macmillan has got it, and I am to finish it off by March. Meanwhile I am unable to live. Macmillan's firm will not back me on with any advance on a novel not yet written, and my only hope of making a fine thing of it is to appeal to some member of the literary guild of which I am a humble member for temporary assistance. *My brother* is quite out of the question. Pray never hint to him about this letter. As my wife and I sat with blank faces looking at one another and wondering what would become of us, she said suddenly, 'Write secretly to Lord Houghton and ask him whether he will help us over the style [!]. Tell him in a manly way how you are situated and how you refused to relieve yourself of your difficulties by law, but insisted on working them off, then ask him what he can do for you.' I have done so.

£40 would be a perfect godsend to us now my Lord: we shall inherit about £12,000 in a few years: *I could not undertake to repay such a loan out of my next novel*, but I could bind myself to do it within a year. If you could help to keep me alive and slightly free from worry until *Oakshott Castle* is done, I honestly venture to think that you would have served literature by £40. Whatever you do let the secret of this application remain in your own bosom. How bitter it has been to make it even to *you*, you may guess

Yours ever my Lord,

HENRY KINGSLEY

A receipt for £30 was sent to Lord Houghton on January 2.

It was some months before Charles Kingsley began to realise in what manner his brother Henry was trying to raise money. For some reason he began by assuming that Mrs. Henry Kingsley was the writer of the begging letters. On hearing that Henry had asked Lord Houghton to support his application to the Royal Literary Fund for a grant, he wrote:

I have reason to believe that my brother's wife, Mrs. Henry Kingsley has been in communication with you on a subject on which she is wont to have communications with many persons and that you have behaved with your accustomed kindness and generosity. If this be so let me entreat you not to do so again or to entertain any proposal either from her or from her mother Mrs. Hazelwood (who is equally likely to trespass on your good nature) without referring to me, who am intimately acquainted with the true state of my most industrious, but most unhappy brother's affairs, and also have known all about these two women for some 20–30 years.

Lord Houghton in replying to this letter stated that he had personally lent Henry Kingsley money and that it puzzled him exceedingly to know that his writings did not supply him with an income big enough to live on. Charles Kingsley at once wrote:

> Your letter filled me with grief and astonishment. I was alluding to what must be quite a different matter, having heard that you had helped him to obtain a grant from the Literary Fund.
>
> You had a right to express your astonishment that his writings do not supply him with the needful comforts of life. The only persons who can solve the mystery are the two women who have both him and his earnings in their power.
>
> Let me entreat you to tell me the amount of what you were so kind as to lend him. My honour and conscience will not be satisfied until it is repaid.

Two days later Kingsley wrote again thanking Lord Houghton for his reply to his communication and then continued:

> But in justice to my poor brother and others I must assure you that neither he nor any one of the family mentioned the Literary Fund to me. The matter came out *vi necessitatis*, in enquiry into certain affairs, and I was quite unaware that such secrecy attended the transactions of the Fund. I therefore only am to blame. I have spoken of it to no one but you; and I, of course, shall not do so.

The Royal Literary Fund made no difficulty about coming to the assistance of Henry Kingsley. In all, three separate grants were made to him of which the society holds record.

Chapter 20

WESTMINSTER ABBEY

When all the world is old, lad,
And all the trees are brown;
And all the sport is stale lad,
And all the wheels run down,
Creep home, and take your place there
The spent and maimed among
God grant you find one face there
You loved when all was young.

CHARLES KINGSLEY

ONE August day in 1871 the smiling face of the Prince of Wales looked over the gate at Eversley rectory. He had come from Bramshill which at the moment was being used as a camping ground by the 10th Hussars. The informality of his visit and his genial friendly greeting gave the rector enormous pleasure, for he had the feeling of a family retainer for his 'young master'. When, a few weeks later, the Prince was struck down by typhoid, Kingsley called his flock together in daily intercession for his recovery. So anxious did he become during the critical period of the illness that he found it impossible to remain at Eversley and went to Lynn whence he could walk over daily to Sandringham to get the latest news which he at once telegraphed to his wife, who in her turn posted it up as a bulletin in the village shop.

The great anxiety and sympathy shown by the public and their relief when the Prince was pronounced out of danger were alluded to by Charles Kingsley in a sermon preached at the Chapel Royal, which he made the occasion of a plea for sanitary reform. Since the Prince Consort had died of the same illness eleven years earlier, more than 200,000 persons had been swept away by this preventable fever. He reminded his congregation that no one could be said to be immune no matter what their position or worldly circumstance. The Prince had sickened as poor men sicken, he had been brought to death's door like any pauper, and, because of the danger to which the heir to the throne of England had been subjected, it became an imperative duty to deliver his countrymen from dirt, overcrowding, insanitary conditions, and needless death. No fetid alley or malarious ditch must be left to poison cities, his congregation must see to that. A precious life will not have been imperilled in vain if they will all act promptly according to their opportunity. England must somehow be transformed into a cleaner country for it would then become a happier one for all.

As one of the chief spokesmen of the better health for the people campaign, Kingsley was at this time asked to compose a hymn to be sung at the laying of the foundation stone 'with masonic rites' of the working men's block of the Queen's Hospital at Birmingham. The following lines were written for the occasion:

> Accept this Building, Gracious Lord,
> No temple though it be;
> We raised it for our suffering kin,
> And so, Good Lord, for Thee.
>
> .   .   .   .
>
> Oh hasten Lord that perfect day,
> When pain and death shall cease;
> And Thy just rule shall fill the earth
> With health and light and peace.
>
> .   .   .   .
>
> When ever blue the sky shall gleam
> And ever green the sod;
> And man's rude work deface no more
> The Paradise of God.

The verses were made on a well-worn pattern, but they were much liked and enthusiastically sung by a choir of 1000 voices. So much impressed were the citizens of Birmingham at Canon Kingsley's success in inoculating his flock at Chester with a conviction that sanitary reform was an essential factor in civic life and Natural Science the most important of modern studies that they persuaded him to become President of their Midland Institute.

As an interesting speaker and a public figure Kingsley was at this time called on to address all sorts of gatherings. At

Woolwich he spoke at the commandant's request and chose 'what the Germans call *Erd-kunde*' as his theme. By these words he did not mean collecting weeds or butterflies, but the history of Nature herself, 'to show for example that no man can now be a first-rate botanist unless he be also no mean meteorologist, no mean geologist, and—as Mr. Darwin has shown in his extraordinary discoveries about the fertilisation of plants by insects—no mean entomologist likewise.'

For military men engaged in bush warfare or exploring expeditions it would be a great advantage to know something of botany, to know which plants are poisonous, which edible, which are styptic, which preventive of scurvy. The same might be said of geology and mineralogy in building roads, finding water, and selecting healthy camping grounds. He reminded his hearers that the greatest philosopher of the old world had been the tutor of the greatest captain of the old world, in short that Aristotle was the tutor of Alexander. Scientists should be honoured by soldiers, for the two categories of persons who will have most to say in shaping the coming world will be the soldiers and the scientists, and the man who can combine both roles at their highest will be the real ruler of men. Kingsley's key-note was always the same, 'Science is on the march—listen to her divine words, for what is she but the Voice of God, *Deus revelatus*?'

In January 1872 the Canon went to Chester to attend the reopening of the nave of the Cathedral which had been closed for repairs. The ceremony he found magnificent and the Cathedral looking wonderfully beautiful. Two months later a great blow fell, for Maurice, the man he revered above all other men, died. In writing of his death Kingsley remarked again on the great beauty of his face, his extraordinary personal charm, and his saint-like characteristics. It was close on thirty years since he had consulted the Master over 'Elizabeth of Hungary' and twenty-four since they had stood shoulder to shoulder in support of Chartist demands. What a friendship it had been!

Most of this year, with the exception of the three months' residence at Chester, was spent at Eversley, but Charles managed to put in a holiday in the Lake district and to go yachting with Lord Carnarvon. Present at Bramshill at a meet of the foxhounds he wrote one of his last sets of verses, *The Delectable Day* founded on domestic experience.   The first three quatrains describe the meet, the gallop, and the home-coming of a boy on a grey pony, and the last three run like this:

> The climb homeward by park and by moorland,
>   And through the fir forests again,
> While the south-west wind roars in the gloaming,
>   Like an ocean of seething champagne.
>
> And at night the septette of Beethoven,
>   And the grandmother by in her chair,
> And the foot of all feet on the sofa
>   Beating delicate time to the air.
>
> Ah, God! a poor soul can but thank Thee
>   For such a delectable day!
> Though the fury, the fool, and the swindler,
>   To-morrow again have their way!

During the summer of 1872 a Canon of Windsor died, and Fanny, who had never been really satisfied with provincial life at Chester, insisted that Charles should write to Dean Wellesley to find out whether it was possible to get recommended for the vacancy.   Canon Wellesley replied as follows:

I must wait till Mr. Gladstone chooses to consult me and I should only do you harm by suggesting your name till he asked my advice.

You know that the names submitted to him are referred to me before being finally agreed to.   If they are good in themselves I cannot, on account of any friend of my own whom I might wish for in preference, object to them.   I could only help you as occasion offered—meanwhile October is far off and it appears to me very indecorous that poor old Garnier [?] is not allowed to die out naturally rather than legislatively.   I cannot think that Wilberforce can mean Walpole for the post, a respectable man, but nothing more.   He might mean Woodford of Leeds for whom he is always looking out, but I should doubt whether Gladstone would be guided by him, but try Lord Lyttleton.   I cannot quite understand about Lord Eversley—if he has been 'consulted' it must be by someone with authority.   Gladstone, however, never lets any of the colleagues interfere. Lord E., as an independent nobleman, would have no object of his own, yet is a constant supporter of the Government. If he, as a Hampshire authority (first rate as to Winchester), would write and recommend you to G. this would do you more good than anything.

I can only assure you of my readiness to aid you if the opportunity offered. You have always had a fancy for Windsor and there is no post to which your works do not fairly entitle you. Otherwise I should have thought that you would have been in a position of more freedom and better off—if you kept Eversley and could exchange your inferior stall for one of a thousand a year.[1]

Kingsley forwarded this reply to his wife with the note:

Beloved, You will read this and form your own conclusions. *Mine are* that he is quite right and that he probably wants me to wait for the Windsor stall in which case we could be six to nine months in that glorious air and keep H. here as curate on as good or better terms than an average rectory. . . . Of course I had far sooner be Canon of W. than Dean of the other W.[inchester].

Meanwhile Mr. Kingsley arranged for Grenville (the boy on the grey pony) to be coached for a public school by a German who came to live at the rectory. When the time came for this boy to enter Harrow, Charles Kingsley obtained leave from his Bishop to quit his 'charming but unwholesome house' and move nearer the school. This arrangement was to hold good for a year, and the condition on which he was granted permission to reside out of his parish was that he took the Sunday services at Eversley. It is noticeable that from the date on which Charles Kingsley was made a Royal Chaplain Sir William Cope treated him with far more geniality than before. He went so far as to express delight in his conversation, and when the Kingsley family had moved to Harrow entertained him as a *persona grata* at Bramshill during week-ends in order that he might conduct the Sunday services at Eversley. Sir William, though a clergyman, never officiated save in his private chapel because he could not accept the Archbishop of Canterbury's ruling in the Denison case.

Sometimes Fanny became depressed and thought that they would never escape from their most unhealthy residence except

[1] Add. MSS. B.M.

THE STUDY WINDOW AT EVERSLEY RECTORY

by renting houses outside their parish.   But on Lady Day 1873
there reached the Kingsleys at Harrow a letter from Mr. Gladstone proposing,

> with the sanction of Her Majesty, that in lieu of your canonry at
> Chester, you should accept the vacant stall in Westminster Abbey.
> I am sorry to injure the people of Chester; but I most sincerely
> hope your voice will be heard within the Abbey, and in your own
> right.

The appointment was welcomed by the whole family—by
Charles who was automatically freed from having to write for
money, by Fanny who looked forward to the periods of residence in London, by Charles's mother whose pride in him was
intense, by Grenville the schoolboy, and by Maurice just returned
from Mexico.   As for the newly appointed Canon he walked on
air, for to him going to Westminster was like coming suddenly
into an inheritance of rare treasures.   Amidst the general satisfaction a serious note was sounded by Maurice who had not seen
his father for some time.   He thought he had gone downhill
in his absence and was anxious to get him on board ship at once.
But the Canon though freed from summer duty at Chester
had to take London duty in September.   This, he thought,
would make it impossible to do as Maurice advised till about
Christmas time.

Kingsley's periods of residence at Chester had been three,
nine months in all spread over the years 1870, 1871, 1872.
Considering how very short his connection with the city was he
made a great impression on the life of the place.   His botanical
class of 1870 became the Scientific Society of 1871, and developed into the Chester Natural Science Society of 1872 with
Lyell, Huxley, Hooker, and Tyndall as honorary members.
The Canon had led ever increasing and ever more enthusiastic
bands on excursions by train to places of interest in the neighbourhood and had thoroughly enjoyed having his ideas taken
up so warmly and by such intelligent people as the citizens of
Chester proved themselves to be.

Kingsley churned many subjects round in his mind at this
time, and his journeys about the country gave him plenty to
cogitate about.   Fishing on Deeside in the late summer of this

T

year, for example, made him study what he called 'the evils of peasant proprietorship', which his Irish experience of the cottier system had led him to regard as a system devised to keep people in a state of permanent barbarism.   The crofter of Scotland was in no better case.   With the theories of John Stuart Mill who favoured uneconomic tillage because it exterminated the squires who 'propagated the military class', he found himself in strong disagreement.   To Kingsley's thinking this was exactly what the cottier system did not do, for it kept the landlord in permanent possession of the land and gave the cottier the status of a squatter, who in return for permission to squat must cultivate the soil surrounding his hut, or cottage.   Kingsley collected statistics to show that if a farm were divided among smallholders its productive capacity was at least halved.   In his eyes the feudal system was the highest form of civilisation that Europe had yet seen, but, as it could not be reimposed on society, the important business was to make the landlords efficient, to instruct them how to administer their heritage for the welfare of all, and oblige them if need be to sit for examinations on the organisation of production.   There was a dangerously old-fashioned tendency among property owners to think they could do what they liked with their own, and this was responsible for perpetuating what Charles Kingsley never ceased to regard as 'our really barbaric social system'.

It struck him too that the tendency of those in authority was in some degree to make bad use of their power.   For example the bishops of the Church of England ever since the resuscitation of Convocation in 1852 had become disposed to try and increase their prestige by investing nominees of their own rural deans and archdeacons with powers which, if fully exercised, would destroy 'the manly freedom' of the English rector.   If bishops were ever allowed their way in the nomination of canons it would be a bad look-out for the Church as they would always promote the organiser rather than the scholar.   Personally he would like to see all appointments to canonries as well as deaneries and bishoprics vested in the Crown.

The first sermon preached by Charles Kingsley at the Abbey after his appointment was in April 1873, and he wrote to Dean Stanley for sanction to advocate the opening of the British

Museum on Sunday. He would like to take the wind out of the sails of the ignorant, well-meaning Sunday League and show that the Church of England was a socially progressive body. Mrs. Kingsley tells us that during his period of duty— September, October, and November—he spoke to large congregations twice 'a day'. This must be a misprint for twice on Sundays. She enjoyed being able to give luncheon and dinner parties, but unfortunately prints no list of the people entertained and it is only from the diaries of outsiders that we find, for instance, that Mark Twain was one of their guests of honour. Writing to Fanny at Eversley at the end of his three months' residence Charles says, of the Little Cloister:

> This house is charming—the mere feeling of room in it is most pleasant, and the beauty outside under this delicious gleamy weather quite lifts my poor heart up a-while. . . . I regret much I am leaving just as I seemed to be getting hold of people. But I do not think I could have stood the intense excitement of the Sundays much longer.

The last sermon he preached before returning to Eversley was on 'The Beatific Vision'. After a kind of petition that both he and his hearers might have their souls gladdened by the vision of God and live in a spirit of adoration for the glory of His justice and the glory of His love, he concluded:

> And now friends—almost all friends unknown—and alas never to be known by me—you who are to me as people floating down a river; while I the preacher stand upon the bank, and call in hope that some of you may catch some word of mine, ere the great stream shall bear you out of sight—oh! catch at least this one word —the last which I shall speak here for many months, and which sums up all that I have been trying to say to you of late.
>
> Fix in your minds—or rather ask God to fix in your minds—this one idea of an absolutely good God; good with all forms of goodness which you respect and love in man; good as you and I and every honest man understand the plain word good. Slowly you will acquire that grand and all-illuminating idea; slowly and most imperfectly at best: for who is mortal man that he should conceive and comprehend the goodness of the infinitely good God? But see, then, in the light of that one idea whether all the old-fashioned Christian ideas about the relation of God to man; whether a

Providence, Prayer, Inspiration, Revelation, the Incarnation, the
Passion, and the final triumph of the Son of God—whether all
these, I say, do not seem to you, not merely beautiful, not merely
probable, but rational, and logical, and necessary, moral consequences from the one idea of an Absolute and Eternal Goodness,
the Living Parent of the Universe. And so I leave you to the
grace of God.

Dean Stanley says that the vergers and everyone connected
with the Abbey were very proud of Kingsley's fame as author
and preacher: it delighted them to know how much he enjoyed
Westminster 'just as if he had never had anything else to enjoy'.
His power of attraction, said the Abbey staff, was unusual in a
Church dignitary: there was something about him that fascinated
one and all.

Back at Eversley, he began preparing for his American
journey, devoting himself in the first place to writing the lectures
that were to cover his out-of-pocket expenses.   These would
be rather heavy as Rose, his eldest girl, was accompanying him.
They sailed on January 29, 1875, and after a quiet, comfortable
voyage sighted the Nantucket light on February 10.   They
were met at New York by emissaries from a literary club who
passed them painlessly through the customs, fed them, and then
despatched them to stay with Mr. F. G. Shaw at Staten Island.

From Staten Island, Kingsley wrote to his wife that the air
was like champagne and that there was a slight powdering of
snow made sparkling by sunshine. He attached a log and
chart of his voyage for Grenville to whom it should prove in-
structive. He also said that Thackeray's old friend Curtis,
editor of *Harper's Weekly*, had given him valuable advice on
lecture fees. He should insist on $300 for each lecture.

On February 14 he was invited by the Lotos Club of New York
to meet Ward Beecher and then travelled on to Boston to stay
with the Fields. Everyone in those days enjoyed their hospitality and one of the legends of the time is that Mrs. Fields
became infatuated with Charles Dickens during his visit to her
house at Boston. She certainly showed him the kindest hospitality at a time when he was very ailing and within a few months
of death. Charles Kingsley too stayed with her in Beacon
Street, Boston, and at their country place at Manchester-by-the-

Sea. In this frame-house with its deep verandah I lived for some months in 1928 and found relics of the Field occupation in various drawers and shelves—among them a fragment of Cortez's shroud and an incomplete set of Shakespeare that had been given to Leigh Hunt by Shelley containing many under-linings and marginal comments in the poet's writing.

From Boston Kingsley went over the river to Cambridge to stay with Dr. Wharton, who invited Longfellow to meet him at dinner. The two authors had already made friends in England and the American poet gave a dinner in Kingsley's honour. 'Dear old Whittier', says Kingsley, 'came and called on me and we had a most loving and like-minded talk about the other world. He is *an old saint*.' The distinguished botanist, Asa Gray, for whom he had long cherished admiration, entertained him for a whole delightful morning. Altogether Kingsley could report that he found himself in excellent company and in excellent spirits.

At Springfield, Massachusetts, he stayed with Samuel Bowles of *The Republican* and on his return to New York met William Cullen Bryant whose poetry he had read and liked as a boy. In the Philadelphia Opera House he delivered a lecture on 'Ancient Civilisation' to an audience of four thousand hearers who listened intently to a nebulous address on the development of man and the goal of freedom.

The ideal form of human society [said Kingsley] is democracy —a nation—and, were it even possible, a whole world—of free men, lifting free foreheads to God and Nature; calling no man master—for one is their master, even God; knowing and obeying their duties towards the Maker of the Universe, and therefore to each other, and that not from fear, nor calculation of profit or loss, but because they loved and liked it, and had seen the beauty of righteousness and trust and peace; because the law of God was in their hearts, and needing at last it may be, neither king nor priest, for each man and each woman in their place, were kings and priests to God. Such a nation—such a society. What nobler conception of mortal existence can we form? Would not that be, indeed, the kingdom of God come on earth? And tell me not that that is impossible—too fair a dream ever to be realised—tell me not that the dream is impossible. It is so beautiful that it must be true.

Though there were many people in the audience who could not make much of his doctrine, it did not deter huge crowds from listening to him wherever he lectured. Charles Kingsley might have no message for them but he was famous, he was new, and he was a bird of passage, and no educated American wanted to have to admit that they had not seen him.

In Washington he was received by President Grant and invited to open a sitting of the House of Representatives with prayer.

> The President was delighted with 'The Abbey' and seems to have taken a great fancy to me. Sumner's death has been an awful blow here. I do not wonder, for with all his faults he was a *magnificent* man. He and I were introduced to each other in the Senate an hour before his attack. He was most cordial and we had much talk about Gladstone and the Argylls.

After leaving the capital the usual criss-cross journeyings arranged for English lecturers took place—to New York, to Hartford, to Boston again, to New Haven, and then the delight of a private visit to Mark Twain, whose *Innocents Abroad* had so delighted him in England. At the end of March he crossed into Canada where he found himself highly praised by the French Canadians for his '*tacte infinie et sympathie profonde pour les Canadiens et la France*'. What he had said or done to deserve this eulogy does not transpire. From Quebec he was taken to see that one-time link with Madame de Pompadour's world and old France, Sainte-Anne-de-Beaupré, as well as the Falls of Montmorency. Colonel Strange, who accompanied him, tells how Kingsley stood on a little platform over the abyss looking down at the boiling cauldron with its cone of frozen foam, and how he left him in silence to commune with the Nature he loved so well. 'I was afraid somebody would shout above the roar of the torrent how many cubic feet of water per second went down or something of that sort'. A little time afterwards Kingsley said, 'Thank you, you understand me. I would as soon a fellow talked and shouted to me in church as in that presence.'

Easter was spent with the Dufferins at Ottawa and then the traveller returned to Washington to stay with Senator Potter

and dine with the President.   This time his lecture was advertised by printed post-card:

> Sir Canon Kingsley, LL.D. of London will deliver his great
> lecture on the Norse Discoverers of America at the First Congrega-
> tional Church.   Wednesday evening, April 8, 1874. . . . The
> Boston papers speak of it in terms of high commendation.   The
> Canon has yielded to an urgent request and returns to Washington
> solely for the sake of giving this lecture.   Admission 74 cents.

With great enjoyment Kingsley told his hearers about the
discovery of Iceland, Greenland, Labrador, Nova Scotia, by the
Norsemen, and of their finding of New England which they
called Vinland, and how they brought back from that fertile
region timber and raisins.   And somehow or another all these
real adventurings had been forgotten and turned into sagas.   The
lecturer proceeded with great gusto to describe the deeds of the
Norsemen in other spheres, the invasion of England by Harald
Hardraade, and the better-known invasion by William of Nor-
mandy which had been the making of the English people—of
the Free Commons of England.   'By the bitter woes of the
whole population Dane, Angle and Saxon, earl and churl, freeman and slave, crushed and welded together into one homo-
genous mass.'   People found his lectures exciting and intangible.

In lecturing on Westminster Abbey, he said that he had been
touched, strangely touched, at the way in which Americans with
a deep reverence for antiquity hurried from Liverpool to the
'quaint old city of Chester' to gaze on its girdle of walls and
towers and its modest little cathedral.   Praise of Longfellow
followed; he did not happen to have written on the Abbey, but
his muse was instinct with all those lofty and yet tender emotions
which the sight of that great Abbey should call out.   'As long
as the poet who could write *The Belfry of Bruges* and *The Village
Blacksmith* is read among you there is no need for me to bid
you reverence the past.'   He likes to tell them that their
exquisite poet has exercised an influence in Britain as great as
any he has exercised in his native land.   There is another
American author who has described the Abbey better perhaps
than any living writer, and that is Washington Irving.   What
could be better than this?

The sun was pouring down a yellow autumnal ray into the square of the cloisters, beaming upon a scanty spot of grass in the centre, and lighting up an angle of the vaulted passage with a kind of dusty splendour. From between the arcades, the eyes glanced up to a bit of blue sky, or a passing cloud, and beheld the sun-gilt pinnacles of the Abbey towering into the azure heaven.

Or again this of Henry VII's Chapel?

The very walls are wrought into universal ornament; encrusted with tracery, and scooped into niches, crowded with the statues of saints and martyrs. Stone seems by the cunning labour of the chisel, to have been robbed of its weight and density; suspended aloft as if by magic; and the fretted roof achieved with the wonderful minuteness and airy security of a cobweb.

The Abbey, Kingsley went on, was not venerated as the sepulchre of kings and the scene of coronations, but rather as the resting place of famous Englishmen of every rank and creed, and every kind of genius. To him it was Rheims and St. Denys in one, Valhalla and Santa Croce. Chatham gesticulates from the northern transept, Pitt from the western door, Shakespeare leans on a column in Poet's Corner, and Wolfe expires near the chapel of St. John. Within those hallowed walls 'Life is a frost of cold felicities'. Some have found the atmosphere mournful, but to him it speaks only of content and peace. Peace from toil, peace from their fellow men. No more mistakes, no more quarrels. Pitt and Fox, Warren Hastings and Macaulay, they can afford to be near each other for they understand each other now elsewhere; and the Romish abbot's bones do not stir in their grave beside the bones of the Protestant divine whom he, it may be, would have burned alive upon earth. Elizabeth, lastly, lies in the same vault as Mary Tudor. Kingsley makes no comment on this strange double sepulture except to observe that everything proves the Abbey to be a place of peace. It is awful but never sad. Awful as the symbol of both worlds, the seen and the unseen; and of the veil, thin as a cobweb, yet opaque as night, which parts the two.

An American as well as an Englishman would find himself in right good company in the Abbey, for common cousins, common ancestors are there. Yes, the great Abbey with all its

memories of 800 years does not belong to Englishmen alone or
her Colonies or her Empire but to America also.   For the
American it is ancestral ground, sacred for him as for us, out of
which should blossom common respect and affection.   Is this
all sentiment? he asks in conclusion.   'Remember by well-used
sentiment and well-used sorrow great nations live.'

It was after listening to Kingsley's lecture on Westminster
Abbey that Hurlbert, editor of the *New York World*, wrote to
his affectionate friend Lord Houghton:

> Kingsley's lecture here [New York] ought to make a temperance
> man even of his mad novelist brother.   He is all tear-mists and
> winds of God and gushing to that degree that women cry out for
> a cockfight as an alternative.   He has openly yearned for a dead
> American to bury in Westminster Abbey and I go in fear of having
> him propose Chiffinch, or some other easily spared corpse from the
> Abbey, for Sumner's embalmed remains.

In May Kingsley travelled via Detroit and St. Louis to
Omaha, where he joined an expedition organised by Cyrus
Field.   At Salt Lake City, Brigham Young hastened to place
his Tabernacle at the English preacher's disposal, but the
Canon's passion for monogamy and Christian marriage made
him view Mormonism with such horror that he did not even
trouble to decline the well-meant offer.   Perhaps Brigham Young
was among the packed congregation that listened attentively to
Kingsley in the Episcopal Church of St. Mark, which had been
consecrated only the day before he preached in it.   From Salt
Lake City Charles wrote to Fanny: ' What horrors this place has
seen!   Thank God it is all breaking up.   The tyrant is 70 and
must soon go to his account and what an awful one!'   A painful
talk with an ex-Governor on the habits of Mormons shocked
him badly and caused him to thank God that we at least know
what love and purity is!   Cyrus Field having given them 'the
freedom of railway and telegraph service they can do exactly
what they please and in the way and at the time they please'.
Reno and Sacramento were visited and then the party went to
the Yosemite Valley and on to 'the Big Trees'.   These giant
Sequoias gave Kingsley a great thrill.   Such glorious works of
God, he said, 'could not fail to strike awe into all hearts'.

In the damp sea-fog of San Francisco the Canon caught a

severe cold and was so ill that the doctor there advised him to leave for a drier climate as soon as possible. They went to Denver in which city Dr. George Kingsley joined them. He found his brother suffering from a severe attack of pleurisy and advised him to go south to Colorado Springs as soon as possible. Taking Dr. Kingsley's advice they travelled by the narrow gauge railway that Maurice Kingsley (now married and set up in America) had helped to construct a year or two previously. At the Springs the invalid was most carefully nursed in Dr. Bell's house and five weeks later was well enough both to preach and to lecture.

While giving a repetition of his Westminster Abbey address, a beetle alighted on his manuscript and he kept an eye on it without checking his voice. Presently the beetle opened its wings preparatory to flight and Kingsley caught it in his hand, examined it carefully, and then let it go. This was reckoned a great point in his favour for the ordinary man, it was said, would have brushed it aside, but 'the great English divine, trained to such close habits of observation and thought, could not forego the opportunity, even in the midst of his lecture, to study the points in a new species of beetle, his mental discipline enabling him to carry along in his mind two trains of ideas at the same time'.

At Colorado Springs Kingsley composed the last ballad he ever wrote, *Lorraine, Lorraine, Lorrèe*, with its refrain in onomatopoeic imitation of a horse galloping on hard ground.

Are you ready for your steeple-chase, Lorraine, Lorraine, Lorrèe?
   Barum, Barum, Barum, Barum, Barum, Barum, Baree,
You're booked to ride your capping race to-day at Coulterlee,
You're booked to ride Vindictive, for all the world to see,
To keep him straight, and keep him first, and win the run
     for me.
   Barum, Barum, Barum, Barum, Barum, Barum, Baree.

She mastered young Vindictive—Oh! the gallant lass was she,
And kept him straight and won the race as near as near could be;
But he killed her at the brook, against a pollard willow tree,
Oh! he killed her at the brook, the brute, for all the world to see,
And no one but the baby cried for poor Lorraine, Lorrèe.

Some critics after Kingsley's death were in favour of cutting the refrain out, but Froude on being consulted said, 'I am in favour of keeping the refrain. The music of the song will be incomplete without it. As the words went drumming through his head, the refrain pounded along with them. 'It presses,' he observed, 'like an inexorable destiny and makes you feel the iron force with which poor Lorraine was swept to her fate.'

Charles Kingsley reached home in August. The weather was warm and there was much sickness in the parish. He tried, in the absence of his curate, to cope with the work, but as he was already a very tired man it did him no good to go suddenly into harness. In September he had to take duty at the Abbey, but before he could preach a sermon at all was attacked by a sharp bout of congestion of the liver. When he recovered he could only preach once instead of the usual twice on Sundays. Mrs. Kingsley also fell ill and the anxiety about her crippled his own recuperative power. People said he looked old, bent, and broken, but he could not shunt responsibility on to other shoulders for Dean Stanley was detained in Paris by 'great anxiety'.

A recurrence of the liver trouble laid him low again in October and he was greatly depressed at being told that his Fanny, who was very ailing, had angina pectoris. Autumnal residence in the picturesque but sunless Little Cloister did not invigorate either of them. Kingsley preached his last sermon on November 29 and heavily becolded took his wife back to the rectory on December 3. That night Mrs. Kingsley had a heart attack. To Charles, Fanny did not seem so very ill, but the doctors told him bluntly that there was no hope of her recovery, and in consequence he excused himself from obeying the Queen's command to stay at Windsor.

Fanny, when told how seriously the doctors had reported on her condition, asked her beloved Charles whether he thought it cowardly of her to tremble on the brink of the dark river and shrink from parting even for a while from the protecting love that had made her life so happy. 'Cowardly?' he echoed. 'Don't you think I would rather someone put a pistol to my head than lie on that bed there waiting. But it is not darkness

that you are going to, for God is light. It is not lonely, for
Christ is with you. It is not an unknown country, for Christ
is there.' And he was thanked by an adoring look from the
eyes that meant the world to him.

For three weeks they lived together on the borderland of life
and death in their own private world of joint experience, re-
living happy scenes from the past, reviving common memories
enjoyed in common. He read aloud their own most favourite
poems—*Intimations of Immortality*, *The Buried Life*, and the
Ode to Time.

> Then long Eternity shall greet our bliss
> With an individual kiss;
> And joy shall overtake us as a flood.

And those further lines:

> Attir'd with Stars, we shall for ever sit,
> Triumphing over Death, and Chance, and thee O Time.

Charles did not shake off his cold, his cough racked him day
and night and though the weather was arctic he seemed to be
utterly indifferent about his health. Pneumonia at last declared
itself, a nurse came down from Westminster Hospital and kept
him strictly in bed. He was lying in the room next to Fanny.
Opiates were prescribed and under their influence he was heard
to ramble of the West Indies. One day when the nurse was
off duty and he supposedly asleep, he slipped out of bed and
stumbled to Fanny's bedside. When the nurse returned she
found him holding his wife's hand and saying, 'Don't speak,
don't speak, this is heaven.' The nurse insisted on helping him
back to bed where he lay exhausted and half-conscious for the
rest of the day.

To the surprise of the anxious family Sir William Gull
suddenly appeared at the rectory, having been sent down by the
Prince of Wales to see if anything could be done to save his old
tutor. Having delivered the oracular verdict that recovery was
possible, the royal physician left. Almost as soon as he had
driven away there was a bad return of haemorrhage and Charles
cried out to his doctor, 'Heynes, I am hit! this last shot has
told—did Fanny tell you about the funeral? We settled it all.'

On the day of his death, January 23, he was heard repeating the words—'Suffer us not, in our last hour, for any pains of death to fall from Thee.' Those watching by his bed got the impression that he believed his Fanny to be already dead. By midday he was obviously sinking, but became so quiet that Rose and the nurse hardly knew when the moment he had longed for all his life had at last come.

At luncheon that day in his house, Park Corner, John Martineau sat grieving over the illness of the master he had adored from boyhood up. When from the window he saw the rectory boy riding up to the front door astride a white pony, he knew that he must be the messenger of death. As soon as the news was known in London, Dean Stanley telegraphed to Fanny, 'The Abbey is open to the Canon and the Poet'. But Fanny knew that neither in life nor in death would her Charles wish to be separated from her. In the days of his courtship he had written verses that had seemed at the time almost morbid in a man of twenty-three, but which now she found pacifying and consoling in so far as they expressed a life-long frame of mind and an inalterable conviction. In the heart of the runic cross that she ordered for his grave a spray of passion flowers must be carved as a symbol of their love and the inscription for the plinth of the cross must consist of three words chosen by Charles as summing up their wedded life—*Amavimus*, *Amamus*, *Amabimus*.

.   .   .   .   .   .

Some few years before Charles Kingsley's death, what were known as 'confession albums' made their appearance in country houses, and guests were suddenly pounced on to give truthful answers in writing to a number of searching questions. The fashion persisted into my childhood and I was given just such an album by my grandmother. I note that her own reply to the enquiry 'What is your favourite beverage?' was 'Water from Petrarch's fountain at Vaucluse', and that when asked what was my favourite motto I wrote in a large copy-book hand, 'Be what you seem to be'. Fanny Kingsley preserved her husband's plain and revealing answers to similar questions. To 'Your favourite reminiscence?' he wrote, 'July 1839'; to 'Your favourite place?', 'Clovelly'; to 'The character you most dislike?', 'Myself!'; to 'Your ambition?', 'To die'; to 'Your favourite motto?', 'Be strong'.   There is something engaging about the candour of these answers, and it seems extraordinary that a man so fundamentally simple and consistent in certain respects should present himself so kaleidoscopically in life.   Nietzsche once observed that the people of his day were not so much creative as reactive.   Charles Kingsley's mind was of the reactive type, and this may well be the reason that the effect he produces is unprofessional.   Never, in spite of his other-wordliness, was he a typical clergyman, nor, in spite of his often admirable writing, was he an innately literary man.   Though his interests seemed to embrace the world and his desire to see social justice done was strong, he was no lover of humanity as such and no advocate of rose-water philanthropy.   Like Alfred Tennyson, he suddenly came to regard war as the short cut to the reforms he advocated and the solvent of a rigid society devoted to the worship of money.   Charles Kingsley's career was unpredictable for his star traced no recognisable orbit.   As a parson, he seemed like a lay-man in disguise; as a reformer, like a half-trained pugilist; as an author, like an enthusiastic amateur.   He had no respect for convention and up to the time he was forty his own generation looked askance at him as a revolutionary.   In his life he seemed to achieve little, but when we look back on the nineteenth century, so well padded for the money-spinners and those in authority, his real greatness becomes evident, and we see the gaunt figure of the clerical missionary of Socialism and com-pulsory education towering above the prosperous dignitaries who ruled the Church of England in his day.   Propelled by irresistible spasms of sympathy to lavish his energies on one objective after another, Charles Kingsley lived so reactively and in such complete oblivion of his own interests as to involve himself in a succession of dilemmas during the course of a uniquely experimental life.

The theory that a personality is like a nest of Chinese boxes in the innermost of which lies the secret that animates the whole being does not hold good in practice.   Personality, however closely analysed, can, in the long run, only be sensed, not grasped. Individual lives are composed of tissues and filaments so varied in their fragility and toughness, their dimness and their gleam, so interwoven with the problems of their day, so integrated with their proper background, that a biographer after setting down the chronological order of a life, examining work accomplished, introducing the affections woven into the pattern of existence and the interests and activities to which they gave rise, must be deeply conscious that there is still the enigma of personality to be pondered over—the intangible something that reaches out to the stars, fights in the arena of diurnal conflict, and is capable of distilling from ambience or event, essences that may be blended into an immortal expression of individual humanity. Charles Kingsley from boyhood up felt himself to be utterly unlike other men, and the story of his career serves in most respects to support his life-long conviction, that in acting on impulse he caused his flesh to obey and act in harmony with his spirit.

Index

PRINTED IN GREAT BRITAIN
BY R. & R. CLARK LIMITED
EDINBURGH